The Concept of the Avant-Garde

The Concept of the Avant-Garde

Explorations in Modernism

by JOHN WEIGHTMAN

A Library Press Book
Open Court ○ *La Salle* ○ *Illinois*

First published in the United States of America in 1973 by
Library Press Incorporated, LaSalle, Illinois 61301

Printed in Great Britain
by Watmoughs Limited
Bradford and London

Second Printing March 1974 in
the United States of America

International Standard Book No: 0-912050-40-3
Library of Congress Catalog Card No: 73-83003

To the memory of J. R. Morris
who taught French and ideas

Acknowledgements

I am grateful to the publishers and editors for permission to reprint the following:

The Concept of the Avant-Garde *(Encounter)*; In and Out: Ruminations on Fashion *(Twentieth Century)*; Gide and Sexual Liberation *(20th Century Studies)*; The Solar Revolution *(Encounter)*; Surrealism and Super-realism *(The New York Review of Books, October 28, 1965. Copyright © 1965 NYREV Inc.)*; Saint Artaud *(Times Literary Supplement)*; The Play as Fable *(Encounter)*; A Pad in Paddington *(Encounter)*; Bald Remarks on *Hair (Encounter)*; Plays or Psycho-dramas? *(Encounter)*; God's Bodikins! *(Encounter)*; Rites at the Round House *(Encounter)*; The Outsider Rides Again *(Encounter)*; Flesh in The Afternoon *(Encounter)*; Flashing the Old Job *(Encounter)*; All Flesh is Trash *(Encounter)*; A French No-Play *(Encounter)*; Centre 69? *(Encounter)*; Modalities of Sex *(Encounter)*; The Light and the Dark *(Encounter)*; King Phallus *(The New York Review of Books, August 26, 1965. Copyright © 1965 NYREV Inc.)*; Sartre versus Flaubert *(The New York Review of Books, April 6, 1962. Copyright © 1962 NYREV Inc.)*; Céline's Paranoid Poetics *(The New York Review of Books, June 5, 1969. Copyright © 1969 NYREV Inc.)*; O'Brien's Sexy Cross *(Encounter)*; O is for Orifice *(The Observer)*; Myth of the Butch Bitch *(The Observer)*; Omelette à la Ponge *(Times Literary Supplement)*; Genet's Black Chivalry *(The New York Review of Books, August 24, 1967. Copyright © 1967 NYREV Inc.)*; Nathalie Sarraute *(Encounter)*; Robbe-Grillet and the Ludic Novel *(The New York Review of Books, June 1, 1972. Copyright © 1972 NYREV Inc.)*.

Contents

Preface

Instead of a series of essays on *avant-garde* themes, I would have preferred to offer a full and properly structured analysis of modernism. I dream of such an analysis, because I am old-fashioned enough, in both mind and sensibility, to want to escape from incoherence and weave all the threads into a rationally satisfying pattern. But I am also sufficiently modern to be obsessed by the fragility of language, at least as I myself am able to use it to cope with this rich confusion of intellectual and emotional attitudes, involving time, history, nature, religion and sex. I have managed only a few forays across the field, and each—to borrow T. S. Eliot's admirable phrase—is no more than "a raid on the inarticulate". After each attempt, the inarticulate reverts to its mute, mysterious processes, over which even the would-be rationalist has no control until the next sortie, and little enough even then. The most I can claim is that the principles explored in Part I may throw some light on the practical criticism in Parts II and III.

It will be obvious from the first essay that I approach these matters as a student of French. Avant-gardism, though international, is, in some important respects, a French invention, and I hope that the emphasising of such figures as Rousseau, Gide and Sartre will seem useful.

My thanks are due to Mr Melvin Lasky of *Encounter*, who encouraged me to put this volume together on the basis of articles published in his review. Three of the items—1, 3 and 6—were originally public lectures given at Westfield College and Goldsmiths' College; I have left them in the lecture form.

I

ASPECTS OF THE MODERN

1. The Concept of the Avant-Garde

I have chosen to try to explore the phenomenon of the *avant-garde* for two reasons. In the first place, it has been my lot to find myself involved in the discussion and criticism of contemporary French literature during the development and temporary predominance of an *avant-garde* with which I have been unable fully to sympathise. I am referring to the literary movement known as the *Nouveau Roman*, or New Novel, that has now been superseded to some extent by the *Nouveau Nouveau Roman*, with which, alas, I also have some difficulty. It is a disturbing experience for a critic or a teacher to have to adopt a rather negative attitude towards the material he is supposed to be expounding. Given the general atmosphere, he is bound to ask himself if culture is not marching on into the future and leaving him behind among the fossils of the past. And even though my reservations about this particular *avant-garde* are shared by a number of people whose opinions I respect, I confess to having experienced feelings of guilt and inadequacy, which have led me to reflect on the general nature of *avant-garde* attitudes.

But there is also a much broader and more important reason. For a century-and-a-half, at least, the history of literature, especially in France, has been marked by the emergence of new literary movements—which we may, or may not, wish to call *avant-gardes*—each normally accompanied by a theory of literature. Their succession has gradually led not simply to the belief that literature is subject to change, which is a self-evident fact, but to the rather different conviction that the principles according to which works of literature are composed must undergo continuous alteration if literature is not to stagnate. For instance, a prominent member of the New Novel Group,

M. Michel Butor, argues that a writer who works according to the conventions of the preceding generation or generations, instead of inventing new ones, is actually poisoning the mind of the public. In other words, the validity or virtue of literature is made to depend on the repeated invention of something new in form or content, this new element being meant to be particularly appropriate to the stage that culture has reached.

It is only a step from this attitude to the view that literature is subject to obsolescence, and that works of art, even good ones, are fully appropriate only to the period at which they are produced. This is part of the thesis that M. Jean-Paul Sartre developed so brilliantly in his essay *Qu'est-ce que la littérature?* (1948) and that he illustrated by an unusual comparison. He said that books are like bananas; their flavour can be properly appreciated only if they are consumed on the spot. It follows that the works of the past must be rather like old bananas; they must have died, partly or completely, with the past, *i.e.*, must have become too commonplace or too incomprehensible to retain much interest for us. This view may seem paradoxical in an age when knowledge of certain aspects at least of the past seems to be more detailed than ever before. Nevertheless, it has been expressed very forcibly by certain famous exponents of *avant-garde* attitudes. Marcel Duchamp drew a moustache on a copy of the Mona Lisa to indicate an irreverent approach to traditionally admired works. In a book published not so long ago, the painter, Jean Dubuffet, poured scorn on the idea that any present-day reader or theatregoer might sincerely enjoy the tragedies of Racine. Even more explicit is a remark by Antonin Artaud, a greatly revered figure at the moment in certain literary and theatrical circles. He declares in his major work *Le théâtre et son double:*

> *Les chefs d'œuvre du passé sont bons pour le passé; ils ne sont pas bons pour nous.*
>
> (The masterpieces of the past are good for the past, or appropriate to the past, they are no good for us.)

If this doctrine were taken literally, museums, libraries, and most theatres and concert-halls could be closed down, the discussion of literature in the universities would come to an end, and there would be no occasions such as this one. However, I don't think we are meant to consider it as being wholly serious. After all, Artaud himself was inspired by Elizabethan drama and traditional Balinese dancing, both of which are relics of the past. It is, presumably, partly a reaction against undue reverence for the past and an extreme and vivid way of making the point that the past should be subordinated to the present and the future. But the fierce insistence on the present and the future to the detriment of the past has by now, I think, led to a curious situation, not only in literature and art but in other fields too. In France, more perhaps than elsewhere, what we might call the *avant-garde* approach is evident in literary criticism, philosophy, politics, and indeed in all branches of intellectual and artistic activity. Many people now have a strong tendency to accept a given attitude and to find arguments in its favour precisely because of its supposedly up-to-date character. In this way, the fashion of the moment becomes, as it were, a temporary absolute.

But the tendency can go a stage further still. It may lead to the conviction that the most up-to-date phenomenon is the one that has not yet been discovered, but is *just about to be.* This means that the existing state of affairs is always, by definition, expendable and inferior to the future—provided, of course, that the future is being brought about by people who have a suitable contempt for the past. This is the intellectual equivalent of the declaration made by Artaud on the aesthetic level. It is a way of saying not only that we have no need of the masterpieces of the past but also that we can, and should, dispense with the realities and ideas of the past.

In case this sounds like an exaggeration, let me take a recent example from French university life. Among the many people who have given accounts of the student revolt of May 1968 is a professor of the University of Nanterre, who writes under the pen-name of Epistémon, and who is, I am told, a former classical scholar, now a teacher of psychology. In his little book, *Ces idées qui ont ébranlé la France* (1968), he tells us that the events of May introduced him to what he calls *le non-savoir*, non-knowledge.

(This, presumably, is why he calls himself ironically Epistémon, "the knowing one" or "the learned one".) He says that through being challenged by his students, apparently for the first time, he suddenly realised that he wasn't absolutely sure of anything, that in effect he knew nothing, had no knowledge to impart, and could only step down humbly from his pedestal, as he puts it, and discuss his ignorance with his pupils. This he presents as an exciting and indeed lyrical experience, a sort of revelation or conversion. As I read the passage, I was reminded of the old fable about the Emperor in the invisible robe; it was as if the Emperor himself had discovered he had no clothes on and was delighted with his nakedness. Admittedly, in the context, "non-knowledge" is to some extent a play on words. What Epistémon seems to favour is the rejection of all existing knowledge, in the conviction that something new and better will emerge spontaneously from the resulting vacuum. It is as if he were counting on the approaching moment to provide him with a superior truth, as if the mere fact of moving forward nakedly in time were bound to constitute progress. However, he doesn't explain on what basis he will judge the new truth when it occurs; he just tends to assume that because it will be new, it will be better. And he seems to be so caught up in the excitement of the moment that the possibility of the new truth being a re-issue of an old error never crosses his mind.

Actually, I think that Epistémon's attitude is a mixture, possibly a muddle, of at least three different things. First, it is undeniable that, in the arts subjects as opposed to the sciences, knowledge is relative, and that there are moments when any arts specialist may feel that he knows nothing. This is for the obvious reason that, in an arts discipline—and I count Epistémon's psychology as an arts discipline and not yet a fully established science—the part of the subject which can be fully and finally known is less important than the other, speculative part, which is always doubtful. If we are studying French, for instance, we can learn the genders of the nouns and the rules of grammar, and no theory about the uncertainty of knowledge will excuse us if we get them wrong, just as, in dealing with literature, we mustn't commit factual mistakes, such as confusing the Baron de Montesquieu with the Comte de Montesquiou, or mis-reading a text. There are enough ascertainable details of this kind to keep us endlessly busy, so that no one who is trying to learn French can ever complain of a vacuum of non-knowledge. But, of course, the essential part of the subject, the study of French culture, consists of theories about the facts, and here we enter a field where everything is provisional. We are dealing with a shifting mass of hypotheses, and it is a commonplace that there is no final consensus of opinion about any of them. In other words, the arts subjects are concerned ultimately not with verifiable facts but with moral and aesthetic judgments which are never completely settled, since they are not yet definable in scientific terms, and we who make these judgments are organic creatures living in time. But if Epistémon didn't know this already, I cannot imagine how he functioned as a university teacher before the events of May, since it is the business of such a teacher always to be distinguishing between the known and the unknown, and to be assessing degrees of plausibility of the probable.

Secondly, he may have been half-remembering the well-known procedure of the *tabula rasa*, which consists of making a clean sweep of one's opinions until one can test them again according to a new set of criteria. There are two distinguished exponents of this procedure in French history—the philosopher Descartes and the poet and thinker Paul Valéry. However, the procedure is not compatible with non-knowledge, since its aim is, precisely, to reconstruct all knowledge, past or present, on a sounder basis. It is very close to the technique of Socrates, the first university teacher, who went on failing to understand and proclaiming his ignorance until, by a process of elimination and development, he hit upon a provisionally satisfactory formulation, or to the sceptical attitude expressed by Montaigne's *"Que sais-je?"*, which conveys a sense of the fluidity of thought. Socrates, Montaigne, Descartes and Valéry may have been doubtful about the stability of knowledge, but they spent all their time trying to arrive at knowledge.

Since Epistémon makes play with the term "non-knowledge", I think that, in his case, there is a third element which is more important, and this is what I would call the *avant-garde* itch to jettison the past because it is the past and to hurry on the future, even though the future may be so vague as to be quite formless. This, one might think, is carrying imprudence to the point of irrationality. It can be seen as a kind of intellectual catastrophism, an urge to throw the baby out with the bath-water. But for a long time now, *avant-garde* attitudes have been marked by an extremism which is deliberately irrational. This is indicated, amongst other things, by the contemporary American expression "way-out", which seems to mean both belonging to the extreme *avant-garde* and remote from the norms of reason.

If I had time,* I could quote an indefinite number of other examples to show how the obsession with movement in time is often linked with irrationalism and extremism—in the French New Novel, in poetry, in the *avant-garde* theatre, in the fine arts and architecture, in the cinema (especially the so-called Underground cinema), and even in what is called the new theology. However, I would like to take the precaution of stating at this point that although I am critical of some *avant-garde* attitudes, I am not proposing to launch a general offensive against the

---

* Since I wrote the above comment on Epistémon, the *Guardian*, as it happens, has published an article by Roger Poole ("Universities of the Future," 31 Jan. 1969) which explains the English "students' revolt" in terms very similar to those of Epistémon. Many sentences are a direct echo of *avant-garde* attitudes I have just referred to, *e.g.*:

" 'Facts' are much-despised, lower-order munitions of the universities, as out of date as the rifles of the Crimean War. These arsenals of facts should be kept discreetly in the background and the University should not 'impose' these facts upon the students if they don't want to be told about them."

"The University is there to study the future. What students really want are facts about the future, and teachers are judged harshly if they cannot supply them."

"Who needs the Odes of Horace, of Marvell, of Keats? The absolute effective model of beat poetry or guitar poetry has made their pretended virtues only too relative . . . the teacher of poetry should himself be first and foremost a poet . . . he does not exist as a teacher, for there is, strictly speaking, nothing to learn."

"The text is there to be *felt*, to be *experienced in the here and now*. Historical

avant-garde. It so happens that I have a great admiration for certain parts of it, and I count myself a progressive, not a conservative. Nor am I going to make another last-ditch plea for rationalism at all costs. Although at this moment I am trying to think rationally, I would not commit myself to a simple preference for reason over all forms of the non-rational.

What I have said so far is really by way of introduction to my theme: how has it come about that there is now such an obsession with change, such an urge to hurry it on, often in extreme and irrational ways, such a desire, as it were, to soup-up time's wingèd chariot? After all, there have been cultures based on the opposite assumption, that is on the belief that change should be resisted as far as possible and that civilisation consisted precisely in protecting certain values and monuments against erosion by time. Indeed, Western civilisation itself was like this over a considerable period of its history, and a majority of people may think that it still should be. But the opposite attitude now appears to be widespread in those circles where art and ideas are being created, that is in the various *avant-gardes*. Therefore, if we make an effort to understand them, we inevitably raise the whole tangled problem of our relationship to time. Obviously I am not going to solve it in a few pages. I

---

comment upon it is valueless."

It is not clear to me how far Mr Poole himself accepts the views he summarises. I should say that they show the usual confusion between genuine criticism of the University as the home of dry-as-dust learning and an impossible romanticism about starting the world anew with no reference to the past. No doubt the University itself is very much to blame for being as dry-as-dust, through a mistaken belief in "academic objectivity" about matters on which one can only have opinions. The University exists to discuss life, and there is no reason why it should be dull, if life is not dull. But to despise all "facts" is stupid. I have come across "students" who would have liked to know French without actually learning it and to be acquainted with the contents of books without ever opening them. There is not much to be done for these abstentionists until knowledge can be injected with a syringe. Similarly, the assertion that "historical comment is valueless" is nonsensical. What we did and thought yesterday is already a subject for historical speculation, and every use of language is bound, in a sense, to be reflexive and historical. My thesis is that the *avant-garde* belief that the past can, and should, be rejected *en bloc* is itself a tradition by now, and a very questionable one.

can only comment tentatively on certain aspects of it in the light of my reading of French literature.

The French word, *l'avant-garde*, is of course a military term, a very old one which is found in medieval French. No one seems to know when exactly it was first used as a metaphor, but I have been unable to find any examples before the 19th century. According to an Italian scholar, the late Renato Poggioli, whose book *The Theory of the Avant-Garde* (1968) is an extremely valuable and exhaustive account of various *avant-garde* manifestations and doctrines, the expression was first used metaphorically from about 1845 by French political movements in referring to themselves, but it was only during the very last years of the 19th century that the metaphor was transferred from politics to literary and artistic activities, to which it has since been mainly attached. Poggioli therefore argues that the *avant-garde* in the modern sense is quite recent, and that the first intimations of it go back only as far as the Romantic movement.

I agree that the *avant-garde* mentality, in its exacerbated form, belongs to the last seventy-five years or so. But if we look at the matter in the context of French literary history, I think it is possible to suggest that what we are dealing with is not an absolutely new and separate phenomenon; it is rather the latest effect of a long and extremely complicated process, which is, of course, the general change-over from the static or cyclical view of human existence to the evolutionary view. Evolutionism is, fundamentally, a scientific concept. Therefore, if my suggestion is correct, the term *avant-garde* is not simply a military metaphor, used first in politics and then transferred to literature and art; it is basically connected with science, and with what is sometimes called the scientific revolution, the replacement of the medieval belief in a finished universe by the modern scientific view of a universe evolving in time. The scientific view affected political and social thinking long before it penetrated into literature proper and the fine arts; this is why the metaphor is political before being literary and artistic.

In France, the first real signs of the modern evolutionary view occur in the 17th century at the time of the Quarrel of the

Ancients and Moderns, but the beginnings of the development can, of course, be traced back to the Renaissance and, beyond the Renaissance, to Ancient Greece where most things existed in embryo. In 17th-century France, the first pale dawn of the scientific view seems to have had little or no effect on the aesthetic attitudes of creative artists, or at least on those attitudes that were part of their conscious make-up. The extraordinary flowering of French neo-classical literature is contemporaneous with the Quarrel of the Ancients and Moderns, yet owes practically nothing to it. The works of Corneille, Racine, Molière, Mme de la Fayette and La Bruyère are brilliantly original, but, strangely enough, are not accompanied by any definite doctrine of originality. On the contrary, the prevailing note is one of subservience to antiquity. The eminent Racinian scholar, Raymond Picard, claims that Racine's tragedies were, in their day, *des œuvres d'avant-garde*, but this was true only objectively, not subjectively. Racine clearly had a static view of human nature. He wasn't trying to say anything new. He thought he was creating timeless aesthetic objects, embodying permanent and universal truths. And even the famous thinkers of the earlier part of the *grand siècle*, Descartes and Pascal, who made mathematical and scientific discoveries, were not looking forward to the future in the modern manner. It is true that as they tried to put their conflicting ideas in order, they made many explosive statements. But we have no reason to believe that they themselves knew just how explosive their thought was. In 17th-century France, the Counter-Reformation and Counter-Renaissance atmosphere was so strong—on the intellectual if not on the aesthetic level—that it seems to have caused an eddy in the stream of historical consciousness, with strikingly beneficial results for literature because, other things being equal, literature is easier to produce in an atmosphere where the general values of society appear to be settled.

However, in the 18th century, there was a dramatic change that has often been commented on. Although scientific evolutionism was not yet fully established, the major thinkers of the French Enlightenment foresaw, or sensed, its implications.

Montesquieu, Voltaire, Diderot and Rousseau, all of whom had some knowledge of science, were in a sense sociologists, trying to understand human life as a dynamic process in time, and as a secular process, which cannot be accounted for in religious terms, and more especially not in terms of the Christian revelation. This is true, I think, even in the case of Voltaire and Rousseau who were technically deists, and not agnostics or atheists. Their deism, although they themselves may have sincerely believed in it, was only a kind of surface dressing over what is essentially a secular enquiry into the nature of man and human history. Like their fellow *philosophes*, they were thus brought into conflict with orthodox Christian theology, which is based on the belief in a relationship, which can be called static, between man inside time and God outside time. The great controversy between science and religion, which was not to occur in England until the middle of the 19th century with the formulation of evolutionary theory by Darwin, had, to all intents and purposes, run its course in France by the end of the 18th century.

This, I think, is the fundamental reason why the conditions favouring the development of the *avant-garde* mentality were present earlier in France than elsewhere and why the phenomenon was French before becoming European and American. In France, by the end of the 18th century, the modern evolutionary and secular view of the world had pervaded the consciousness at least of the intellectual élite. The situation that Nietzsche was going to express so dramatically in the 19th century in the phrase: "God is dead", already existed before 1789. In fact, most of the great 19th-century themes are already present in the French Enlightenment: there are intimations of Hegel and Marx in Montesquieu, Diderot, and Rousseau; of Darwin and Freud in Diderot; of Freud and Sacher-Masoch in Rousseau; and of Freud, Sacher-Masoch, and Nietzsche in the Marquis de Sade. We might even say that the Marquis de Sade was the first great modern figure to go mad through the death of God, and that this is why he has been resuscitated so fervently during the last half-century or so as the darling of a number of different *avant-gardes*.

In other words, the intellectual watershed, as I see Enlightenment; French Romanticism, when it occur 1820s, was only an episode, although a flamboyant of post-Enlightenment history. Romanticism brushed away a great deal of the neo-classical aesthetic which had survived, in spite of the intellectual changes, until the early years of the 19th century. It developed the Promethean element that was inherent in the Enlightenment, but it was also in many ways retrogressive, and was much affected by its coincidence with the Restoration, which was an attempt to put the clock back socially and politically. However, by now, a century-and-a-half later, it is undeniable that not only France but the whole world is living to a very considerable extent according to post-Enlightenment attitudes, which co-exist alongside remnants of pre-Enlightenment attitudes. During this century-and-a-half, many sincere, ingenious and elaborate attempts have been made to effect a compromise between the modern scientific view of the universe and the old Christian view, and the French themselves, from Auguste Comte to Henri Bergson, Father Teilhard de Chardin and Simone Weil, have been particularly active in this field. But it seems obvious to me that no reconciliation has been brought about. The two different ways of looking at things exist side by side, and the extremely tangled aesthetic history of the last 150 years—not to speak of the social and political history—can be seen in terms of the tensions between these attitudes and of the growing predominance of the scientific world-view, which is often apprehended more emotionally by non-scientists than by scientists.

What the Enlightenment did was to see history as the continuously unfolding tale of human life on earth, backed, of course, by the much greater time-scale of the evolutionary development of the universe. This view presents human life as a process in time, which we can elucidate to some extent as we look back or speculate about as we look forward, but which has no definable relationship to anything that might exist outside time, *i.e.* to eternity or God. Indeed, eternity becomes increasingly unthinkable; there is only the ribbon-like process of time which is secular in the full sense, *in saecula saeculorum*. This is what is meant by "the death of God", and this is why those theologians like the Bishop of Woolwich, who are disturbed by the scientific view of the universe and cannot keep their religious beliefs and their vision of the material world in separate compartments, are trying to evolve what is called "a theology of the death of God". The death of God means not only that there is no personal entity behind the universe to provide us with a moral law, but also that human life can only be given a meaning, if it has any, within the flux of history. And, if I may be allowed my largest generalisation, I would say that the increasing prevalence of *avant-garde* attitudes is a growing effect of this feeling that we live only in time and have to find our values in time. (I say "feeling" deliberately, because in many cases it is not a clear philosophical awareness and it doesn't need to be to produce the effects we see around us.)

Avant-garde artists and thinkers sense the problem of finding values in flux and they are trying—often perhaps neurotically —to espouse what they think is the movement of history by anticipating the crest of the next wave *(la nouvelle vague)*, or alternatively they may be trying to escape from the dilemma of perpetual movement by finding some substitute for eternity, *i.e.* some God-substitute. Quite often, I think, they are trying to do both things at once, and this is why so many *avant-gardes* have both a progressive and a non-progressive aspect. In so far as they are non-progressive, the metaphorical expression, *avant-garde*, is a misnomer, because the movement is not forward, but to the side, or even backwards in time to pre-Enlightenment attitudes. It occasionally happens, for instance, that the *avant-garde* artist is consciously reconverted to Christianity, and usually to old-fashioned Catholicism, because it offers the best escape from flux.

I might add here, incidentally, that the *avant-garde* syndrome is much less noticeable in scientists than it is in artists and intellectuals. Although it is ultimately a result of science, it doesn't seem to affect the scientist *qua* scientist. I suppose this is because, in his work, he is in the happy position of not being concerned with human emotional values at all, and can take an optimistic view of time. He carries the past with him in the form of agreed, accumulated knowledge, and he can look forward to the future as a continuously deeper or more extensive reading of the book of nature on the level of verifiable fact. Scientific truth is, in itself, an escape from time, because it is cumulative, and because the effectiveness of any part of it can be demonstrated at any moment. But the artist and the thinker are concerned with works of art and intellectual theories, about which there is by no means the same degree of cumulative agreement, and they cannot collaborate with each other in the production of an impersonal truth in the way that scientists can. When George Bernard Shaw said that he stood on the shoulders of Shakespeare, he was deluding himself with a false analogy between science and art. Lavoisier stood on the shoulders of Joseph Priestley and Einstein on those of Newton, but artists and thinkers cannot build a progressive monument in this way.* They are almost totally involved in flux, and their situation has become steadily more critical in this respect since the 18th century.

Before the Enlightenment, that is in the days of Old Western Man, whether pagan or Christian, the work of art could be looked upon as a monument embodying permanent truths and existing in a sort of eternity, outside the life-span of the individual artist who had created it. *Exegi momentum aere perennius*. Fashions might change, but they did so unconsciously, and it was tacitly assumed, by cultures which did not look at themselves historically and scientifically, that their views about moral truth and aesthetic beauty were constants. Then, during the first phase of the Enlightenment (which continued well into the 19th century), there could be, and there was, considerable optimism about the possibility of arriving at the permanent

---

* I am leaving out of account, for the moment, the fact that there is such a thing as the evolution of artistic forms. Racine, for instance, did not invent French neo-classical tragedy from scratch. He had predecessors whose example helped him. But his success did not in any way help the writers of tragedy who came after him. For a hundred years they tried in vain to imitate him or to do something rather different in the same form, and their works are a graveyard of wasted effort. In other words, literary masterpieces are not elements in a continuous construction, as any great scientific invention is, but they may be end-products in a limited series.

truth of human nature, and it was thought that art might be used as an instrument in this search.

The French *philosophes* had looked back over history, had seen it as a record of success or failure (but mostly failure), and had assumed that, by taking thought, they would evolve a concept of man that would allow them, or their successors, to correct the course of history. If history was such a record of crime and injustice, this was because it had not been conducted in accordance with the true nature of man. Once man had been defined as a natural phenomenon like other phenomena, without all the mythical accretions of the past, society would right itself, and the generations of the future would find themselves in a social context that would allow the full and harmonious expression of their inherent possibilities. Actually, this theory takes two rather contradictory forms, which are still very much with us today.

Rousseau popularised the view, although he did not wholly believe in it himself, that the true state of human nature had existed at some time in the past, that man had strayed from it by misadventure, and that the problem was how to return to it. In this hypothesis, movement towards the future involves peeling away layers of supposed civilisation, in order to get back to the purity of man's original being. I suspect that this is not a modern idea at all but an adaptation of the Jewish myth of the Garden of Eden and the classical Myth of the Golden Age, both of which have been present all through Western history in the pastoral tradition. It is an idea we all subscribe to more or less, even though some of us may limit our return to nature to eating whole-meal bread and taking brisk walks over Hampstead Heath. However, although a very tempting idea, it is an impossible one to handle coherently, since there is absolutely no means of deciding what should, or should not, be included in original human nature. Yet, at any given moment, someone is always asserting the supposed "natural" quality of a particular human feature or condemning some other feature as "unnatural," and the tendency is by and large anti-cultural, because if man ever had an original nature, it was presumably an animal one, and culture is something that has been added to it, or has grown out of it. We thus arrive at a paradoxical situation in which culture itself, which is trying to return to a supposed human nature, becomes anti-cultural.

Now it is undoubtedly true that, in a sense, long hair is more natural than short hair and a certain degree of grubbiness more natural than cleanliness. It is also an interesting and instructive exercise to move back from culture into the animal world and to consider man as a naked ape. But is it a fact that animality is always truer than culture, as far as human beings are concerned? I don't think so, but ever since the Marquis de Sade, certain individuals have tended to assume that it is, and quite a lot of them have belonged to various *avant-gardes*. Egoistic self-assertiveness may be thought more natural than collective altruism, instinct and impulse more natural than reason, accident and randomness more natural than deliberate arrangement, inarticulate noises more natural than speech, and the body more natural than the mind. It is not uncommon to come across modern artists who are convinced that the less they know and the more empty they can make their minds, the nearer they are to the unsullied purity of human nature.

I once heard Dylan Thomas say, for instance: "The bigger the fool, the better the poet." This could be a way of asserting that the functioning of the poet's imagination should not be hampered by his intelligence, which is true. But this, and similar statements, can also be taken as justification for the belief that the way to get the creative imagination working is deliberately to blunt the intelligence, and the intelligence may be blunted without the creative imagination ever really beginning to operate—with a consequent drift into randomness and irrationalism. And once randomness and irrationalism have been accepted as principles, anything goes; naturalness and unnaturalness can be combined in any mixture. Thus, a belief in the naturalness of long hair can be combined with a fashion for wearing wigs, or one can organise a happening at which one deliberately takes off one's clothes in order to be spontaneously natural. In England at this very moment, curiously enough, in the matter of dress, three quite distinct degrees between naturalness and unnaturalness are almost equally fashionable—total

27

nudity, deliberate unkempness, and exquisite dandyism. And all three are found more or less in the same *avant-garde*, or in over-lapping *avant-gardes*. I am not complaining about this; such complexities have their charms, as well as their occasional disadvantages. I am merely trying to emphasise the uncertainties introduced by the idea of original human nature. One can never tell whether the next wave of the *avant-garde* is going to insist on naturalness or unnaturalness. Baudelaire, in his day, wrote beautiful poetry about the ideal original human nature, at the same time as he declared that nature was hateful, and that women were particularly abominable because they were particularly natural. Huysmans, who was also a major *avant-garde* figure in his time, began by being a naturalist and then produced his famous book, *A Rebours* (1884), which is a systematic denunciation of nature in favour of artificiality. It is a rare case of an *avant-garde* book with a retrogressive title, directed against nature.

However, I think the more serious version of the evolutionary theory assumes that human nature has never existed in any perfect form in the past, but will do so at some point in the future. This, it may be thought, is just an adaptation of another myth, the myth of the Millennium, and indeed the ideal society foreseen by some of the 18th-century thinkers has been dubbed the Heavenly City of the Philosophers. Still, the myth of the social millennium is a noble myth; since it is genuinely progressive, it fits in to some extent with the scientific world view; it has induced a great many artists to put their shoulders to the wheel of social progress, and it has sometimes even enabled them to produce good art. At the same time, of course, it has had deplorable effects both in art and in life. It has often caused the present to be demolished for the hypothetical good of the future, and, in France particularly, it has led generations of artists to assume that, since the ideal society lies in the future, they must maintain an attitude of unrelenting hostility to the existing state of affairs.

Needless to say, there are always very good reasons for criticising the present, especially if society is as firmly entrenched in certain philistine attitudes as the bulk of French society was in the 19th and early 20th centuries. I am not asserting that the attitude of extreme negativism which begins, let us say, with Baudelaire and continues through Rimbaud, Alfred Jarry, the Surrealists, Artaud, Sartre, and others, is unmotivated; far from it. But the forward-looking self-righteousness of the *poète maudit*, who is alienated from his average contemporaries, and will only be appreciated by posterity, has become just as much a cliché as the conventions against which he is supposed to be revolting. It has long been axiomatic in France that the artist has to be a rebel, an outcast, a demolisher of old forms, a hater of the bourgeoisie, an exceptional individual who lives according to his private anticipation of the laws of the perfect society of the future, not according to the *defective* rules of existing society. In practice, he can rarely achieve this standard completely, and he may not achieve it at all, so that in fact he is often not really a *poète maudit* but that very common French type, the anti-bourgeois bourgeois, who accepts society more or less as it is, while at the same time entertaining a set of intellectual and aesthetic notions which are contradicted by his actual behaviour. I get the impression that a comparable type is becoming increasingly common in England and America and often provides both the artist and the public for certain kinds of *avant-garde* art. The novelty of the situation is not in the contradiction itself; in the old days there was a permanent contradiction between behaviour and Christian doctrine. The new feature is that religious values have been replaced by emotional and intellectual assumptions, often unanalysed, about the relationship between the present and the future. The contradiction was clearly illustrated two years ago by the success of the play *Les Paravents* by Jean Genet, a powerful and nihilistic denunciation of society, which was brilliantly staged by the French National Theatre. This was an almost perfect example of a society applauding its own negation.

I now come to what I think is the crux of the matter. The fundamental development that has taken place in recent times is that the Enlightenment's hope of achieving a definition of human nature has come to seem more and more illusory, at least to a number of important thinkers and artists. When the *philosophes* assumed that it would be possible to define the nature of man and create the perfect society, they imagined they were looking towards the future, but in fact they were falling back on to a static conception. The accumulation of knowledge has shown not only that man is part of the evolutionary process, but that, being an animal with culture, he is an exceptionally mobile part. It is possible to talk about the nature of the non-cultural animals, such as the lion or the tiger, because it hasn't altered appreciably in the course of recorded history. But the more we learn about man, the more we realise that his so-called nature has included such a bewildering variety of customs, attitudes, beliefs, and artistic products that it is impossible for any one person to comprehend more than a very small part of the possible range. Moreover, we are more aware than ever before of the complex and mysterious forces at work within ourselves, and which we do not wholly understand. Consequently, it would take a very confident man today to echo the line from Terence which was a slogan of 19th-century humanism: *Homo sum, humani nihil a me alienum puto.*

In other words, as some modern thinkers—particularly French ones—like to put it, the death of God is now being followed by the death of Man. However much some people may wish to reject the past, precisely because they find it so difficult to contemplate, the knowledge of it weighs upon them as an immense repository of largely unassimilable data, while the future stretches ahead as a vista of endless and ultimately meaningless change. The sheer fact of living in time becomes then an existential anguish, because history is no more than a succession of moments, all in a way equally valid or invalid, and human nature ceases to be a unifying concept and is no more than the name we give to the successive appearances of man.

And, of course, this anguish of living in time is accompanied by the twin anguish of contingency, which is the sensation of scientific law running through animate and inanimate nature, without any intelligible reference to the human consciousness and emotions. Hence a metaphysical dizziness or a nihilistic despair about the very concept of human nature which can combine in all sorts of complicated ways with both the pastoral myth of original human nature and the millennial myth of future human nature.*

Let me indicate very briefly some of the consequences of this in *avant-garde* art.

It is because man has been trying, since the Enlightenment, to understand things rationally and scientifically that he has arrived at these dilemmas. Hence a widespread disgust, often a fascinated disgust, with the idea of science and a further justification for the flight from reason. Hence also a search for methods of producing a sensation of mystic depth, in other words, an apparently meaningful, although incomprehensible, relationship with something beyond average existence, *i.e.*, the transcendent. The use of alcohol and other drugs for this purpose has been widely publicised recently, but it has been a commonplace since Baudelaire invented the expression "artificial paradises". It is also paradoxical, because it is a scientific method, although a crudely applied one, of blurring the scientific vision. It has occasionally helped—but always, I think, accidentally—in the production of imaginative masterpieces, such as *Kubla Khan*, but it is also responsible, I suspect, for a vast output of so-called works, which are really examples of psychological randomness, and must be incomprehensible to the authors themselves, once they have emerged from their drugged state, and to other people, whether *in* or *out* of the drugged state.

Even without drugs, randomness may be turned into a sensation of mystery. If nothing can be given a meaning in the general flux, everything can be given a sort of mystic weight, through being contemplated in a state of Existentialist awareness, which may range from hysterical euphoria to nausea. In its extreme form, this awareness even eliminates the need to create a work of art. Anyone can be his own artist, simply by

* A student has pointed out to me that what I call the pastoral myth and the millennial myth may be just the old opposition between Platonism and Aristotelianism: the belief in the pre-existing ideal *versus* the belief in development from the embryonic to the ideal. If these are two basic modes of functioning of the human mind, the fact that neither can be fully accepted nowadays would in itself be enough to cause intellectual panic.

picking up a stone or a found object or drawing a line around some fragment of the given world and seeing it as an embodiment of mystery. This helps to explain *collages*, cut-outs, and the ramifications of the Cult of the Object amongst Surrealists, Existentialists, and other *avant-garde littérateurs*. Two or three years ago, I had the experience, in an art gallery, of finding a heap of sand on the floor and having to ask the proprietor whether it had been left behind by the builders or was meant as an exhibit. In this particular case, it was an exhibit. Obviously, a heap of sand, however beautiful and mystic, is not meant as a permanent work of art. It cannot be picked up and carried away in its heap-form. It is simply a momentary object of attention that can be replaced by others. Therefore this attempt to see eternity in a heap of sand links up with the sense of cultural and social mobility which led Sartre to liken books to bananas. The two attitudes come together to make works of art part of the flux in which we live, instead of would-be permanent monuments. Hence the development of what is sometimes called "throw-away art": the work of art is like a flower that wilts after a day, or a culinary masterpiece that is eaten, or a dress that goes out of fashion after a week or so. It has constantly to be replaced by something new, although the new may be a haphazard revival of the old. The latest evening dress may be grandmama's petticoat that has been rediscovered in an attic, or a uniform from the Boer War. In this case, it is also, of course, by its very nature an ironical—but perhaps unconscious—comment on the fact that we exist only in terms of ephemeral fashions.

Randomness is also connected with the dream on the one hand and, when it becomes frantic, with madness on the other. Both are forms of unreason that have been much cultivated by different *avant-gardes*. The interesting point here, I think, is that while medicine and psychiatry, which are scientific in intention, try to interpret dreams and madness in rational terms, some *avant-gardes* have reverted to the medieval attitude and accept the dream or the madman's perception as a truth that is higher than the truth of the waking mind or of sanity. This is particularly noticeable among the Surrealists and their descendants, who have taken Rimbaud's prescription about *le dérèglement de tous les sens* very seriously, and who use Freud as an excuse for an irrationalism that Freud himself would not have approved of. It seems to me that they often confuse unreason with the imaginative faculty, both in their doctrines and their works. I agree that reason is not enough. Reason cannot invent. Invention is a leap into the future which depends on imagination or intuition, whatever we may mean by these words, and reason can do no more than test the results of invention. But I remain convinced that all genuine works are connected ultimately with the rational faculty, and indeed feed the reason and help it towards truths that it can eventually define in its own terms. Many *avant-garde* productions, I suspect, are altogether beyond the reach of reason, and therefore lie in an area of random meaninglessness.*

But here again all sorts of contradictions occur. For instance, the *avant-garde* playwright, Eugène Ionesco, professes a conscious belief in the dream and randomness, yet his early plays are for the most part examples of imaginative order that can be discussed rationally, *i.e.* his practice is, in my view, much superior to his theory.

* Another student has objected that the concept of the random makes no sense. All impulses must be determined; therefore, whatever the artist produces corresponds to something in his psyche, and it is presumptuous to judge this something in the name of "reason", which may be no more than a system of bourgeois conventions dating from the 18th or 19th centuries.

I agree that "random" is to some extent a metaphor; I am not using it in the sense of "totally undetermined". I mean that the phenomenon is momentary and has not been satisfactorily fitted into any overall pattern by the artist himself. Nor am I defending a static concept of reason. "Bourgeois reason" is just as unsatisfactory a cliché as any other, since reason is a continuous process of digestion and ordering of data (*cf.* Lalande, *La raison et les normes*).

The problem in artistic production and criticism is:

(*a*) that the artist himself can never be absolutely sure that he has succeeded in creating a valid imaginative pattern. Past examples show that he is not necessarily an impeccable judge of his own work;

(*b*) that the critic can never be absolutely sure of the rightness or wrongness of his reactions. Again, past examples show that he is sometimes right, sometimes wrong.

There is no way of avoiding the perpetual debate between the artist and himself, the critic and the work, and the critic and himself. "Culture" is surely bound to be this endless dialogue between imagination and reason.

Since language is normally the vehicle of articulate meaning, it is in connection with language that the problem of meaning *versus* meaninglessness occurs most acutely among *avant-garde* writers, but in a form that I, for my part, find rather surprising. I would have thought that anyone wishing to appease his thirst for mystery has only to contemplate language as we use it every day. Since no genius has arisen to explain to us how language works, there is a sense in which even reasonable statements are extremely obscure and can give rise to mystic wonder; at least they do so in me. If I had to establish a hierarchy of mystery, I would say that imagination is more mysterious than reason, but reason much more mysterious than unreason. However, many *avant-garde* writers do not see linguistic phenomena in this light. For some, all the ordinary uses of language are too comprehensible, and so they adopt various methods of breaking through language, as it were, to a mystery which is supposed to lie beyond it, or of putting words together in a fashion which is meant to provide an escape from flux, yet without being an expression of any permanent human nature, as the classical work was supposed to be.

At one end of the scale are those poets who dispense with the existing languages altogether and replace them by collocations of more or less onomatopoeic sounds. These sounds are perhaps intended as a return to the voice of man's original pastoral nature, like the barking of dogs or the mooing of cows, or perhaps they are supposed to make us feel that all language is futile, since no language provides the key to the meaning of the evolving universe. Then come those poets who treat words as objects, like the objects of the *avant-garde* painter or sculptor, and try to dissociate them from the articulate meanings they might have in a sentence. Of course, poets have always been aware of words as objects with a shape, a rhythm and a feel in the mouth, but traditional poets combined this sense of words as tangible entities with the elaboration of more or less coherent statements. Coherence is now such a despised characteristic that many writers try to eliminate it, as the so-called literary element has been removed from painting and sculpture. The poem is meant to be a sheer juxtaposition of words which doesn't allow the mind to pass through it in the usual way and so slip back into the flux of time. The normal comprehension of any sentence is, necessarily, an act in time, so that if you can halt comprehension, the words become, or may appear to become, ultimate fragments of the universe, producing a semblance of eternity. Hence the modern American saying: "A poem does not mean, it just is." Hence also the title of Susan Sontag's book of essays on various *avant-garde* phenomena: *Against Interpretation*, although it is again paradoxical to write interpretative essays to show that genuine modern art is impervious to interpretation.

However, I think there is a profound truth embodied in this kind of remark, and the attitude behind it has produced both good and bad poetry. It helps to account, for instance, for the qualities and defects of two very important French poets, Mallarmé and Valéry, who were *avant-garde* in their day, and of one minor contemporary *avant-garde* poet, Francis Ponge. In all three poets, the deliberately opaque use of language can take the form of preciosity, which has been very prevalent in recent years in various departments of French literary and intellectual life. Preciosity may be a valid and brilliant means of extending the possibilities of language, but it can also be a facile and ostrich-like way of arriving at gratuitous mystery, especially in discursive thought. If a critical comment on a hermetic poem is as hermetic as the poem, how does one know that one is not dealing with a poem and a pseudo-poem, or perhaps even with two pseudo-poems?

Finally, and connected with what I have just been saying, there is the use of language to create a puzzle, a conundrum, or a game. This is not quite the same thing as a sheer object, since it allows a kind of circular movement of comprehension within the terms of reference of the game itself. When the chief exponent of the *Nouveau Roman*, Alain Robbe-Grillet, declares that a writer is someone who has nothing to say, I think he means that life is non-significant and that we know very little about human psychology. Therefore the writer produces a construct, put together according to his own arbitrary rules, or to rules founded on the unexplained realities of his particular temperament, and we are intended to enjoy it as a sort of metaphysical *trompe-l'oeil*. It has an appearance of meaning, since the language of which it is composed conveys sense up to a point, but it is really a self-sufficient linguistic labyrinth, from which the mind is not intended to escape. It offers no exit on to any reality other than itself. In short, in my opinion, it is often no more than an ingenious, sterile, solipsistic fruit on the tree of literature. Its over-deliberate arrangement is, in the last resort, equivalent to the randomness of some other *avant-garde* works. One can see why certain writers have felt compelled to move in this direction, without being convinced that they have found the best solution to their problem.

I have been able to indicate only a few of the ramifications of this vast subject, but I must now conclude. If this were an *avant-garde* lecture, and not a lecture on the *avant-garde*, I could end by mooing like a cow, or letting off fireworks or uttering *Ubu*-like expletives to emphasise the meaningless of the evolving universe. But I cannot quite bring myself to do this, and so I must assume that I am still not altogether convinced by the more extreme forms of the *avant-garde*, as I understand them. I am not saying that these forms of the *avant-garde* should not exist. I am strongly in favour of everybody producing whatever kind of art they can, as long as we are all free to say what we think about it. But, granted that the intellectual dilemma underlying many *avant-garde* manifestations is genuine and even tragic, I have doubts about the consequences that are sometimes made to flow from it.

I think that dramatic phrases such as "the death of God" and "the death of Man" can breed a great many misconceptions. If God is dead, for instance, this is not a new tragedy. The phrase must mean that God never existed, that he was always an anthropomorphic projection on to the backcloth of the universe and that man never had any relationship with eternity. It follows that the Book of Job or Lucretius may be making much the same point as the atheistic New Novel, only more forcefully, and this may be a cheering thought rather than a depressing one. It is surprising how many old literary bananas still have a lot of flavour. Thirty years ago, M. Sartre himself produced a notable banana, entitled *La Nausée*, which is still remarkably fresh. Similarly, although we cannot embrace all the manifestations of man, I don't see why we should therefore proclaim a humanism of the death of man. Even though we live in the flux of history and have no fixed and clear basis for our moral and aesthetic assumptions, I still cannot feel that they are arbitrary, and if they are not arbitrary, they have to be treated as mysteries, which we can go on trying to understand. Perhaps they correspond to something that might be called an evolving human nature, and that we might accept as a sort of open-ended working hypothesis.

And if all time is equal, there is no more need to rush impetuously into the future than there is to cling stupidly to the past; in any case we can only live in the present by borrowing from the past; we *are* the past which is living in the present. Indeed, the evolutionary view makes partisan attachment to any one segment of time rather vulgar. In short, although the universe may appear to be meaningless, I don't see why we should try to imitate this apparent meaninglessness in art or in thought, or try to palliate it by methods which fail to satisfy all our faculties.

2. The Obsessive Object

It was in 1962 that I first noticed how the term *l'objet* had established itself as a catchword in France. I had been to see François Truffaut's charming film, *Jules et Jim*, and had been struck by a tiny episode in it. Jim encounters a friend in a Parisian café. This friend is sitting at the bar-counter with a pretty girl who says nothing, but smiles in a Mona-Lisa-ish way. She never speaks, explains the friend; she is not stupid, she is hollow, and he adds, giving her a little tap: *"C'est la femme-objet."* The film was based on a novel by Henri-Pierre Rocher, who had been born more than seventy years before, and the episode was supposed to take place in the 1920s. When I checked, I was unable to find the phrase in the book; Truffaut had added it as an appropriate joke for the 1960s.

About the same time, one of the *conservateurs* of the Musée des Arts Décoratifs at the Louvre, M. François Mathey, organised an exhibition entitled simply *"L'Objet."* It consisted of everyday objects—pieces of furniture, lampstands, stoves, chairs, etc.— designed, and in some cases actually made, by painters and sculptors at the invitation of the Louvre authorities. It seemed strange that non-figurative artists, who were not interested in putting objects into their pictures, should have agreed to create objects. It is true that Georges Mathieu, in a letter included in the catalogue, gave a reason. He said that, for the first time in French history, there was no contemporary *style of living* in material things acceptable to the élite, and implied that such a style ought to be created. General de Gaulle did not live among Gaullist furniture, as Napoleon III had lived in a Second Empire setting, or Louis XV in Louis Quinze. The point was a valid one, but granted that industrial art might not constitute a style, it was difficult to imagine General de Gaulle living in a setting composed of the objects in the Louvre exhibition, which were for the most part feathery, spindly, twisted, oblique and non-functional. M. Mathey said that, to his surprise, they had turned out to be mainly baroque. I was impressed by their resemblance to accidental natural objects, such as flotsam and jetsam, bulbous fruits, stick-insects and sea-bed growths. Nothing was firm, simple, and neat, as in industrial design. There was frequent, ambiguous hesitation between animate and inanimate forms, and a definite preference for the weathered, damaged or unfinished work; for instance, the ornamental hangings of a four-poster bed were literally rags. Since 1962, of course, in both Europe and America, it has become quite a common sign of a certain type of avant-gardism to prefer the worn, the cluttered, and even the inconvenient in both dress and furnishings. This may be a naturistic reaction against the supposed soullessness of technological gadgets; certainly, these particular French objects showed a definite rejection of utilitarianism. But I suppose we shall never know whether the artists were spontaneously echoing the archaic, mystic element in Gaullism, or reacting against the authoritarianism of the bourgeois Gaullist state, or translating some other, more obscure, collective urge.

Another pointer was that M. Mathey had persuaded the writer, Francis Ponge, to compose an introduction to the catalogue. Ponge, then in his sixties, was enjoying a considerable vogue for the first time in his life, because Sartre had written an article on him and the younger generation of writers had become interested in his peculiar treatment of pebbles, insects, fruit and other non-human objects, which was thought —rather too hastily, perhaps—to predate a notable feature of the New Novel, especially as practised by Alain Robbe-Grillet: this was the apparently impersonal descriptions of pieces of string, lamp-posts, cardboard boxes and severely, indeed mathematically, objectified landscapes.

This tendency had also moved into the cinema with *L'Année dernière à Marienbad*, made by Alain Resnais and Robbe-Grillet, in which the characters have the petrified look of statues or figures on a chess-board, and a statue is treated almost as if it were more alive than the characters. *L'Année dernière à Marienbad* was responsible for the fact that several other film directors, who had no obvious connection either with the spirit of the New Novel or with the tradition of documentary film-making, began to let the camera dwell interminably on certain objects, such as the staircase wall in Bresson's *Pickpocket*, or on parts of the body considered as objects. This fashion was eventually to reach its climax in America, in Warhol's early films, where the camera was left running in front of a single object or a set of objects, such as floating balloons or a sleeping body. Meanwhile, in France, two Anglo-American films, *Goldfinger* and *My Fair Lady*, which might seem middle-brow or positively low-brow, were given a surprisingly enthusiastic, and even philosophical welcome, because they were thought to be full of awareness of the object, the first being a treatment of the Midas story, which is perhaps the most powerful myth about objectification, while the second is based on the Pygmalion myth of de-objectification (statue into woman); Eliza, *la femme-objet* (lower-class, uneducated, manipulatable), is worked upon until she becomes *la femme-sujet* and is faced with the problems that afflict subjects, but are unknown to objects.

The object also found its way into critical parlance. For a long time, Gaston Bachelard had been preparing the way by writing, although in a fairly traditional manner. about the symbolism of air, fire, earth and water and their importance as imaginative, pre-scientific categories. Continuing a similar line of enquiry, Roland Barthes and Jean-Pierre Richard produced stimulating studies of the psychological significance of the materialistic obsessions or concrete metaphors used by a number of writers. Barthes was one of the first critics to take an interest in Robbe-Grillet, and he praised him for inventing what he, Barthes, called *la littérature objectale*, that is a form of literature which makes a special use of objects. As for Richard's big doctorate thesis on *L'Univers imaginaire de Mallarmé*, it promised (my italics):

> . . . une psychanalyse des *matières* favorites de Mallarmé: glaces, feux, gazes, écrins, eaux limpides . . . On saisira à travers les pages de cet essai l'intention poetique des *objets fétiches* tels qu'éventail, miroir, danseuse,

lustre, grotte, diamant, foule ou papillon. . . .

(. . . a psycho-analysis of Mallarmé's favourite *material themes*: ice or looking-glasses, fire or brilliance, gauzes, jewel-boxes, limpid water . . . The present study will bring out the poetic intention of those *objects with a fetish quality*, such as fans, mirrors, ballet dancers, chandeliers, grottoes, diamonds, crowds or butterflies. . . .)

Actually, Richard included a good deal more than objects but his preoccupation with them was in keeping with the trend.

By 1968, the concept of the object was beginning to be referred back on to other artists of the past, so that the novelist, André Pieyre de Mandiargues was able to write in the English edition of *Réalités*:

People have come to realize that what is likeable about Ingres is what I may call the objective character of his art. The salient feature of modernism is the increasing attention devoted to objects. In poetry, as in films (Godard's for instance) and painting (pop art), the artist's gaze is fixed upon objects . . . Ingres reduces everything to the status of objects, even the women who appear in almost all his paintings. In this respect he reminds me of Robbe-Grillet and particularly of certain scenes in *La Maison de rendez-vous*, in which we find an obviously ambiguous treatment of woman-as-statue.

Even if one doubts the truth of these remarks as applied to Ingres and Godard, they at least offer additional evidence of the fact that the object was becoming a cliché. In ordinary conversation, people could be heard talking about *la civilisation de l'objet*, although this was often only a slightly nobler phrase for *la société de consommation*. In short, for ten years or more, *l'objet* has been, or was, a common theme, linking the plastic arts, poetry, the novel, the theatre in a number of its *avant-garde* aspects, the cinema, literary and artistic criticism and everyday conversational exchanges. By now, its frequency has declined and the craze is probably over, except for an occasional rejection of *la femme-objet* by the French supporters of the Women's Liberation Movement.

In England and America, if I am not mistaken, the term *object* has never enjoyed anything like the same popularity; its use has been restricted mainly to the plastic arts, and even in that field may to some extent be a borrowing from the French. It has also occurred a little in connection with the

Anglo-American manifestations of the Theatre of the Absurd, but there again the French influence has no doubt been very strong. When, a few years ago, the BBC organised a debate on "The Cult of the Object", most of the speakers referred only to the phenomenon as it existed in France. However, my impression is that the web of attitudes and emotions connected with the concentration on *l'objet* is not unknown in the English-speaking world, although it has not been given such vigorous expression here; with us it exists, as usual, in a more diffuse and less explicit form, except perhaps in dress, where England, for a while at least, seemed to take the lead in variegated dandyism or anti-dandyism; dress is, of course, object expressing the subjectivity both in its relationship to itself and to others. It follows that whatever one can say about the situation in France has some relevance for the Anglo-American world.

Two obvious preliminary points need to be made, to clear the ground. First, there is nothing new about the mere presence of objects of various kinds in literature, art and daily living. Since objects, either man-made or natural, have always existed, they have always figured largely in all cultures. They have been functional, like pots and pans; aesthetic, like pots and pans that are carefully shaped and adorned to be things of beauty; socially significant, like pots made of silver or gold, which are not simply functional or aesthetic but also convey the status of the users or the solemnity of the occasion; and, finally, symbolic or emblematic, like pots which express concepts of excellence or spiritual value, such as prize-cups, loving-cups, chalices, and the Holy Grail. There is no lack of any of these in French art or literature, from the Middle Ages to the end of the 19th century. It is true that during the neo-classical period, roughly from 1650 to 1800, their range was rather limited, because of the conventions of respectability and the emphasis on sublime abstraction, but they came into their own again at the Romantic period and during the subsequent Realist movement. All 19th-century French poetry is full of symbolic objects, from Lamartine's *Crucifix* or Vigny's *Bouteille à la mer* to Rimbaud's *Bateau Ivre* or Mallarmé's swan. The novels of Balzac and Zola are crammed with functional and socially significant objects, as well as large symbolic ones, such as the Château de Clochegourde in *Le Lys dans la Vallée* or the coal-mine in *Germinal*. The same can be said of natural objects; the 19th century is the great period of the pathetic fallacy, whether nature was thought to be in sympathy with man or hostile to him. Lamartine asks the lake and the rocks to preserve the memory of his love; Baudelaire, in some moods, sees nature as being full of mystic intimations or bracing anthropomorphic parallels, and in others laments its indifference; in the majority of cases, his objects—the sea, the forest, the decomposing carcase in *Une Charogne*—are treated traditionally; only in his most original poems, such as *Dans ma cervelle se promène* or *La mort des amants*, does he move on from Romanticism or Parnassianism to the truly modern mood.

In 20th-century culture, objects continue to have all the old characteristics and functions, at least in certain areas and when handled by certain artists; but in addition they have acquired some unprecedented attributes, and it is the latter that I am concerned with. To anticipate my main point in a phrase, they have become existential and phenomenological. For instance, a non-figurative painter is rejecting the object in the Balzacian social or symbolic sense, as being too obvious and external, but he is no doubt trying to turn his total canvas into an aesthetico-existential-phenomenological object.

Secondly, we have to leave out of consideration another kind of object that has become very popular everywhere since the turn of the century—the object as Freudian symbol. Hunting the symbol has long been an enjoyable and useful pastime, and there is hardly a writer of classical status who cannot be reinterpreted in terms of Freudian imagery. Occasionally, we find Freudian symbols mixed up with the specifically modern uses of the object; in his novel, *La Marge*, Pieyre de Mandiargues, whom I have just quoted as one of the object-obsessed, has an obtrusively phallic tower, which he describes in openly Freudian terms and links up with certain New Novel characteristics. However, through letting the reader see too easily that the tower is phallic, he nullifies its effectiveness and merely exemplifies a paradox of contemporary literature, which is that

Freudian symbols, once they are known about, cannot be used any more, except in remote and distorted ways. Consequently, I don't think the obsessive object has any direct link with the vulgarisation of Freudian notions in France.

The main immediate source is clearly Existentialism, as it has been popularised through Jean-Paul Sartre's literary works and his easier theoretical writings, with some help, perhaps, from Albert Camus and Simone de Beauvoir. Here, I think, we can distinguish at least two meanings of the term, although there may be connections between them. The first is represented by the most memorable instances of the object in Sartre, those that occur in his novel, *La Nausée*: the pebble, the door-handle, the narrator's hand, the tramcar-seat, the café-proprietor's braces, and the chestnut-tree root. All of these produce a feeling of nausea in the narrator, because his awareness of the absurdity of the world is concentrated on them at certain times. We are not told why these particular objects should carry the full weight of the Absurd rather than others, and their choice is presumably dictated to some extent by the accidents of Sartre's life or temperament. Logically, if creation is absurd from the point of view of contingent man, any object can be taken as representative of the incomprehensibility of the universe, and this is implied in *La Nausée*, if not actually stated. Everything outside Roquentin's consciousness is loaded with absurdity, beginning with the body in which that consciousness finds itself. I would suggest, incidentally, that Sartre's puritanical hatred of the flesh might be explained not as a last remnant of a religious taboo nor as an unhappy consequence of early training, but as intellectual exasperation at this fact that the body is an organic object, in relation to which the consciousness is, or seems to be, just as contingent as it is to the rest of the world. Sartre is a Cartesian, in that he believes in the duality of consciousness and body; but whereas Descartes, as far as we can tell, was able to accept the division quite cheerfully, Sartre is permanently scandalised by it, in much the same way as Samuel Beckett is. To relieve the weight of all that brute matter weighing on the consciousness (in his terms, all the *En-Soi* or Being-in-Itself pressing on the *Pour-Soi* or Being-for-

Oneself), he, like Beckett, thirsts to translate the universe into pure intellectual concepts or words, as the title and the contents of his autobiography, *Les Mots*, suggest; but the universe is linguistically inexhaustible, and in any case there is always a vertiginous gap between one sentence and the next. If the whole of creation outside the mind is *En-Soi*, that is object, as soon as language stops, consciousness, then reduced to its simplest and most immediate form, is no more than dumb or numb awareness of this state of affairs.

Consciousness, as numb awareness of the object, is a characteristic of a great deal of recent French writing and of some manifestations of modern art, both in France and elsewhere. It is a theme which recurs repeatedly in the writings of Paul Valéry, who died in 1945; and Valéry could be cited as a precursor of Sartre in this respect, although Sartre has never shown much interest in him. It is present in the first part of the early novel by Camus, *L'Etranger*, which shows the whole landscape of the world, rather than individual objects, as being opaque to the observing consciousness of the hero, although not always unhappily so, since Camus's temperament was capable of enjoyment in a way which seems impossible to Sartre's. This early part of *L'Etranger*—"the first fifty pages", as Robbe-Grillet has said—was an inspiration to some practitioners of the New Novel; no doubt they also stemmed directly from Sartre too, and they may even have discovered numbness for themselves. Whatever the mixture of causes, there is a large number of books by Robbe-Grillet, Michel Butor, Robert Pinget, Claude Ollier, Jean Ricardou, Jean-Pierre Faye, etc., in which a dominant feature is this tendency to present the world as incomprehensible, irreducible object or objects.

The same point might be made from a slightly different angle. To use Sartrian terms again, consciousness is an anguish, or at least a tragic or lyrical *malaise*, because of the impossibility of coincidence with being, *i.e.* the consciousness can never catch up with itself, as it were, because it is living from moment to moment in time. When one is looking at a real-life scene, for instance, the details are too numerous to be taken in at a glance; they are, in fact, philosophically infinite, and we have no *necessary* means of choosing which ones to concentrate on. At the same time, while we may get relief through translating the reality of the contemplated object—a chair, for instance—into language or art, any such rendering is unfaithful to its irreducible density as object. The use of line or paint or words is bound to betray it, by making it appear more comprehensible and so, in effect, humanising it. Ideally, the object should just be given as it is: a chair is a chair is a chair, as Gertrude Stein might have said. Of course, if strictly adhered to, this principle leads to the suicide of art, since the "artist" merely points to the chair, thus representing reality by itself. This paradox means that a lot of modern art, including perhaps the New Novel, tries, as it were, to contain its own suicide. The object becomes dense, nutty, obsessive and "significant", precisely because it resists meaning and is, in the deepest sense, non-significant.

What I have said so far might seem to suggest that the consciousness is passive and simply reflects or registers the absurdity of the world; but if we look at the second meaning of the word *objet* in Sartre, we see that this is not so. It is true that the pebble picked up by Roquentin, or the door-handle he happens to take hold of, are *given* objects, but Sartre's conception of the consciousness, which comes ultimately, I suppose, as much from Hegel as from Descartes, is dynamic. The object, though given, is perceived to be there, because the consciousness goes out to meet it, is thrown against it—*objectum*—in fact, creates the object by discovering that it is there, although the effect of the creation is, as I have said, that the object reacts on the consciousness to produce an impression of incomprehensibility. This view of the consciousness as a perpetually renewed outgoing act is fundamental not only to Sartre's conception of the relationship between the consciousness and the material world but also to his treatment of human relations. He sees each consciousness as being initially a subjectivity which tends to turn other subjectivities into objects, or to turn itself into an object—either to escape from the perpetual strain of being a genuine subjectivity and having to choose amongst non-necessary data, or to submit masochistically to other subjectivities.

If I have understood Sartre correctly, his hated social type, the bourgeois *salaud* or swine, is at once a subjectivity which is oppressing the proletariat by turning it into an object, and an object with regard to itself, because the bourgeois who is guilty of *mauvaise foi* accepts his bourgeois conventions as given objects and objectifies himself by means of them. His subjectivity then appreciates itself as object, through a mirror-like process. A further development of this idea is that the bourgeois strengthens the objectivisation of his subjectivity by surrounding himself with objects which confirm the patterns of his *mauvaise foi*. Hence the bronze statue of the bourgeois notability that Roquentin is so satirical about in *La Nausée*, and the picture gallery of civic worthies which he comments on at length, as if it were a kind of temple of bourgeois *mauvaise foi*, full of deplorable ikons. Hence also, I suppose, the Second Empire drawing-room which is the setting of *Huis Clos* and the statuette, *le bronze de Barbédienne*, on the mantelpiece, and the porter's joke about the toothbrush being the object most expressive of human dignity; the toothbrush is essentially a bourgeois object, perhaps because it represents the insistence on scientific, or pseudo-scientific, hygiene, the superstitious cleanliness by which a fundamentally secularised class replaces Godliness. (It occurs again, of course, with great effectiveness in Beckett's *Happy Days*.)

La femme-objet fits into this context, because, in a male-dominated society, woman is an object of the male subjectivity both in the act of copulation and in general social behaviour. Simone de Beauvoir complained, long before Germaine Greer, that woman is only too willing to accept her role as object. Woman, as it were, is doubly objectified within the already existing objectification of bourgeois *mauvaise foi*. So true is this that the smiles on the middle-class women's faces during the Sunday morning social parade at Bouville in *La Nausée* are a form of object that they put on or take off according to their husband's instructions (or rather that they cannot take off quite quickly enough and which remain congealed on their faces), whereas the lower-class women are not called upon to use what we might call *le sourire-objet*, since at their level they do not need to exchange these social signs. *Le sourire-objet* is just as much part of the bourgeois *civilisation de l'objet* as a mink coat or a diamond ring. The object has such automatic importance for the bourgeois woman, as we see in *Huis Clos*, that even when she is in Hell she cannot sit down on the sofa assigned to her, because its colour clashes with that of her dress; even in an extreme metaphysical situation she is still operating according to the social-cum-phenomenological conventions of colour-matching.*

I repeat that these two main forms of the object in Sartre seem to me to be different, although they may appear in the same context and be perceived almost in the same mood. The metaphysical-existential object is redolent of the absurd incomprehensibility of the world, and the social-phenomenological object symbolises conventions which, from Sartre's point of view, may also be absurd, but in a rather different sense.

It can happen, of course, that the same object has both a metaphysical and a social function; the statue that Roquentin sees simultaneously as a representation of a bourgeois *salaud* and as a piece of weather-beaten metal probably has the two functions, whereas the pebble and the door-handle are purely metaphysical. The social object is more ordinary than the absurd metaphysical one, and is really a more sophisticated form of the object in Balzac and Zola. This object belongs to the tradition of rationalistic discourse about man, whether Christian or humanist, and is used to confirm or illustrate what are basically political judgments.

Now the metaphysical object, such as the pebble or the door-handle, also depends on the reason, because the perception

* To comment again on Shaw's *Pygmalion* in the light of the object: Eliza is at first treated as an object by both her father and Higgins and then, paradoxically, through her training as an object, acquires the dignity of an educated subjectivity, only to discover that love is a struggle between two subjectivities. When, at the end, she fetches Higgins's slippers, she is presumably carrying objects to signify her own reobjectification.

Whether the original Pygmalion myth is about the relationship between men and women, I don't know. It may be a myth about pure creation, that is, a way of saying that the subjectivity can only appreciate itself in the object it creates and that it longs to be able to transfer its own life to that object.

of the Absurd is by definition a function of reason; but at the same time it is connected with the anti-rationalistic tradition in art and literature, which has been gathering force since the second half of the 19th century. Sartre himself, I think, would claim to be a rationalist, but he has borrowed certain things from the anti-rationalist current and, in return, has had some influence on it. I see the anti-rationalist tradition as running, say, from Rimbaud, with his *dérèglement systématique de tous les sens*, through Alfred Jarry, with his anti-rationalist doctrine of *la pataphysique* and his Id-like character *Ubu Roi*, to Raymond Roussel and the cult of chance, through the Surrealists and their successors in abstract art, pop art and the Beat and Hippie movements, to Artaud and the Theatre of Cruelty, the Theatre of the Absurd and, with some qualifications, to Gaston Bachelard and Francis Ponge. Most of these phenomena —including the Theatre of the Absurd, if we take it as beginning originally in the 1920s and 1930s with Artaud and Roger Vitrac—pre-date Sartre and obviously helped to prepare the atmosphere in which Existentialism was popularised. As far as I can discover, the term *l'objet* was not a catchword until Sartre became famous, but it was certainly used on occasions by the Surrealists, without the adjective "absurd" being attached to it. *"Choses"* was a common synonym and indeed is still used in this sense. Ponge called his early book, *Le Parti Pris des Choses* (first published in 1942, but containing texts written long before), and did not start using the word *objet* until later.

The Surrealists, in their heyday, were much more radical than Sartre in their revolt against traditional rationalistic humanism, because they proclaimed that reason itself was a bourgeois convention, and they tried to free themselves from it by various means, including automatic writing and the deliberate cultivation of frenzy, a procedure that had been recommended first by Baudelaire and then by Rimbaud. It is arguable that, in literature, they did not produce many works of great merit, but in art they certainly evolved a number of memorable absurd objects. Dali's picture of a watch slopping over the edge of a table like a fried egg, Juan Gris's cup-and-saucer made of fur or any of Magritte's compositions bring home to us forcibly that, in our commonsensical moods, we think in categories which we take to be universal and stable, but which the imagination can call into question or reject. A kindred fact, which has perhaps been driven home more completely now by the development of science than by Surrealism, is that the sensory apparatus with which we apprehend the world receives only a limited range of signals. The Surrealist pictures just referred to jolt us out of the commonsense view that we understand reality, or can apprehend more than a fraction of it, by deliberately confusing the organic and the inorganic, the human and the animal, the dream and the waking state. A metal and glass watch is changed into the consistency of rubbery flesh, and hygienic china is changed into fur, which we tend to think of as unhygienic.

A similar uncertainty may explain the cult of the found object, *l'objet trouvé*, which the imagination can work on indefinitely; for instance, bicycle handlebars can become the horns of a bull. The psychological implications of such changes can be developed in various ways; the essential point about them, as regards the Absurd and the object, is that they engender a feeling of insecurity about ordinary sense data. There may be something similar in Sartre's obsession with the viscous, which is half-way between solid and liquid and has an adhesive, organic quality. It will also be remembered that Roquentin is bothered by the café-proprietor's braces because they are neither one colour nor another. His excitement about the chestnut-tree root may be connected with the fact that a tree is an especially powerful object, and is used again and again in myth and literature, through being a static representation of dynamic growth. If there is any difference between the Surrealist object and Sartre's, it is probably that the Surrealists use theirs in the first place to create a social scandal, whereas Sartre's opens out much more clearly on to inhuman metaphysical nothingness or unknowingness.

The two main exponents of the Theatre of the Absurd, Ionesco and Beckett, form a neat structural contrast as regards their general attitudes towards universal object or *En-Soi*, at least in some of their most characteristic works. Ionesco shows an obsession with claustrophobic proliferation, whereas Beckett has a passion for emptying out, eliminating, or paring down. It may be that these are two basic possibilities. Either the *Pour-Soi* gives way to hysterical nausea, or it tries to establish a temporary, illusory authority over the *En-Soi* by means of language, that is, words are used to hold the *En-Soi* at bay by creating an impression of Non-Being.

In Ionesco's early plays, apart from *Les Chaises*, where the multiplying chairs are straightforwardly representative of the imaginary audience, the objects have a slightly Surrealist character. There is a bride with two noses; eggs, which even in their literal form are intriguing because they are at once mineral and organic and contain the dynamic mystery of generation, are used lavishly with reference to human breeding; in *Comment s'en débarrasser*, a corpse grows into a giant, a horrific imaginative conception which reverses life and death as simply as Dali and Juan Gris reverse the organic and the inorganic. But from *Rhinocéros* onwards, the objects seem to change into pure symbols and to become less interesting. The Rhinoceros itself is, of course, to some extent a ready-made Surrealist object. Although an animal, it has an absurd single or double horn, and a hard stone-like exterior as if it were inorganic. It is reminiscent in fact of a crab or a lobster, and these two crustaceans—similar to eggs in that they are flesh inside an apparently inorganic shell—also figure largely, we are told, in Sartre's nightmares; it is a commonplace that dragons and the supposed monsters of outer space should be given a similar organic/inorganic appearance. But as a symbol of totalitarianism, the rhinoceros is rather too vague to be quite satisfactory.* The play is most effective if we suppose that it is not so much about Nazism or Communism as about Ionesco/Béranger, the isolated consciousness, having a vision of all the other people in the world turning into incomprehensible, animated objects. If this is so, Béranger is very close to Roquentin, because he is reacting to the whole of the human world as Roquentin reacts

* Ionesco has said in an interview that he should have used a sheep, but he was probably just talking at random. A sheep would have conveyed no sense of menace.

to the inanimate world or to the self-objectified bourgeois. Even so, the rhinoceros is as much a symbol as an absurd object; by now Ionesco has reverted almost completely to symbolism, with the curious result that the later plays are more old-fashioned than the early ones. It is tempting to look upon the rhinoceros, the symbol of paranoiac horror, as a simple inversion of the blue-bird, the symbol of ideal happiness in Maeterlinck's *L'Oiseau Bleu*, once a world-famous play of the Symbolist Theatre.

As for Beckett, most of the relatively few objects he admits on to his almost empty stage are also symbolic in a traditional way, although he may display modernism by being deliberately ambiguous. In *Waiting for Godot*, the mysterious tree is polyvalent, perhaps gratuitously so, but the boots, the bowler-hats, the carrot, etc., come from the music-hall, no doubt by way of Charlie Chaplin. However, like all stage properties, they can be re-interpreted in terms of Existentialist psychology or phenomenology. The Chaplinesque boots and bowler have an immediate social significance as tragi-comic signs of alienation. They are ill-fitting, bourgeois cast-offs worn by the outsider, and therefore correspond to the wry acceptance of class differences and social injustice in the old music-hall; Chaplin, with his splayed feet, tilted hat and twisted, twirling cane was a broken-down version of Burlington Bertie. At the same time, footwear and headgear are material extensions of the human biped, *homo sapiens vestitus*, and, like all articles of dress, take the imprint of human experience or parody human nature, since they are *En-Soi* modified by the *Pour-Soi*. It is not necessary to be a foot- or shoe-fetishist to see that boots can be full of character (*cf.* Van Gogh's well-known painting)*, and that a bowler hat is a second, domed cranium, a solid and solemn casing for the *Pour-Soi*. Similarly, in *Happy Days*, Winnie's handbag contains the essential instruments for living, and enables her to execute her therapeutic daily routine. A woman's handbag allows her—in the admirably phenomenological

* Both Peggy Ashcroft and Dora Bryan have declared independently in television interviews that once they have hit on the right kind of shoes for a given character they feel they know how to play it.

French phrase—to *se donner une contenance*, *i.e.* a way of holding herself without embarrassment in the eyes of others and in her own; perhaps, *la femme-objet* needs to carry such narcissistic reassurance around with her in order to play her subordinate part with a semblance of dignity, or perhaps, more generally, all *Pour-Soi* needs some bit of *En-Soi* as a temporary resting-point: a security-blanket, a teddy-bear, a cigarette or a pipe, a glass to hold, a walking-stick or a steering-wheel.

Apart from this, Beckett seems to do all he can to emphasise the mind/body division in an ultra-Sartrian, neo-Cartesian way, by progressively crippling and maiming his characters, so that they are reduced to limbless hulks with talking heads. He puts them into wheel-chairs, dust-bins, and jars, buries Winnie up to the neck in sand and submerges the figures of *How It Is* in mud. Ionesco is paranoiac. His *Pour-Soi* is afraid of the threat from all other *Pour-Soi*, objectified into *En-Soi* and therefore lost to human discourse (although he detests Sartre, he obviously shares the feeling that *l'enfer, c'est les autres*, but—we could add—*les autres réifiés*). Beckett seems to hate the immediate *En-Soi* of the body even more than Sartre does. He wants to disguise it by merging it into the general object or matter of the universe, leaving only language as a live, intangible creature still functioning inside the almost inanimate carcase. Language becomes then pure essence of *Pour-Soi* surviving inside *En-Soi*, from which it is almost totally divorced. One could argue that this is a variety of romantic pessimism. For language to exist at all, there must, at some point, have been a profitable exchange between the "spirit" and its fleshy setting, and, in so far as Beckett is a born writer, he must be enjoying the resonance of language in his own body.

Bachelard and Ponge, perhaps because their attitudes were formed well before the development of Existentialism (Ponge is now over seventy, and Bachelard would have been ninety, had he still been alive), stand in sharp opposition to Sartre, Ionesco, and Beckett, in that their conception of the object is, on the whole, a happy one. Instead of expressing the permanent and anguished divorce between the consciousness and inanimate or animate nature, they wish on the contrary to celebrate a sort of marriage. Camus, too, as I have suggested, could sometimes take a cheerful, lyrical view of the object, especially in its extended form as sea and landscape, and indeed one of his early volumes of poetic prose is entitled *Noces* ("Nuptials"). It may be that the choice between feeling tragic or enthusiastic about the gap between the consciousness and the world is a temperamental accident. What some people see as an appalling abyss may be perceived by others as mystic depths, or the same person may switch from one approach to the other in different moods. Camus is a sort of dualist, since he establishes a polarity between *l'amour de la vie* and *le désespoir de la vie*, much as Baudelaire did between *l'extase de la vie* and *l'horreur de la vie*. Since the difference can exist independently of any overt manifestation of "good" or "evil" that would explain attraction or revulsion, the reasons for it are presumably hidden in the mysteries of micro-biology.

A rather different dualism is to be found in Bachelard. During the early part of his career, he was a philosopher and a historian of scientific ideas and, as he himself explains, he was suddenly converted to a conscious appreciation of the concrete, physical aspect of the universe, because science does not offer a stable home for the imagination. His thesis is, briefly, that no one can live his ordinary, everyday life according to the concepts of modern science, since these are infinitely complex, always provisional and, in any case, beyond the range of sensuous apprehension. We should then return, with a clear conscience, to pre-scientific categories, from which we cannot really free ourselves. We all feel inevitably that the sun rises and sets, that the four essential elements are earth, air, fire and water, that flame is an image of passion, and so on. This is the stuff of poetry and of satisfactory living, and always will be. Let us recognise the fact and "make the images happy". The way to do this is to accept them willingly as the subject-matter of our day-dreams, and to cultivate day-dreaming as a healthy exercise of the psyche.

In discussing the use of objects as centres of contemplation, Bachelard makes some charming suggestions. In *La Psychanalyse du Feu* he dwells at length on the importance of having an open fire—and, what is more, a wood-fire—in one's living-room; fire is an image of vitality and sexuality and therefore our eyes need to dwell on it when we are in a state of creative musing. In *La Poétique de L'Espace*, he stresses, in a Jungian way, the importance of having a house with both a cellar and an attic; the cellar corresponds to the dark, unconscious forces within us, while the attic is an image of elevation and spirituality, and we need to have this polarised reflection of our being in the area we occupy. Bachelard is undoubtedly right in asserting that we need to dream the world at the same time as we live in it; but he may be mistaken in insisting so definitely on his archaic, naturistic categories. Had he been born some fifty years later, he might well have evolved some poeticisation of central-heating as vertebrated fire and of the motor-car as a sleek, mobile shell. Also, in his very last works, he himself does not seem altogether satisfied with the gap between his scientific thought and his policy of day-dreaming. Perhaps he quoted so many minor poets because he, like they, was still in the aftermath of Symbolist dreaminess. One part of his mind is attuned to the treatment of nature or object in the manner of Einstein or Heisenberg; the other may not be so far removed from Maeterlinck.

Ponge is an equally cheerful but more astringent exponent of the object. He starts from a sense of wonderment. This is not simply the kind of awe that poets have always felt, but is tinged with the modern awareness of the Absurd that he seems to have discovered for himself. Because of the universality of the Absurd, he doesn't deal with traditional, dignified objects, or only comes upon them incidentally, as it were. He says that he had to write poems, because he wasn't intelligent enough to make intellectual statements. But I suspect he means by this that no one is intelligent enough to make such a statement, which would suppose that we were understanding or assimilating the Absurd. All one can do, when faced with a fragment of creation—a pebble or a wasp, say—is to react to it with words taken not as elements of an intellectual formulation but as verbal objects, almost as if they were the pigment or clay used by an artist. Ponge sees much more clearly than Sartre, and just as clearly as Valéry, that words themselves are given or acquired historical objects within the consciousness and not a direct emanation of it. They are semi-abstract objects, of course. Each word is an act which takes place in time and its use is an incomprehensible intellectual phenomenon. It is also a complex of sense-data, the uttering or hearing of which is a physical experience. We might translate this into Sartrian terms by saying that language is uniquely poised between the *Pour-Soi* and the *En-Soi* (*i.e.* is embodied, or objectified, spirit). Thus, words are poetic objects in themselves, and this is why Ponge, with characteristic paradoxicality, maintains that Littré's dictionary is one of the greatest works of literature in the language. It may be that, by deliberately turning his back on all intellectual structures, Ponge has condemned himself to write nothing but whimsical prose-poems; but he is enjoyable to read precisely because he takes the Absurd as a source of fun and a poetic challenge. Actually, he does sometimes make what amounts to an intellectual statement; the poem, I have already referred to, *L'Objet c'est la poétique* (the title is a quotation from Georges Braque) is really a manifesto in favour of the object:

> *L'homme est un drôle de corps, qui n'a pas son centre de gravité en lui-même.*
> *Notre âme est transitive. Il lui faut un objet, qui l'affecte, comme son complément direct, aussitôt.*
> *Ne serions-nous qu'un corps, sans doute serions-nous en équilibre avec la nature.*
> *Mais notre âme est du même côté que nous dans la balance.*
> *Lourde ou légère, je ne sais.*
> *Mémoire, imagination, affects immédiats, l'alourdissent; toutefois nous avons la parole (ou quelque autre moyen d'expression) : chaque mot que nous prononçons nous allège.*
> *Dans l'écriture il passe même de l'autre côté.*
> *Lourds ou légers donc je ne sais, nous avons besoin d'un contre-poids.*
> *Il nous faut donc choisir des objets véritables, objectant infiniment à nos désirs. . . .*

(Man is a queer creature, a body which doesn't contain its centre of gravity within itself.

Our soul is transitive. It needs an object to serve as its immediate and direct object.

Were we pure body, we should no doubt be in a state of equilibrium with nature.

But our soul is on the same side of the scales as we are.

Is it heavy or light? I am not sure.

Memory, imagination, immediate impressions weigh it down; however,
  we have speech (or some other means of expression): each word we
  utter makes us lighter.
If we *write,* it even moves to the other side of the scales.
Are we heavy or light? I am not sure, but we need a counter-weight.
We have, then, to choose real objects, which object indefinitely
  to our desires. . . .)

I end with a few remarks on the New Novel, because it
presents the most enigmatic treatment of the object, one which
I am not sure I understand and have never seen adequately
explained. I have already mentioned the fact that the New
Novel often conveys a numb awareness of the surface of the
world, which is close to the sensation of the Absurd; however,
this awareness is neither an anguish nor a lyrical experience.
Robbe-Grillet has said that if he knew why he described objects,
he would not want to describe them. He is the New Novelist
who has produced most theoretical writing on this subject, and
he is very emphatic in his rejection of the absurd as being a
form of the pathetic fallacy. He is particularly scathing about
Roquentin's meditation on the chestnut-tree root, which he
considers to be too self-indulgently dramatic. Material creation
is not absurd, it just is.

This leads Robbe-Grillet into a discussion of realism and
language in which, I think, he is patently mistaken. He seems
at times to imagine that a novelist can describe objects impartially, as they are *(Das Ding an sich?),* without imposing any
interpretation on them. When he made these claims, he may
have read the first fifty pages of *L'Etranger,* but he had obviously
not seen Camus's excellent analysis of the impossibility of
realism in the penultimate section of *L'Homme Révolté.* He was
also wrong about language, because he seems to have supposed,
in flat contradiction of his own practice, that language is a
neutral instrument by which reality can be grasped, that is, he
had not understood, like Ponge, that language is a concrete
intellectual/emotional entity.

But, of course, a writer may be quite mistaken in his theories
and effective in his practice. What are we to make of the india-
rubbers and the swing-bridge in *Les Gommes,* the women, the

loops of string, the sea-gulls in *Le Voyeur*, and so on? As Robbe-Grillet describes them, they do not seem to fit into any of the categories I have defined. They are not absurd metaphysical objects perceived with anguish, like Sartre's pebble; they are not similar objects perceived with lyrical excitement, like Ponge's pebble, in the poem of that name; they are not social objects in the ordinary sense, although the sumptuousness of the décor in *L'Année dernière à Marienbad* may operate as social object for some spectators; they are not neo-Surrealist horror-objects, nor Freudian symbols, nor symbols of any other kind, because Robbe-Grillet has specifically stated that he does not wish them to be considered as such. In connection with some of them, and particularly the beetle which is crushed on the wall in *La Jalousie*, he has accepted Eliot's term, "objective correlative", which was suggested to him by the Canadian critic, Bruce Morrissette.

The crushing of the beetle is not a symbol of sexual desire, but it is an action which is loaded with the significance of the sexual relationship between the adulterous couple. We might call the beetle and its crushing a referential object within the social group of three people: husband, wife and lover. This presents no problem and is, in fact, quite traditional. In Proust, the exotic flower, the cattleya, is used in exactly the same way as a referential object in connection with the love-affair between Swann and Odette. But most of the objects in Robbe-Grillet are not referential, or if they are, it is impossible for the reader to guess what they are referring to. They may not be gratuitous from Robbe-Grillet's point of view, since he may have some good personal reason to be obsessed with india-rubbers or swing-bridges or lamp-posts; but all the reader can be sure of is that, in each book, the objects are arranged to form a kind of labyrinth, which seems to be compulsively organised, as if the author were using them to work off some obsession that he was unable or unwilling to express explicitly. If this is so, and if the labyrinthine pattern is valid for a lot of readers, then the books are very original, because Robbe-Grillet is using language, and what is more, a form of the novel, to produce something like an abstract painting or a piece of abstract sculpture, that is, something which is aesthetically effective without being rationally articulate; the whole book becomes a genuine impenetrable object. But unfortunately, the pattern produces no effect on me, and so I cannot be sure of this; and no criticism that I have read has enlightened me.

However, in the case of some of the minor exponents of the New Novel, I suspect that the preoccupation with the object can be explained all too easily. The minute describing of the external world without the attribution of any meaning to it is an easy formula to imitate. I cannot see much more than this kind of facility in the works of Ollier or Ricardou, however neatly they may write. Sometimes, as in Pinget's *L'Inquisitoire*, I wonder if the New Novelist himself is not holding up the whole tendency to ridicule. One wonders what other reason there can be for the rather mischievous description of all the furniture in a country house which is contained in that novel; it is almost as if Pinget had decided to make an inventory of all the appurtenances to be found in the castle of *L'Année dernière à Marienbad*. They are all antiques, of course, and antiques are a special kind of object with ambiguous connotations; they are works of art or craftsmanship in their own right; they are social objects expressive of wealth and class tastes; they are also imaginative poetic objects allowing a flight from the prosaic present into the exotic past. However, if there is an intellectual point to this conducted tour of all the objects in the country house, it probably is that past civilisations leave behind them a sort of litter of humanly modified *En-Soi* in historic buildings and museums and that this litter is at once awe-inspiring, because it is tangible evidence of past endeavours to make sense of the universe, and blank, because in all cases the direct connection with the *Pour-Soi* which created it has evaporated. Objects continue to exist as silent witnesses to new forms of life with which they have nothing to do. Or, if this way of speaking about them personifies them too much, we can say that the police officer carrying out his interrogation is having a lot of *En-Soi* served up to him, since the *Pour-Soi* of both the creators and the temporary owners is completely beyond his grasp. The deafness of the servant under interrogation is symbolic of the inevitable deafness of any present trying to listen to the extinct voice of any past.

What it amounts to, then, is that during the last decade or so the term *"l'objet"*, through being used as a catchword, has developed such a range of overlapping meanings that, like "nature", it has come to signify almost anything that the consciousness cares to refer to, or to find repose in. The object can be part of the given world, or part of the man-created world. It can be animate or inanimate, concrete or abstract, or, like words, an intermediary phenomenon between the abstract and the concrete. It can be symbolic or non-significant, or significant in its non-significance. It can be aesthetic, or anti-aesthetic, disquieting or indifferent, hated or loved. In short, the subject has been able to re-phrase the whole gamut of his intellectual and emotional functioning in terms of the simple opposition between himself, in his purest form, and the object. Nothing strictly original may have been discovered, but the apprehension of the external and internal worlds has at least gone through a new and interesting phase.

3. Rousseau
and the Concept of Nature

Jean-Jacques Rousseau is the outstanding case of a modern European thinker who made the concept of nature one of his basic principles and a point of reference in all his works. He is still important, because the attitudes he expressed about nature continue to be prevalent today; they can be found in an extreme form in certain contemporary groups, and at the same time they are so interwoven with the general fabric of living that most people in the Western world are more or less Rousseau-istic, often without knowing that they are, or without even having read a word of his writings. There is nothing very surprising about this; most people are also to some extent Marxist or Freudian, without having read either Marx or Freud. The comparison with Marx and Freud is not an idle one, because Rousseau is a phenomenon of the same order. After he erupted on to the European intellectual scene in the middle of the 18th century, people almost everywhere began to imitate his assumptions, and although he was subject to a lot of criticism and some persecution, he remained a dominant influence on European sensibility for fifty or seventy-five years, and my impression is that he had a deeper effect, say, than either Voltaire or Goethe.

Yet it may well be, as some people have maintained, that there was nothing really original in his thought. His concept of nature was certainly not a brand-new invention. Something very like it can be found in many earlier writers and indeed—as I shall argue—can be traced back through the whole of Western culture to Ancient Greece. Moreover, it had begun to be prevalent in France during the early part of the 18th century, just before Rousseau emerged. Rousseau's peculiarity is that he gave it tremendous emotional force and applied it in startling ways over a very wide field, from art to education and from everyday living to political theory. The results were many and varied. People began to go for walks, to discover mountains and lakes, to listen to the nightingale, to breast-feed their babies instead of farming them out to wet nurses, to consider their children as children instead of defective adults, to have cottages in the country, to deplore pollution, although they didn't call it that, to collect folk-songs, to see their love-affairs as marriages in the sight of God, to doubt the reality of blue blood and to foment revolutions.

None of this naturistic philosophy, however, is quite as simple as it may at first appear. The history of Rousseauism is extremely complicated, for two main reasons, I think. In the first place, the concept of nature on which it is based is profoundly ambiguous; and in the second place Rousseau himself both believed in the concept of nature and didn't believe in it, and this helps to give his writings their characteristically passionate yet equivocal quality, which has been communicated to many of his followers.

Let me try to explain first what I mean by the ambiguity of the concept of nature. So far as I know, no one has yet written a complete semantic history of the word "nature", tracing it back through the modern languages to the Latin *natura*, which presumably came into use as a translation of the Greek *physis*. C. S. Lewis made a useful attempt in *Studies in Words*, but he did not go very far. However, if you look at some of the notable modern books on the idea or concept of nature, you will see that there has been a vast amount of philosophical and scientific discussion of the meaning of nature, with which Rousseau has little or no connection. For instance, his name is not even mentioned in one of the most interesting modern English studies, R. G. Collingwood's *The Idea of Nature*. This is because the majority of philosophers and scientists have been concerned with speculations about the *general* nature of the universe. Does it consist of one basic substance or of several? What is the relationship between the organic and the inorganic and, within the organic, between mind and matter? If God exists, is he co-extensive with nature or is he outside nature? If he doesn't exist, is nature finite or infinite, cyclical or evolutionary, teleological or random, and so on?

Rousseau is not much interested in this kind of speculation, because he is not primarily a philosopher or a scientist. It is true that, like many of his contemporaries, he dabbled to some extent in science as a young man, and all his life he was in the habit of botanising; but his botany, I suspect, was for the most part an emotional experience, a way of communing in detail with the natural landscape. He was, first and foremost, a moralist, or what we might nowadays call a moralising sociologist, and his characteristic feature is that he takes nature as a moral touchstone. Although he rejected Christianity, he remained a deist, and he saw nature as an expression of God's goodness. However bewildering the incidental complexities of his thought—and I must say, they are bewildering—he constantly reverts to the view that whatever is good is natural and that whatever is natural is good: evil is unnatural and is to be eliminated by a return to nature.

It is fair to say that this apparently simple principle is behind most of his major works. The early publication which brought him instant fame, the *Discours sur les Sciences et les Arts*, created a sensation precisely because, in the heyday of the Enlightenment, it upheld the paradoxical thesis that the arts and sciences had done more harm than good through corrupting the original purity of natural man. The *Discours sur l'Inégalité* sought to trace the growth of social differences as a consequence of the institution of property, which was seen as a departure from the natural state of non-ownership of land. *La Lettre sur les Spectacles* denounced the theatre as a sophisticated source of corruption and advocated its replacement by ceremonies more in keeping with a natural way of living. *Emile*, which is a treatise on education, tries to work out the natural principles according to which a child should be reared; how can he be made to experience things naturally, and thus grow up in such a way that his inherent nature is not distorted? The novel, *La Nouvelle Héloïse*, is a story about the clash between natural virtues and social conventions, and attempts to evolve a compromise between the two, and even to suggest a possible Utopia. The very last work,

Rêveries d'un Promeneur Solitaire, tells how the elderly Rousseau, to console himself for the buffetings he had received from society, retired to the bosom of nature and led a simple, frugal life, consisting of walks and communion with natural phenomena.

There are only two important books which don't follow this pattern. The *Contrat Social* begins as if it were going to use the argument from nature in order to define the proper functioning of society, but in fact proceeds to do something rather different. The *Confessions* makes frequent reference to nature, but doesn't develop any systematic use of it as a principle. And to my mind, it is no accident that these are the two books which have the richest content of thought, because they recognise—at least by implication—complexities in the moralistic idea of nature that the other works disregard or even conceal beneath layers of emotion.

The ambiguity of the idea of nature arises from the fact that, if the word means, as it must do fundamentally, everything which exists or has existed or will exist—*i.e.* if it is a single term to denote the totality of being—nature is not reducible to human rules of morality, because these rules are inevitably based on a choice *within* nature. For instance—to take an elementary example—if you are suffering from a cold, this is undoubtedly a natural phenomenon, although, from the human point of view, it is by and large thought of as a bad thing, that is as a manifestation of evil which one ought to try to cure. (Rousseau, incidentally, disapproved of doctors and counted on nature to cure itself.) I suspect that most people are tempted to say to themselves: I wouldn't catch so many colds if I got more fresh air, if I led a more hygienic life, that is, if I behaved more naturally, and they equate natural living with health, and may even feel guilty at their lack of health. Some naturists, of course, introduce a reassuring variation by saying that a cold is nature's way of periodically ridding the body of its toxins, but this simply moves the problem one step back, because you then have to explain how, if nature is good and you have tried to respect it, the toxins got into your body. But in either case, the question is being looked at from the human angle.

Obviously, from the point of view of the cold virus or the toxins, the iller the human being is the better. An epidemic is a golden age in the history of a microbe. And God, if he exists and loves his creation, must love microbes as much as he loves men, since there is no evidence that he has a hierarchy of preferences.

The same remark may be extended from the common cold to any manifestation of what we may be tempted to call evil. If we take the example of social inequality—and it is very relevant, since Rousseau's main historical importance, perhaps, was that he was understood to be proclaiming the principle of natural equality—it is clear that inequality is at least as natural as equality, and certainly more frequent. Practically all known societies have had what the students of animal behaviour call a pecking order, but the difference between animals and humans is that in human societies the pecking order can, and does, pass from one generation to another, and in the process develops ramifications and complexities that are unknown in the animal kingdom. Rousseau happened to live during the last phase of the *Ancien Régime*, when inequality had reached an extraordinary pitch, so that society was largely based on what one might call the *natural* fiction of the colour of the blood —superior blue or ordinary red. But this fiction had developed in Europe by perfectly comprehensible stages from feudal times onwards, and since the production of fictions is a natural characteristic of man as contrasted with the other animals, one can consider the belief in aristocracy as a natural consequence of a certain historical evolution. Nature itself produces those things which some people condemn as being unnatural.

In short, everything is in nature. It is by definition impossible for creation to be unnatural. When the Incas of South America turned human sacrifice into an everyday institution, this was natural. When the Nazis tried to liquidate the Jews, this again was natural. It was a specialisation of a certain human tendency and couldn't be other than natural.

There can be little doubt, then, that Rousseau was intellectually mistaken in assuming, as he so often did, that one has only to remain faithful to nature to be in the right, and that any occurrence of evil must be a betrayal of nature. But in

E

making the mistake, he was far from being alone. As I suggested earlier, this partial definition of nature had been present in the European atmosphere for a long time, before he seized upon it and gave it such powerful expression, and it is interesting to see how his great French contemporaries also juggled with it.

Diderot, for instance, played about with it quite a lot and even boosted the idea of the noble savage; but he also recognised the amorality of nature and, in his most characteristic works, expressed a kind of tragic view of the mystery of the cosmic process, which is close to the agnosticism of some contemporary scientists. Voltaire, on the other hand, was a great believer in the virtues of civilisation and he made fun of Rousseau, saying that Jean-Jacques wanted people to crawl on all fours and eat acorns; but Voltaire too was caught in a contradiction. He always professed to be a deist, but he never managed to reconcile the necessary goodness of God according to deism with the manifest imperfections of God's universe; and this is the dilemma behind his masterpiece, *Candide*, which gives him a similarity to the modern exponents of the Absurd.

Then, in the generation following Rousseau, there occurred a fascinating juxtaposition of opposite views, which is a perfect illustration of the ambiguity of the concept of nature. Bernardin de Saint-Pierre, the author of *Paul et Virginie* and *Les Harmonies de la Nature*, and the Marquis de Sade, whom the 20th century has canonised as a genius, were exact contemporaries; they were born within three years of each other and died in the same year. Bernardin was a friend and a disciple of Rousseau, whereas the Marquis never met him but had obviously read his works and showed how his arguments could be turned upside down. Bernardin puts forward the most naïve views about the beauty and moral perfection of nature. He has remained famous in France, not only as the author of the pastoral tale *Paul et Virginie*, but as the person who declared that melons are easy to cut up into portions, because they were obviously meant to be eaten *en famille*. This is what we might call the white view of nature. The Marquis de Sade takes the black view, but it must be admitted that he does so very gleefully. He argues that since nature, and particularly organic nature, *i.e.* life, consists of temporary arrangements of matter condemned to an endless process of cannibalism—this is a premonition of Tennyson's "nature red in tooth and claw"— any individual has the right to do what he likes provided he can get away with it. A homicidal maniac is expressing his nature by indulging in the ecstasy of murder, and in any case by killing his victim he is helping nature to proceed to a new arrangement of the matter of which the victim was composed, and is thus identifying with the natural process. It is rather significant, I think, that historically Sadism should have been a subsidiary and inverted or specialised development of Rousseauism. This helps to explain the apparent paradox, very noticeable during the Revolution and common again today, of the link between pastoralism and violence. The Charles Manson/Sharon Tate murders, for instance, seem to have both a Rousseauistic and a Sadistic aspect, as indeed has the whole hippie movement.

Since I have just used the word pastoralism, this is no doubt an appropriate point at which to explain where I think the moralising view of nature really originated, and how Rousseau came to voice it so strongly.

As I have already emphasised, the idea that we should return to nature, because nature is good, is not at all a recent invention. Strangely enough, it goes back at least to the ancient Greek civilisation of Sicily, since Theocritus, who flourished 300 years before Christ, is generally considered to be the inventor of the pastoral genre in literature, and there are grounds for thinking that the pastoral was more responsible for the spreading of naturistic ideas than the philosophical revival of the Renaissance. The pastoral is a commonplace in Latin literature and it runs right through European litera- ture up to the 19th century. All through the Middle Ages, the pastoral was strongly reinforced by the fact that the imagery in the Bible—particularly in the New Testament—is entirely pastoral, as it was bound to be, since it emerged from a pastoral culture. We have the parable of the Good Shepherd, which is a very important image, and the story of the Prodigal Son, who returns to his pastoral setting after a period of riotous living, presumably in the urban centres of the far country.*

The interesting problem from our point of view can, I think, be formulated as follows. Why did people who were living what seems to us to have been a very pastoral life, nevertheless invent an ideal of the pastoral? It is easy enough to understand that European town-dwellers should have had a longing for the country from the 19th century onwards, after the Industrial Revolution was well under way, but why should poets have been nostalgic about it in Ancient Greece or Medieval Europe? The answer must be that even in those remote periods, civilised individuals who spent some of their time at least in towns, felt that they had lost contact with the original truth of nature, and so *imagined* a state of natural harmony centring on the shepherd. However, it is difficult to believe that they didn't realise that they were indulging in a myth comparable to the conceptions of the Golden Age or the Garden of Eden. Anyone who has had any dealings with sheep knows that lambs are charming but that the grown animals are very dull, and offer little or no basis for communion between man and beast. The shepherd is usually closer to his dog than he is to his sheep. In any case, the whole pastoral concept, and even the parable of the Good Shepherd, is riddled with hypocrisy. The shepherd looks after the flock and protects his charges from other predators in order to prey upon them himself. The destiny of a sheep is to be eaten, but this is not often mentioned in pastoral works, where the animals are usually a woolly decoration on the landscape. A farm is not a symbol of the harmony of nature; it is organised exploitation by man of the animal and vegetable kingdoms. The Golden Age, whether in the past or the future, when the lion lay down, or will lie down, with the lamb, could

* Incidentally, the sexual connotations of the pastoral show curious fluctuations, which would be worth exploring.

In the Ancient non-Jewish world, the pastoral is almost entirely male homosexual. In the Middle Ages, it becomes heterosexual and links up with courtly love, which is an important element in Rousseau's make-up, since he absorbed it through *L'Astrée* and other neo-courtly works. In the modern world, the pastoral is homosexual again in André Gide, and heterosexual (but with a strong homosexual undercurrent) in D. H. Lawrence, and largely bisexual, I understand, in the hippie movement.

only exist in Never-Never Land; nature demands that the lion eat the lamb and so on. In short, the whole pastoral idea is an attempt to re-think creation, leaving out evil. It is an attempt to see human beings as fitting perfectly into their natural background, as if, at some point in the past, there had been a stable and totally happy condition of mankind, from which we had departed through some accident or mistake.

In the Old Testament, of course, this mistake is called the Fall, and it is a consequence, rather surprisingly, of eating that hygienic natural fruit, the apple. To paraphrase the prophylactic saying: "An apple on one day brought the devil to stay." But the apple is from the tree of knowledge and the meaning obviously is that knowledge, or mental activity, is the corrupting force which destroys the purity of nature. Rousseau is echoing this point of view in his famous statement: "The man who meditates is a depraved animal." And, of course, traditional Catholic theology condemned intellectual speculation and what was called the *libido sciendi*, the desire for knowledge, which were contrasted with the innocent ignorance of faith. However, Christianity has always been in two minds about nature. There is the optimistic current of opinion, according to which creation, being God's handiwork, is bound to be good. Nature is all things bright and beautiful, and the only fly in the ointment is the principle of original sin, inherent in the individual man since the Fall. Only man is vile. Then there is the much more sombre current which sees the whole of nature as being shot through with wickedness and as a constant distracting temptation for man, whose attention should be centred not on this world but the next.

Now Rousseau, in so far as he is indebted to the Christian tradition, belongs more to the first current than to the second (although he was born in Calvinist Geneva and therefore shows some traces of the second) and he reinforces this optimistic current—as other people have done—by frequent cross-references to the Bible and to the pagan pastoral tradition which, as I have said, is an attempt to imagine nature with the principle of evil removed from it. Rousseau doesn't really remove the principle of evil, although at times he may appear to be doing so. The truth of the matter is, I think, that he *displaces* the principle of evil. For him, original sin is not in the individual but in society. As long as man lived alone or in very small family groups disseminated throughout external nature, he could be virtuous. As soon as he formed larger communities in towns or cities, things began to go wrong, and society compounded the mistakes by passing them on from generation to generation, until we have all the manifest inequalities, cruelties and inconveniences of the modern world, which is so far removed from the primitive beauty of nature.

This, I think, is the sense of the two celebrated opening sentences, one from *Emile*: "Everything is good as it comes from the hands of the Author of all things: everything degenerates in the hands of man", and the other from the *Contrat Social*: "Man is born free and he is everywhere in chains." The point is reiterated in various forms all through Rousseau's works, and it is extremely important historically because it proclaims the inherent innocence and goodness of the individual, while making the community responsible for evil. In other words, Rousseau was one of the first people *to blame the system*, and he did so most eloquently. What makes him such a representative modern figure is that his paranoiac obsession with the evil effects of the system caused him to express the whole emotional range of alienation, long before the term alienation itself was invented, and indeed nearly a hundred years before Marx. And Rousseau's alienation is, of course, of the most fundamental kind. It is not simply the alienation of certain groups of individuals within society for economic reasons, as in certain forms of political thought. It is the alienation of all individuals from the supposed goodness of nature, in fact from the Garden of Eden or Paradise on earth; and when the Living Theatre, for instance, proclaims the desire to return to Paradise Now, it is being, amongst other things, very Rousseauistic.

It is not difficult to suggest reasons why the sense of alienation should have been so strong in Rousseau, since he has left us an account of his career in his masterpiece, the *Confessions*. His mother died in giving birth to him, so that he was an orphan or half an orphan from the start. He was brought up in the first instance by a feckless, unreliable father, who was not respectable enough to survive within the strict society of Geneva. After the father's disappearance, he was handed over to foster-parents, and then apprenticed to a rather heartless master-craftsman. He ran away from Geneva at the age of fifteen, and from then on until his death he was an exile, a wandering, picaresque figure, a foreigner everywhere, even in his native Switzerland when he returned to it for a short time in later life. He never knew a stable, family background nor received any continuous, formal education. Nor did he ever manage to earn a living in any consistent way. In spite of his phenomenal success as a writer, during most of his career he was a parasite existing on the charity of the privileged people whose social position he theoretically contested, but with whom he felt a snobbish affinity. In addition to all this, he was a chronic invalid, afflicted with a urinary disability that could only increase his social uneasiness and suspiciousness. He never enjoyed a satisfactory love affair nor achieved sexual fulfilment, although he claims to have fathered five children. He was not homo-sexual, like so many modern alienated figures, but he had sexual peculiarities which he explains at length, and he admits that he always tended to fall back into masturbatory isolation. Given all these factors, it is hardly surprising that his mind should have dwelt so passionately on the natural ideal, which had the advantage of offering a single remedy for all his ills. It was a unitary solution and a marvellously adaptable one, since the term "nature" can undergo various changes of meaning to suit the purposes of any argument.

However, I said at the beginning that Rousseau himself doesn't always appear to believe fully in the validity of nature. It is certainly the case that he seems to shift his ground from book to book, or from chapter to chapter or even from page to page. To put it bluntly, his thought is a mass of contradictions. Sometimes he gives the impression of wanting to go back to a simple, countrified existence, a kind of subsistence economy which would be as near as possible to the primitivism of certain savage tribes; this is more or less the concept of the hippie commune. On other occasions, he appears to be taking as his ideal some small republican city state, which is a mixture of Geneva, Sparta, and Rome. Curiously enough, he tends to make this city state disciplined, heroic and warlike, as if the ability to be disciplined and to fight well were admirable attributes of natural man. And then again, in *La Nouvelle Héloïse* or in certain parts of the *Contrat Social*, he falls back on to the concept of a hierarchical, paternalistic society, in which a single individual or a small élite have a correct understanding of nature, which they impose upon the less gifted majority: that is, he returns to the notion of inequality after having vigorously denounced it. It is because of these fluctuations that he has been interpreted in so many different ways: as one of the founders of European socialism, as an originator of the French Revolution, as being responsible for the Reign of Terror and as an embryonic Fascist.

It is tempting to poke fun at him, because of the complexities that the idea of nature involves him in. For instance, in *Emile*, the private tutor who is organising the young hero's education in such a way as always to present him with natural situations on which his brain will work naturally so that he draws the natural conclusions, has recourse to the most artificial devices. On one occasion, he schools an entire village in an elaborate deception for the greater good of Emile. It doesn't seem to cross Rousseau's mind that he is making nature depend upon a very complicated *mise en scène*. Also, probably because he was living under the *Ancien Régime*, he assumes that peasants can be commandeered for the benefit of an upper-class boy. In other words, his belief in equality co-exists quite happily with an assumption of inequality. In *Emile*, he dismisses wine on the ground that it is a product of civilisation; in *La Nouvelle Héloïse*, he admits it into his Utopia, gives a poetic description of the grape harvest and praises his heroine, Julie, for her ability to imitate certain famous vintages in her wine-making. The reason is that Rousseau himself happened to be fond of wine, and in the last resort couldn't bring himself to exclude it from Paradise. (It is interesting to compare this attitude with that of some modern pastoralists who reject, or criticise, alcohol, and yet accept marijuana. Marijuana, of course, is given the perfectly pastoral name of "grass", so that the shepherd consumes the same fundamental substance as the sheep, but in a gaseous and therefore spiritual form, rather than in a material form.)

A still more comic instance of confusion in *La Nouvelle Héloïse* is the episode of the second boat-trip on the lake when the oarsmen catch fish presumably to make a meal for the party. Julie, the heroine, is distressed at the fact that the beautiful creatures of the lake are going to be devoured by men, so she has all the fish thrown back except one. But if you are going to eat one fish, you may as well eat several, because the principle of respect for other living creatures has been broken. In any case, fish to some extent eat each other, just as animals do, so that a human vegetarian is being more squeamish than nature is in general. I personally sympathise with Julie's attitude. I have a spontaneous, *i.e.* a "natural" preference for vegetarianism. But at the same time I find I have to eat fish, eggs and meat to get along, and I can even enjoy them if I manage to shut off part of my mind while I am consuming them. Clearly, on the question of vegetarianism, as on so much else, nature offers us no clear guidance; it is divided against itself.

Nevertheless, after smiling at Rousseau or after becoming irritated with him because of his contradictions, I think we have to admit that he has the great merit of illuminating the difficulties of a problem with which we are still very much involved. He was reacting as best he could against what seemed to him to be the defects of the society of his day, and he used the concept of nature because it was in the air and because it was convenient and probably because he enjoyed believing in it as far as he could. I think we would all like to believe in nature, because if we could do so, this would mean that God was in his heaven and all was right with the world. But there are two senses at least in which nature is not at all reassuring from the human point of view, and Rousseau both sees this and doesn't see it.

The first sense has to do with the operations of the natural universe. Rousseau quarrelled with Voltaire ostensibly about the Lisbon earthquake. Voltaire couldn't understand why, if

God exists and is good, catastrophes like the Lisbon earthquake could occur. Rousseau obstinately refused to see the point, and yet in *La Nouvelle Héloïse* he makes Julie die before her time as a result of a natural accident. The issue of natural accidents goes back at least as far as the Book of Job, but it has certainly been clarified by the modern exponents of the Absurd. The problem is that external nature, *i.e.* everything from cosmic phenomena to the functioning of the human body, is governed by a system of cause and effect which operates with total disregard for human emotions. The rain falls on the just and the unjust, hurricanes slaughter hundreds or thousands of people, plagues come and go, etc. All these acts of God, as they are revealingly called in English legal parlance, are incomprehensible. Science can show that they are physically necessary, that, in a certain sense, they constitute an order, but, from the human point of view, they are a sign of a disorder, of a permanent discrepancy between the human consciousness and the universe, and awareness of this discrepancy is the sensation of contingency or of the Absurd. As far as the human mind can see, the so-called economy of nature is very imperfect. For instance, whole species were wiped out by nature itself, long before man began the process of pollution. Now Rousseau will admit this alien, incomprehensible quality of nature only indirectly and infrequently, except in the *Confessions*, where he shows an extraordinary ability to define in detail all those accidents of nature which go to make up a human destiny, his own. I think that if he hadn't rounded off his stimulating but defective theorising by writing this literary masterpiece, he would have seemed a much less impressive genius to us now.

The second sense has to do with the difference between animal and human nature. Although science tells us that the animal species have evolved over the ages, the time-scale involved is so great that we can, to all intents and purposes, think of animals as being physically and psychologically static, and we can conceive of an ideal natural state for each animal, provided we accept the general rule that animals prey on each other. One could define the perfect life for the lion, the tiger, the antelope, etc., in the economy of the jungle, because that life is what it is and need not be subject to change, except in so far as the whole universe is involved in a slow process of alteration. But it is impossible to define the perfect human life, because man is the one animal with an unstable nature, on both the physical and psychological levels. The reason why Rousseau suggests several different versions of the ideal existence is that we have no means of knowing at which point, if any, in human development it would have been appropriate for man to stop.

We don't know, for instance, if the natural unit is the family, the tribe, the city-state, the nation, or the world community, or a structure including all of them, although historically they have often been incompatible. Would we have been better off without the invention of fire and the wheel? Should we have remained naked and stayed within the tropical zones? Above all, was the creation of language man's greatest achievement, or the fatal step which led to his progressive corruption? To put it in current anthropological terms, how do we distinguish between nature and culture, when the ability to produce culture has always been a special feature of man's nature?

The mere asking of the question is a sign of the immense gap between man and the natural purity of the animals. To think and to express thoughts, however naturistic they may be, is itself a cultural activity. I think it was Goering who said, when he was trying to emphasise the primitive directness of Nazi emotions: "Whenever I hear the word culture, I reach for my revolver", but this is a profoundly unphilosophical statement, because a revolver is a highly sophisticated cultural object, and just as artificial, in fact, as the elaborate rhetoric with which Rousseau attacks the accumulated achievements of society.

What Rousseau helps us to see, then, through becoming entangled in such a web of contradictory ideas, is the impossibility of founding a system of thought on any stable concept of nature, if you are dealing with human behaviour. Man is by definition the unique cultural animal, and he can only correct the mistakes of culture by more culture, not by less. Rousseau himself was obviously adding to culture, at the same time as he was trying to subtract from it. He is wrong to blame society while exonerating the individual, because nothing can occur in society that does not first occur in an individual. But he helped to demonstrate the principle of error inherent in culture. Precisely because man is gifted with an inventiveness which allows him much greater autonomy within external nature than is possible for the animals, he is capable of suicidal blunders as well as of beneficial discoveries. These blunders and discoveries are cumulative from generation to generation and, what is more—this is an aspect of the Absurd—their effects are sometimes interchangeable: a blunder may eventually prove to have been a good thing, just as a positive discovery may produce negative results at two or three removes.

It is the case, I think, that each successive generation, as it awakens to consciousness, gets a fresh view of the advantages and anomalies of the society it is living in, and so can educate its elders—*i.e.* it gets a glimpse of another possible arrangement, which it may tend to think of as "nature". But it is also the case that there is always a reason why things came to be what they are. And while it is important to take practical decisions, whether one is advocating the new or explaining the old, it should be recognised that there can be no dogmatic truth. The one thing we can be dogmatic about is that there is no dogma. In studying the rather ramshackle way in which we move from the past to the present and from the present to the future, I can see no proof that anything in particular was bound to happen or not to happen. All deterministic theories are vitiated by the inbuilt unpredictability of the human animal, just as all grandiose assertions about the ultimate aims of human life— in the manner of Bergson, or Teilhard de Chardin, or any of the religions—can never be anything more than projections either of wish-fulfilment or fear. On the one hand, human nature is not determined in the same way as animal nature is, or if it is, the determinism is so complex that it amounts to a kind of freedom; on the other hand, it is logically impossible for man, who is a creature inside nature, to understand the overall purpose of nature, if there is one. The part cannot understand the whole, and when it invents so-called revelations, these reveal nothing intelligible about the ultimate purpose, although they may throw a great deal of light on the multiple possibilities of human nature within the framework of general nature.

My conclusion must be then, that in so far as Rousseau preached a return to nature, he was wrong. The metaphor doesn't really make sense, because man cannot stray away from nature; he can only develop certain of his natural potentialities at the expense of others, and the pattern or mixture of developed potentialities may vary from individual to individual, society to society and period to period. But in saying this, I am by no means preaching a quietist acceptance of the relativism of all things. On the contrary, I think it is up to all of us to decide as best we can which potentialities we can approve of and which we must reject, so that the perpetual instability of human nature may be made as fruitful as possible. And in spite of the weaknesses of his theoretical terminology, Rousseau made a genuine, if rather muddled, contribution to this task.

4. In and Out:
Ruminations on Fashion

During the last few years, I have found the word "fashion" occurring to me again and again as I have been trying to puzzle out the problems I meet with in my professional life, or to understand what I have seen going on around me.

My job is to talk to students about French literature, and the history of the subject, like the history of any other national literature, can be seen as a series of fashions, with the difference, perhaps, that the changes are rather more marked in France than in some other countries and are expounded, defended or attacked there with greater vehemence. At some periods, "nature" is in and "artificiality" is out. All the manuals tell us, for instance, that aristocratic ladies of the 18th century began breast-feeding their babies because they had read Rousseau's *Emile*, which purports to be a treatise on the "natural" upbringing of children. At other times, "nature" is despised and "artificiality" is put forward as the supreme human conquest. Only a century after Rousseau, Huysmans created a highly influential character called Des Esseintes, a bachelor who would have looked upon breast-feeding as revoltingly crude and who shut himself up in sealed rooms to lead a deliberately imaginative life with the help of drugs, perfumes and other stimuli. The pages in which he announces that he is turning his back on "nature" correspond exactly, but in reverse, to those in which Rousseau sings his hymn of praise to "nature".*

* For the moment, I am neglecting the fact that the differences are, to some extent, illusory. Rousseau's *Emile* is no less artificial a production than Huysmans' *A Rebours*. Indeed, it could be argued that the anti-natural artificiality of the latter is a direct outcome of the pseudo-natural artificiality of the former; primitivism may be highly sophisticated and sophistication within a hair's breadth of primitivism. Yet there is a clear contrast

There are many other simple contrasts. Sometimes, sub-jectivism is damned. Pascal's dictum, *le moi est haïssable*, is often quoted as defining one of the ideals of French neo-classicism of the 17th century and, certainly, there is a straining after impersonalism in certain aspects of the literature of the period (although Pascal himself, of course, remains famous as a highly subjective, and even anti-classical figure). With the Romantics the first person singular became current again, so that Stendhal, in the early 19th century, could allow himself to call a book *Souvenirs d'Egotisme* and, towards the end of the century, Barrès could entitle a trilogy *Le Culte du Moi*. Similarly, the social responsibility of the writer may appear an urgent issue to one generation and of slight importance to the next. Com-mitment was the vogue in Paris some fifteen years ago, but today the doctrine seems as old-fashioned as the "New Look". Or preciosity may hold sway for a time and then be succeeded by a return to plain-spokenness; or rules may be faithfully respected for years as being a valuable guide to composition, and then suddenly rejected as an intolerable limitation. Even the lives and deaths of writers seem subject, to some extent, to fashion. The French writers of the 19th century were remark-ably prone to syphilis, although promiscuity was just as preva-lent among those of the 18th; those of the 20th century show a preference for homosexuality, drunkenness, and car-accidents.

What is true of French literature is also true of all other social phenomena one cares to investigate, as well as of the obvious events of everyday life. Any adult must be aware of having lived through many fashions in dress, speech, dancing, education, ways of thinking, and so on. We apply the term "fashion-conscious" mainly to women, and more particularly to young women who are sensitive to the latest shift in the hem-line and conform to it. Actually, they may not be conscious of fashion as fashion at all, but may sincerely look upon it as a per-petually renewed form of revealed truth. The fashion-conscious are, strictly speaking, those dress-designers who are always

---

between Rousseau and Huysmans, just as the bikini looks different from the crinoline, although both forms of adornment are "artificial" and are interlinked in that they represent opposite swings of the pendulum.

sniffing the air to discover what is likely to catch on next, or the business men who are arranging planned obsolescence, or the politicians who sense that the time has come to make such and such a change, or the artists in any field who develop new styles or, more simply, those many individuals who, with age, become disillusioned about obvious fashions and, through inertia, remain faithful to the last fashion they happened to adopt. Queen Mary's toques were appropriately regal, but do we know that she stuck to them for that reason? She may have seen through fashion, become bored with it and decided to keep pre-1914 costume as a convenient, permanent uniform, since, in any case, it is difficult for a queen to know how far exactly she should be ahead of, or behind, the fashion. Or again, of course, she may have assumed, as many people do who never grasp the concept of fashion, that the fashions which were current in her prime were "truer" than any which occurred later.

Design in dress, it may be said, like design in external furnishings or changes of style in pop songs or dance steps, is a superficial affair, however subtle the psychologists may wax about it. Shifts of mood in literature, or the replacement of one philosophical assumption by another in the general consciousness, are more serious matters, like developments in political organisation or religious conviction. And it will be added that the term "fashion" applied to them is derogatory. If we are to treat them as they deserve, we should put each back into its context and explain it according to the methods by which history normally proceeds.

But this attitude itself, I should say, is a result of an obsolescent fashion—the belief in a hierarchy of seriousness in subjects. I agree with the psychologists that there are no non-serious subjects, only non-serious ways of dealing with them. The disappearance of the bustle can be put on the same level as the rise of the Labour Party, and indeed there might well be some connection between them, if one were learned and perceptive enough to see it. The pejorative flavour of "fashion" is to be explained by the use of the word in connection with subjects that are not only thought to be frivolous but also considered so shallow that the ordinary rules of cause and effect hardly apply to them. In fact, "fashion" is almost equivalent to "chance", with the difference that the latter is a short-hand way of referring to the impact of unknown causes, whereas the former is applied to instances in which the causes are thought to be of little importance and, indeed, to be practically non-existent. "It's only a fashion", people say; that is, "It has no serious causes behind it and will not last." I should prefer to reverse the tendency and say, not only that all fashions are motivated, although we may often be unable to see the motivation, but that probably all human group phenomena are, in a sense, fashions. Some last a few weeks, some a few years, some a generation or more, some for centuries.

If we stand far enough back, we can see a whole civilisation as a large fashion, containing a fluctuating mass of smaller fashions, fitting one within another like Chinese boxes. The worship of Amon-Ra was a fashion which lasted, with variations, for some three thousand years. Christianity has now endured, with variations, for over two thousand years, but a thousand years hence it may appear to have been a fashion. Nationalism, the Western concept of romantic love, Chinese ancestor-worship, the various imperialistic movements, the building of the pyramids or of the medieval cathedrals, the composing of great orchestral symphonies, the writing of certain kinds of tragedy, have all proved to be phenomena limited in time—that is, which can happen in one period but not in another. Notre Dame may not appear as fragile as the medieval coif and Versailles has survived the disappearance of the full-bottomed wig, but this does not necessarily mean that stone buildings are of a totally different order of being from personal finery; since they are made of stone, they outlast the fashion that created them and have, as it were, a posthumous life which varies according to the aesthetic and psychological fashions of succeeding generations. They will be kept up or abandoned, praised or denigrated, as the collective mood changes. The one certain thing is that, when the generation which produced them has gone, they never again stand in the same relationship to human ideas and emotions as they did at

F

the time of their making. *Le buste survit à la cité*, wrote Théophile Gautier, a great believer in the permanence of art. It is true that surviving artistic objects—books, pictures, music—can have a meaning both for subsequent artists and for the public, but this meaning may be as unstable as the significance, say, of a Methodist chapel of the 19th century which was turned into a cinema after the First World War, then into a bingo hall after the Second.

It may still be objected that I have not yet proved why the word "fashion" should be applied to these broad phenomena. Everybody knows that houses rise and fall, that the Middle Ages gave way to the Renaissance, that the Reformation was succeeded by the Counter-Reformation, and so on. The obvious course is to study these things according to the rules of historical determinism, and in many fields the process has now long been under way.*

One reason why I find myself falling back on to the word "fashion" is that, even in study, there are fashions. People used to suppose until fairly recently—when it was still quite fashionable to boost university work—that scholars in the arts subjects

---

* I am not criticising such methods of study, and I try to apply them as best I can. To take my initial example again—Rousseau's naturism (as I have said, very impure and uncertain) can be seen partly as a development of the idea of nature, which had been given a new lease of life from the Renaissance onwards, and partly as the reaction of an unskilled, unadaptable outsider, brought up in Protestant Geneva, against the extreme sophistication of French 18th-century culture. To be thorough, we should go on to explain the history of the idea of nature from the Ancient World up to the Renaissance and the Enlightenment, and we should also show how French society came to be as rarefied as it was when the idea was again in a developing phase. We should, further, discuss Rousseau's extremely complex personal psychology, which helps to explain his desire for communion with, or even dissolution in, nature. As for Huysmans, he occurs as the climax of several generations of anti-bourgeois dandyism, and in a society which was essentially bourgeois and materialistic. Rousseau had been attacking the last phase of aristocratic extravagance in the name of bourgeois common sense; Huysmans was extolling aesthetic individualism against bourgeois philistinism.

In none of this, of course, can there be any "scientific certainty". The whole picture is never anything more than a variable mass of probabilities. But this form of reasoning does not go to the root of the principle of change I am trying to get at; it tends to assume that things stay put until some new, definable, and probably external cause intervenes to alter them.

and in the loosely named "social sciences" were in possession of something objective, a body of knowledge. This is far from being the case in the modern university. It was comparatively easy for a 17th-, 18th- or even 19th-century scholar to go ahead and do his work, using the assumptions that came to hand. The situation is no longer so simple, because we now see all such assumptions as hidden fashions. For instance, it has become a commonplace to talk about the 19th-century's attitude to the 18th, or about the 18th-century's attitude to the 17th, or about the 17th-century's view of the Middle Ages. We then go on to discuss what the 19th century thought of the 18th-century's view of the 17th-century's opinion of the Middle Ages. In other words, the past does not stay put; it is continually in process of reconstruction.*

If the changes were entirely due to "advances in scholarship" or "the progress of knowledge", there would be no need for comment, but these optimistic expressions often refer to fundamental differences of approach, which means that it is not so much the picture that has altered as the eye of the beholder. A clear instance is the new emphasis with regard to the Renaissance. Some 20th-century scholars almost claim, in so many words, that the whole concept of the Renaissance was a 19th-century invention, to be explained in terms of 19th-century psychology.† This makes one wonder what enormous assumptions we are harbouring that will be pointed out by the 21st century. Of course, such speculations land us in an infinite regress, because, even if we could foresee what our successors will think, their attitude would still not provide us with an absolute. However, we have to make the effort because

* There are other reasons, of course, besides fashion, for the uncertainties of history. On all questions, a good deal of the evidence has been lost or was never recorded, and therefore has not survived. That which was recorded may be partial or mistaken, and there may be no means of knowing where the gaps or mistakes occur. We realise, from personal experience, that the imponderables in a given atmosphere may be all-important, and these are precisely the elements that have usually disappeared. All history, to a greater or lesser degree, seems to be like Egyptian history, that is, a series of imaginative leaps from monument to monument.

† *Cf.* Arnold Hauser, *The Social History of Art,* translated by Stanley Godman (1951).

Marxism, Freudianism, and Existentialism, however sketchy our knowledge of them, have accustomed us to be on the lookout for our concealed prejudices. The old Socratic tag, "Know thyself", has taken on a far deeper meaning. Oneself is a shifting pattern of partly temperamental, partly conditioned attitudes, whose relativity is now very apparent; oneself is no longer a definite, solid instrument to be used for the exploration of the past. The knower and that which is to be known are both variables. It is as if one fashion were trying to appreciate and evaluate another. Indeed, strictly speaking, this is exactly what is happening. Of course, if a time ever comes when perfect self-knowledge is achieved and contemporary fashion is totally understood, then fashion will wither away, like the State in the Marxist Utopia, or be brought so firmly under control that it ceases to be fashion. But this is probably an impossible ideal.

By "fashion", as I am now beginning to see, I mean all those temporary, collective crystallisations of behaviour which, at any given moment, represent the current limited choice from among the infinite possibilities of human nature, whether the problem at issue be the design of a hat or a metaphysical interpretation of the universe.* "Tradition" would have been a nobler word,

* The word "collective" is perhaps superfluous. The individual, however individualistic he may be, cannot exist outside the context of society. Even hermits belong to the scattered community of hermits, and it is a well-known fact that such communities are more common at some periods than at others. The isolated tramp or hobo has been a monotonously frequent figure in contemporary drama, which proves that playwrights are in the grip of some fashion.

More generally, individualism has been a flourishing fashion in Western Europe for several generations. But someone who thinks of himself as an individual, and is assertive about the fact, may be doing little more than denying his real social context. In saying this, I am not refusing to attribute any meaning to the word "individual". On the contrary, as I shall argue later, one of the signs of the outstanding individual is that he is a creator of fashion. I am only pointing out that a great many individualists overlook the fact that they are demonstrating their individualism by collective means to the collectivity. Rousseau, for instance, describes himself as sitting utterly alone on the banks of a lake, after renouncing the world. It does not seem to occur to him that his beautifully measured French, which he uses to express his isolation, is not a purely individual creation but also a highly complex social product, and that he is writing to be read.

but it suggests the deliberate or automatic handing on of a system of conventions which very probably developed in the first place as a fashion. Tradition itself is fashionable at certain times and not at others. We are used to thinking of England as a country of tradition but, just at this moment, anti-traditionalism is all the rage, at least on the surface. "Custom" would have been another possibility, but it suggests the accomplishment of a ritual gesture and lays the emphasis more on conservative repetition than on the inherent principle of change. The advantage of the term "fashion" is that it stresses the half-conscious, partly individual, partly collective nature of these group phenomena, while also implying that they are subject to forms of dynamism that have not yet been fully understood. As I have said, there is no absolute. Human nature —and this is its often unsuspected peculiarity—seems to be infinitely variable, not in the sense that man has no limits (until further notice, he undoubtedly has, although he is constantly straining to transcend them) but in the sense that the pattern is always changing within the limits, and on several levels at the same time. It is tempting to suppose that, within a given social context, all fashions are ultimately interrelated, however complex and devious the lines of connection between them may be, but all one can be sure of is that, whether connected or not, they evolve at different rates.

Fashions in teleology have altered more slowly than fashions in headgear. For centuries, the dominant Western European view was that human existence should be considered as the enactment of a trial run for heaven.* This is now a minority view, which may gain a little in one direction or lose a little in another, but has not yet reasserted itself as the reigning formulation. It has been supplanted by the belief in progress here and now, which rests on the assumption that Utopia is an ultimate possibility. The two views have fused together in some minds, and there have been various subsidiary theories,

---

* According to a minority belief which was fashionable for a time, God knew the result of this trial run beforehand and, since he made the rules, could disregard it. However, the gratuitousness of the pseudo-test only made it more awesome still.

e.g. that the processes of world history are circular, or are leading to the gradual realisation of the World Spirit, or can best be understood as the interplay of challenge and response. Another belief, which is always held by a minority but may sometimes become a majority vogue, is that life makes no sense at all and is just a flicker of imperfect consciousness on the surface of vast, inhuman chaos.

I myself, in stating that there is no absolute and in continuing, even so, to cogitate as if there were some absolute to be found, am in the tradition of the more sceptical aspect of the Enlightenment as it has been modified by non-religious Existentialism. The only absolute, according to this view, would be that there is no absolute, only a perpetual search, according to the processes of reason, although we should be hard put to explain rationally what reason is. However, the attempt is made to grasp phenomena impartially and globally, and in terms of their essential mobility. We assume, being hopeful rationalists, that the changing forms have their own logic, internal and external, but we are under no illusions about its endless complexity. Any previous formulation can be brought into play to help with the explanation, because the chances are that even the most remote human fashions—the ceremonial burial of bulls by the Egyptians or the ritual self-disembowelling once practised by the Japanese or the methods by which Dalai Lamas were selected—can have a bearing on those nearer home.

The difficulty of comprehending the shifting truth of such matters can be demonstrated—although the demonstration is probably superfluous—by a few remarks about the most obvious form of fashion, that in dress.

Basically, no doubt, clothes are a protection against the weather and their form is decided, in those primitive societies which need clothes, by the occupations of the wearers and the materials available. But even in the least sophisticated setting, it is difficult to find a simple expression of this fact. Animals only venture by accident beyond climatic conditions for which they are not "naturally" equipped, and their mistakes usually result in death. It is impossible to tell whether man invented clothes because he accidentally found himself living in harmful surroundings or whether, having invented clothes, he hit upon the idea of living permanently in an "unnatural" environment. Whatever the truth of the matter, all of us in the temperate zones only differ in degree from cosmonauts in space-suits. We cannot revert to pure "nature", except on pain of death. However, our earth-suits are never wholly functional, and may at times be positively anti-functional. Or rather, their mysterious psychological functionalism may take precedence over their immediate, physical functionalism.

Clothes are not just a protective skin; they are forms of adornment or distinction, *i.e.* systems of signals by which the wearer addresses the community and also himself. Writers on fashion have often pointed out that, in warm climates, where no protection is needed, clothes are worn as an indication of social status, or on ceremonial occasions to emphasise the break with the everyday atmosphere, or as a means of "helping nature" by bringing out certain characteristics rather than others. A native of Borneo who broadens his shoulders by means of a feather-cape and has a bright, very narrow apron hanging from his navel to his knees, is comparable to the Elizabethan with his ruff, his padded shoulders, and his codpiece. It remains obscure why nature should need to be helped in this way. And still more puzzling is the fact that the attributes that are thus brought out vary from time to time and from society to society. Broad shoulders and general sturdiness of build may be considered desirable in some contexts, whereas leanness, slightness and even fragility may be preferred in others. Phallic emphasis seems a simple enough phenomenon, yet it is more often indirect than direct. Most male dress eliminates the phallus, as if it were non-relevant to the normal business of living or had to be kept sacred by a total taboo. But occasionally it reasserts itself in the most startlingly suggestive symbolism: a sight that an Englishman takes some time to get accustomed to in Edinburgh is that of groups of Scottish gentlemen in full regalia with their skirt-like kilts compensated for by the very prominent sporran* and the slightly more discreet dirk tucked into the stocking.

It is doubtful whether the sporran is now any more functional than the Borneo native's feather-cloak, but it may originally have had some functional justification. One of the commonplaces of fashion in personal appearance is that the useful or the accidental can at once take on a prestige significance or a symbolic quality within a limited context, and the same item may, at the very same moment, have quite opposite meanings in different contexts. During one recent hard winter, men's Russian fur-caps sold like hot cakes in London, and women went in again for Russian boots, as they had done in the 1920s. It was difficult to tell, however, how far the young men in fur-caps were influenced by the cold, the idea of Britain going into the Common Market (and therefore becoming vaguely Continental), the prestige of the Soviet Union or merely by the desire to be different. At the same time, the English press reported that the young dandies of Moscow thought fur-caps very old hat, while their girl-friends were refusing to wear boots and trudging through the snow in court-shoes. Similarly, it is interesting, if hardly comforting, for a balding European to discover that baldness was a prized distinction for a time in Ancient Egypt and in Old Japan; perhaps Yul Brynner could have brought it back into vogue again, if he had been a really good actor or had had any other notable characteristic besides baldness.

These examples show the extreme fluidity of dress or appearance symbolism and its unstable relationship with what might

---

* "*Sporran:* A pouch or large purse made of skin usu. with the hair left on and with ornamental tassels, etc." *O.E.D.*

Lest I be accused of anti-Scottish bias, let me add at once that there are grounds for believing the English striped old school tie to have a good deal in common with the South American native's decorated pudendal sheath. The symbolism of the tie cannot be dismissed as a Freudian exaggeration. The French pop singer, Patachou, used to have (perhaps still has) a night club where part of the fun consisted in cutting off the ties of the male guests and hanging them, as permanent trophies, from the ceiling. This practice could either represent the union of each male client with the proprietress, an ideal night-club arrangement fusing the maternal with the amorous, or it could be a two-way castration complex disguised as a joke. The second suggestion is probably nearer the truth.

be called the materialistic substructure. We can add that, psychologically, dress is at once a proof of similarity, a uniform (*i.e.* as the word implies, a sign common to all the members of the social class or group), and a proof of difference with regard to those people who do not wear the uniform. As Thorsten Veblen pointed out, elaborate costume is not so much an aesthetic production as a form of conspicuous consumption or conspicuous leisure, either on the part of the wearer or, by transference, on the part of the person who paid for it. Quentin Bell added* that any costume can, on occasions, become a form of conspicuous outrage. An extreme dandy is, in his elegant way, being ever so slightly insulting towards all those people who are not so carefully turned out as he is. The bearded, dishevelled, none-too-clean, black-garbed beatnik is aiming at the same effect and, to all intents and purposes, is an inverted dandy. He is in black partly to avoid washing, which would be an acceptance of bourgeois convention, and partly to make it clear that he is avoiding washing, and perhaps partly also to show that he is already in mourning in anticipation of atomic doom. If, as is reliably reported, the beatnik and/or his girl-friend shrink new pairs of jeans to their persons by stepping into the bath with them on, this is presumably to make themselves more significant within their group by emphasising their secondary, or even primary, sexual characteristics, and to increase the public outrage by flaunting them in the face of society. A further complication, of course, is that within the group for which a particular form of dress is a rallying sign, prestige differences develop. I do not know whether beatniks vie with each other in blackness and sheerness; no doubt they do. Or perhaps I am already out of date in thinking they are still black when, in fact, they may well be competing with each other in the introduction of new colours and new shapes.†

But it is no secret that the aim of *haute couture* is to allow rich women to show that they are as well off as the other members of their class, while at the same time, in some subtle way,

* Quentin Bell, *On Human Finery* (1948).
† Since I wrote this blackness has gone out and gaudiness has become the prevailing fashion.

personal and different. And they achieve this not by inventing their own clothes but by accepting the suggestions of largely male dress-designers who, for their benefit, introduce tiny modifications into the prevailing fashion, which has been invented, at least in part, by these same dress-designers. Further, according to one writer on fashion,* the attitude of the dress-designers is ambiguous. They may be narcissistically in love with clothes and, at the same time, hate and despise women and wish, half-consciously, to wreak vengeance on the female sex by distorting the female form. If this is true, something very complicated is happening when, say, a rich business man pays for his wife to be dressed by a *grand couturier*. For the wife, the "creation" is a sign of similarity, of difference and of difference within similarity. For the designer, if he is homosexual, it may be a more or less aesthetic transposition of his sexual tensions. For the husband, it is a social banner; instead of hoisting a flag, he parades the woman. (Ascot is an interesting and peculiar ceremony in this respect because, in the most vulgar way possible, it puts the women on the same level as the horses.) Also, for the heterosexual male, finery, even when not understood in detail, may provide deeper satisfactions. The husband has paid for a lot of surface frills and he is comfortably aware that this is proof of his right to brush them all aside, if he is so minded, and their expensive, ambiguous, perhaps comical quality is no more than a frothy barrier for his vigorous instinct.

These remarks are far from exhausting the subject but they are perhaps enough to establish the point I am trying to make for the moment: practically all the elements in the situation are polyvalent.

An Ascot hat, for instance, is a temporary monument determined by the conscious, half-conscious and unconscious attitudes of the numerous people connected with it, of whom the wearer, strangely enough, may be the least complex or the least vitally concerned. I suspect there is no real difference in kind between an Ascot hat and the Albert Memorial. Both are

---

* Edmund Bergler, *Fashion and the Unconscious* (1953).

collective products, drawing their characteristics from the total fashion of the day, although they may have been ordered and designed by specific persons.* To understand how one kind of Ascot hat can be fashionable in a given year, or why the Albert Memorial was possible at the time of its creation and is no longer so, one would have to estimate the fluctuating interplay of symbols which, at the best of times, are all multi-significant and constantly changing at different rates. And always there is the problem of why the possibilities of human nature have been narrowed down, or extended, to that particular formulation, why the changes are taking place in the way they are and why the rates of change are so uneven at different levels.

In the long run, all this is no doubt reducible to historical determination, at least in theory, because any "explanation" supposes series of causes and effects, but no philosophy that I have come across really attempts to follow the subtle interplay of phenomena, as they flicker back and forth from the material to the psychological, from the substructure to the super-structure, from the collective to the individual, from the narcissistic to the objective, from the linguistic to the actual, from the "frivolous" to the "serious", from the comparatively stable to the completely unstable, from the recurrent or seasonal to the non-repeatable, and so on. It is true that everything cannot be pointed out at once. This, however, is a limitation of human expression not an objective characteristic of the universe, and the usual division of phenomena into "subjects" is a misleading convenience. Nor am I claiming that "fashion" is necessarily the key to the whole problem. I am only confessing that the term keeps suggesting itself as I attempt to follow the patterned mobility of happenings in various fields. To repeat in another form what I have already said, if we knew the total causes of fashion in the deepest sense, we should presumably have an adequate philosophy of human nature.

Another way of approaching the issue would be to compare science, the one field in which fashion is not essential, with all

---

* I say "total fashion" for the sake of convenience, but as I have just suggested, most fashions exist partly in opposition to other contemporary fashions.

others in which it is. There are fashions in science, in the sense that, for more or less obvious reasons, scientists concentrate on certain lines of enquiry at particular times. Individual sciences have their boom periods and their periods of eclipse. Scientists, as a body, are subject to their own collective fashions, which are outside the domain of science: *e.g.* they may show a proneness to mysticism or an interest in politics. Also, science creates intellectual fashions which spread out among non-scientists, as Newtonianism did in the late 17th and the 18th centuries. But since the results of science are cumulative, all its findings are present at once, and are only subject to fluctuation in so far as some formulations may be modified retrospectively in order to bring them into line with later findings. If I have understood the situation properly, Einsteinian physics are not a fashion which has replaced Newtonian physics, in the way that Romanticism replaced Classicism, but a rectification over a given area. Fashion reappears in science only in those departments where facts are relatively few and hypotheses not easily verifiable: cosmology, for instance. It may also be the case—but here I am guessing—that beyond a certain point in microphysics, if the "facts" are permanently outside the range of human apprehension, there will be fashions in suggesting imaginative versions of them.

Outside science, results are not cumulative, and indeed, the use of the world "result" may be quite misleading, because a so-called result can begin to dissolve again as soon as it has been achieved. There are, however, series of developments which continue for a longer or a shorter time and appear to be governed to some extent by their own laws. A short but fascinating discussion of them in one particular field is to be found in an article by Professor E. H. Gombrich, "Psychology and Art",* which has implications extending far beyond the boundaries of art. Professor Gombrich is not dealing with fashion as such; he is concerned with establishing a distinction between the *ad hoc* symbolism of dreams or the random patterns of immediate perception and the more complex symbolism of art. A

---

* In *Freud and the Twentieth Century* (1958).

distinguishing feature of the latter form of symbolism is that, up to a point, it is subject to evolution or progression. "Art has a history", says Professor Gombrich, and he quotes with approval, as being applicable to art, a general statement about the growth of symbolism made by Ernest Jones, which reads as follows:

> If the word symbolism is taken in its widest sense the subject is seen to comprise almost the whole development of civilisation. For what is this other than a never-ending series of evolutionary substitutions, a ceaseless replacement of one idea, interest, capacity or tendency by another? The progress of the human mind, when considered genetically, is seen to consist, not—as is commonly thought—merely of a number of accretions, added from without, but of the following two processes: on the one hand the extension or transference of interest and understanding from earlier, simpler, and more primitive ideas, etc., to more difficult and complex ones, which in a certain sense are continuations of and symbolise the former; and on the other hand the constant unmasking of previous symbolisms, the recognition that these, though previously thought to be literally true, were really only aspects or representations of the truth, the only ones of which our minds were—for either affective or intellectual reasons—at the time capable. One has only to reflect on the development of religion or science, for example, to perceive the truth of this description.

For the reasons already given, I would put science in a separate category, but the passage is helpful in that it suggests the duration of a certain form of symbolism as being the key to a particular fashion. Professor Gombrich develops Jones's idea by quoting a number of examples to show that, at a given point in a given society, the degree of evolution in symbolism may vary from one art to another. For instance, Elizabethan England was far more sophisticated in linguistic than in pictorial expression, so that the stiff portraits of the period are well behind the subtlety of literature. But whereas Jones seems to imply that there is continuous progression or substitution in a given field, Professor Gombrich emphasises that there may be breaks in continuity, for artistic on non-artistic reasons:

> Mature art can only grow within the Institution—as I call it—within the social context of the aesthetic attitude. Where this breaks down, representation must soon revert to the more primitive, more readable conceptual image.

A kindred fact is that, precisely because a form of perfection has been achieved in one direction, the tendency may have to be reversed in order that further "advances" may take place. Cubism can be understood as a revolution against the perfect, formal imitativeness of academic painting, a return to distortion as a relief from the softness of pretty-pretty realism. Professor Gombrich ingeniously illustrates this by showing, by means of photographs, how much a saccharine academic painting can be "improved" for modern tastes by putting it behind wavy glass, which destroys its insipidity. Picasso, who was a child virtuoso in academic art, has repeatedly borrowed the clumsiness of primitive art to produce exactly this effect of hardening and tightening. Therefore, in discussing any particular fashion in art, we have to take into account these internal tendencies, the way the symbolisations are moving to and from certain extremes, as well as the surrounding social situation and its more or less direct impact on the kind of art being produced. Generalising the conception, we can say that a fashion is a temporary balance, a developing or diminishing balance, between all these factors, internal and external.

In all fields, one of the obstacles to understanding is that "chance" is always undoing previous formulations. New materials, new skills, new forces are stumbled on by accident and enter unpredictably into the mixture.

No one could have foreseen, for instance, that the discovery of the beneficial effects of sunlight in the treatment of bone tuberculosis would, within half a century, lead to a universal passion for sun-bathing and to the extraordinary development of the holiday industry. The idea of nature, by itself, could probably not have produced this effect; it had to link up with the survival of sun-worship in Sweden and the medical justification (itself reinforced, perhaps, by the fact that tuberculosis had been a "fashionable" disease all through the 19th century). Eventually, boredom with a universal practice or a need to make the body mysterious again by hiding its shape may reverse the trend so that the pin-up girl of 2000 A.D. is shrouded in black from top to toe, like those peasant women still to be seen today in Mediterranean countries just a little way back from beaches crowded with naked flesh. On the other hand, medical reasons are not always compelling. One would have expected the establishment of a connection between lung-cancer and nicotine to have put a stop to smoking or to have reduced it to the level of a hidden vice. The fact that it has not done so cannot be explained simply by the force of advertising, since advertising itself only exists by public permission. Either people are prepared to risk death to enjoy the soothing effects of tobacco, or they want to commune in self-destruction (a remarkably common tendency), or cigarettes and pipes have meanings unconnected with smoking (it would be easy to suggest more than one such meaning). Even so, there has been a slight change, and if I were the Labour Party's publicity expert, I would advise the Leader of the Opposition to stop being photographed in the act of pulling on his pipe; the sight, instead of being bluffly reassuring, as it was in Baldwin's day, is now ever so faintly sinister and nasty.

One feature of the workings of "chance" is the emergence of the fashion-creating individual. Or perhaps it would be more correct to say that chance lies in the coincidence of the temperament of the operative individual with the immediate possibilities or needs of the collective situation. Napoleon had an exceptional temperament and, in a sense, it exactly fitted the possibilities of France just at the moment when he reached his prime. He could not have soared to power as he did, but for the situation, and the situation could not have evolved as it did, but for him. What is true of him—I quote him because, according to popular mythology, he shares with Jesus Christ the distinction of being the most frequent identification figure among lunatics, and is therefore an archetypal fashion-creator —is true, more or less, of all initiators in politics, literature and the arts. Even when they have to battle long and hard to make their point, as was the case, say, with Florence Nightingale, they are still being partly created by a trend of their times. Florence Nightingale is, for us, a great Victorian, not a great anti-Victorian, or she was very Victorian in her anti-Victorianism. To say this is not to belittle her efforts, which were heroic. It is merely to recognise the interdependence of the individual and the collectivity. A temperament born completely out of its time may never even begin to realise its possibilities and, conversely, a society which does not throw up the right individual at the right time may never develop one of its latent fashions.

All this has been commonplace enough since Gray wrote about "village Hampdens", but there is a tendency to overemphasise one aspect or the other: to say, for instance, if one believes too much in the collectivity, that if Shakespeare had not occurred when he did, someone else would have written more or less the same plays; or, if one believes too much in individuals, that if Shakespeare had been born at some other time he would, inevitably, have been as great an artist. The concept of fashion, if taken seriously, allows us to hold the two factors in balance and to understand how the great man is conditioned by the mass of ordinary men and the mass of ordinary men by the great man. The great man and the mere fashion-designer have one thing in common; both share the qualities of the medium. They sense a collective possibility and bring it into being, rather as an orator reacts to an audience or an actor to his public. This is not to say, of course, that all fashions are created by identifiable, outstanding individuals. The casual inventions of anonymous individuals may catch on and spread like wild-fire, while the deliberate creations of professional designers remain still-born. For instance, very few of the changes in language can be traced to their source and literary artists have surprisingly little to do with them. Even in dress, a field in which a great many people are actively engaged in directing trends for commercial reasons, major innovations occur that no one was able to foresee and that the professional designers can only deplore: *e.g.* the world-wide use of bluejeans as a uniform for youth or the general abandonment of hats, except as occasional ceremonial garb, by men.

Perhaps what I have been trying to get at in probing the subject from these various angles is some form of dynamic, structuralist philosophy. Clearly, "human nature" is not a given set of attributes, statically repetitive like animal nature. The perpetual change of fashion in dress symbolises, and to some extent reflects, the no less constant fluctuation in the realisation of the various human potentialities at all levels. The problem is: can we make positive, reassuring sense of this fluctuation; can we hope, if not to dominate it, at least to understand it well enough to go along with it consciously, as a cyclist rides his bicycle? For this, we should have to know, for instance, when one part of the structure begins to change, what repercussions this is likely to produce in other parts. We should have to grasp how "facts" are constantly being incorporated into fluctuating symbolisms and how different symbolisms interlock, interreact and create new "facts". This is a tall order, and the thinker who tries to fulfil it may lapse into extreme scepticism or despair. Valéry, in his way, did his best, and his conclusion was: *"Nous entrons dans l'avenir à reculons"* (We move into the future backwards), *i.e.* we never fully understand the part of life we are engaged upon and only begin to see it when it has receded into the past and has become remote and unalterable. By then, it belongs to history and is subject to all the uncertainties of historical inquiry. Therefore, non-knowledge oscillating with knowledge is the only truth amid the changing forms of life. But even Valéry was still working away in his note-books on his death-bed; and as long as one has energy left to go on thinking, one wants to know.

Can all the possibilities of human nature be realised at once, or do collectivities have to "set" in temporary, restricted patterns because some of the extremes of human nature are mutually exclusive? Is the fatigue, which often seems to account for the substitution of one pattern for another, a limitation, a sterile oscillation, or a sign of some deeper, more interesting truth? What are we to make of the contradictory human instinct to cling to the known while thirsting for the unknown, which may abolish the known? Anyone who could answer these questions would find sermons in *Vogue* and fashion-notes in *Hymns Ancient and Modern*.

G

5. *Gide and Sexual Liberation*

It is usually taken for granted that André Gide was one of the major spiritual and psychological liberators of the turn of the century and, in particular, that the part he played in breaking down 19th-century sexual conventions in France was comparable to the emancipatory influence of D. H. Lawrence in England.

The parallels between the two men are, indeed, more striking than their differences. Both suffered from tuberculosis and had that passionate interest in living life to the full which is often characteristic of consumptives. Both had forceful mothers who instilled into them moral principles, which they eventually reversed, as it were, and used as a means of self-realisation instead of repression. Although neither professed much conscious interest in Rousseau, they were both uncannily like the 18th-century reformer who relaunched the so-called "philosophy of nature" in the modern world. They were invalids who evolved a doctrine of health. They believed nature to be essentially good, and saw man's unhappiness and suffering as being largely caused by the complexities of sophisticated society and the ramifications of thought. At times it is almost as if Lawrence and Gide were amplifying Rousseau's three most paradoxical and inflammatory assertions: *"L'homme qui médite est un animal dépravé" (Discours sur 'Inégalité)*, *"Tout est bien sortant des mains de l'auteur des choses, tout dégénère entre les mains de l'homme" (Emile)* and *"L'homme est né libre et partout il est dans les fers" (Contrat Social)*.

Lawrence's attack on the intellectualism of the Bloomsbury Group and his use of the gamekeeper in *Lady Chatterley's Lover* as one of Nature's gentlemen and a modified Noble Savage are very Rousseauistic. So are Gide's advocacy of direct experience as opposed to book-learning—although he seems never to have been without a book in his hand—and his violent rejection of social restraint in the famous phrase of *Les Nourritures Terrestres:* "*Familles, je vous hais!*"

Rousseau was not particularly interested in sexual emancipation, in spite of the fact that he was never able to achieve complete satisfaction of his own peculiar masochistic tastes. Perhaps he had no need to make a fuss about sex, since 18th-century upper-class French society was remarkably uninhibited in this respect, and he himself had been initiated at an early age by a mature woman. His problem was rather how to achieve the experience of satisfactory spiritual love, and how to reconcile love with some "natural" form of social organisation, based ultimately on deism; this is the problem he deals with in a rather confused way in his one and only novel, *La Nouvelle Héloïse*.

Lawrence and Gide, on the other hand, made sex the main item in their policies, since they were reacting against the squeamishness and hypocrisy of the 19th century. Neither, in the last resort, is a deist; they are both sex-centred pantheists. They work on the principle that if the individual gets his sex-life straight, if he recognises the nature and strength of his instinct, and speaks about it frankly, everything else will fall into place. Truthfulness about sex is the high-road to authenticity. Lawrence certainly implies that society is disordered because educated people no longer have the ability to be sexual in the proper way, and in *St Mawr* he even goes to the length of turning a horse into a living, phallic idol, whose natural beauty brings out by contrast the tawdriness of sophisticated human relations. Gide is faced with the rather different task of proving that his particular brand of sex—which is homosexuality and perhaps, more specifically, paederasty—is both justifiable in itself and not inimical to the healthy operation of society. His argument has ultimately to be that paederasts are a "natural' subdivision of humanity, and have only to accept themselves as such, and be accepted as such, for their lives to be established on a sound basis.

At first sight, it might seem that Gide put across this message very successfully, and that his own life was an example of complete spiritual and sexual liberation. After years of argument with himself and others, he broke free from the Protestant indoctrination of his childhood and reached a position of agnostic acceptance of the world as it appears to be. At the same time, he had the courage openly to assert his homosexuality, and presumably to live by it. In spite of his early invalidism, he survived to the age of eighty-two, and there is no indication in his writings that he ever showed any signs of recanting. The accounts given by his friends who were with him during his last illness confirm that he died in a state of complete serenity.

By now, of course, his enormous popularity has waned and his direct influence may be small, because the concepts of naturalness and permissiveness have been carried much further than he carried them, or than was generally possible in his day. But it would be difficult to overestimate the effect of his writings, especially *Les Nourritures Terrestres*, in bringing about the present situation. In the 1930s, all young French people with any education at all read *Les Nourritures Terrestres* as a kind of pagan New Testament, and tried to assimilate the message of sunshine, nakedness, freedom and *disponibilité*. It is true that there were intimations of a similar philosophy of liberation in two other famous writers, Montherlant and Colette, but Montherlant s attitude was more complicated and involved Catholic overtones of suffering, while Colette was non-ideological and refrained from didacticism or proselytising. Gide had no rival in France as the apostle of the anti-bourgeois, "life-enhancing" philosophy and, by a curious coincidence, the idea of naturalness in the sunshine, which he had sponsored, was given a tremendous boost in the years after the Second World War by the creation of the myth of Brigitte Bardot and St-Tropez, which brought the Riviera within the system of world-wide pop-culture.*

* The film which touched off the new development was *Et Dieu créa la femme*, made by Bardot's then husband, Roger Vadim, who, according to the gossips, began life as the boy-friend of the film-director, Marc Allégret, who had been the most famous of Gide's boy-friends. So, if the stories are true, Mme Bardot, the symbol of heterosexual naturalism, is slightly more than the spiritual grand-daughter-in-law of André Gide; there is as yet no term in *les structures occidentales de la parenté* to denote the precise relationship.

But although Gide's message is superficially clear and has inspired both homosexuals and heterosexuals alike, obscurities arise as soon as one looks more closely into his life and writings. The inveterate confessionalist, who published his *Journal*, as well as three very outspoken autobiographical documents—*Si le grain ne meurt, Ainsi soit-il* and *Et nunc manet in te*—left a number of important points undiscussed, and gave a confusing account of some others. It is well known that he revelled in ambiguities and fluctuations, which he considered closer to human truth than any settled doctrine, and he lived long enough to go through many different, and perhaps contradictory, phases. However, he certainly tried to be self-conscious, and most of his writings deal with his personal problems, either directly or in a transposed form.

The question is: did he really make out a convincing case for sexual liberation, or at least for the form that he himself preferred, and do his life and writings provide a satisfactory illustration of the achievement of such a liberation? For my part, I now seriously doubt this. I am not sure that his honesty was always very lucid, just as I suspect that he sometimes made a show of frankness when he was not being very honest. His life and writings can be seen as a puzzling, interlocking pattern, the implications of which do not always correspond to what one can legitimately take to be his conscious doctrine.

In *Corydon* and elsewhere, he repeatedly makes the point that homosexuality is such a widespread phenomenon, not only among human beings but also in the animal kingdom, that it must be considered "natural" and blameless. Like all such arguments, his argument from nature is very indefinite. As I have said earlier, everything is part of nature: homicidal tendencies, sadism, incest, etc. If human morality has any meaning, it is essentially a choice among natural possibilities. Gidean and post-Gidean permissiveness is based on the liberal assumption that the wider the choice the better. If homosexuality does no harm, it should be accepted as a legitimate manifestation of the given temperament: "why should I not live according to my nature?" as Gide asks in *Si le grain ne meurt*. The same question could be put by someone who felt an urge towards incest, for example, a practice that Gide does not discuss. (He introduces a slightly incestuous episode in the last chapter of *Les Caves du Vatican*, where the hero, Lafcadio, goes to bed with his half-niece Geneviève, but he appears uncertain about the attitude he should adopt towards it.) However, although he claims to find his own variety of homosexuality "natural", he is not sympathetic to all kinds.

In *Si le grain ne meurt*, he gives a vivid description of a sodomitic episode at which he was present and which filled him with horror, not because such things should not be witnessed by a third person, but because the idea of sodomy revolted him; he is never absolutely explicit about his own form of sex, but one gathers that it must have been mutual masturbation. After describing this scene, in which a friend of his sodomised a young Arab, he expresses his violent repugnance, but does not discuss whether such behaviour should be tolerated or not. One would expect him to add: "This seems revolting to me, but if some people like to do it, good luck to them. What I like may seem revolting to them, and we have to learn to accept each other's peculiarities." Perhaps he assumes that if one is working according to the principle of "nature", this goes without saying; each of us is accidentally disgusted by certain aspects of nature, but we have to hold our disgust in check so as not to interfere with other people's liberties. Still, the situation would have been clearer if he had actually said so, because it is also a "natural" phenomenon that our feelings of disgust should condition our moral principles. As it is, he never explains precisely what he means by "homosexuality", nor does he elaborate on the relationship between morality and sexuality, whatever form the latter may take. Yet there must be a sense in which homosexuality involves morality just as much as heterosexuality does.

In fact, there is an immediate sense, with which he should have been directly concerned. His initial homosexual experiences, and probably many of the later ones too, took place in North Africa and Italy with boys who must be described as prostitutes, either casual or professional. He is attentive, up to a point, to their individual personalities, but he never reflects on their general situation in society, or on the objective quality of his relationship with them, which is that of the wealthy tourist enjoying the consequences of local poverty. Surprisingly enough for one so scrupulous, he has the average attitude of the rich, 19th-century French bourgeois that flesh is for sale like any other commodity. It may be that prostitution is morally defensible, but it needs to be defended in this case, if the facilities of paederasty depend upon it to a large extent, as they seem to do, according to the evidence provided by so many recent novels and films.

Gide occasionally tries to dignify the relationship between the mature lover and the young boy by stressing its educational aspect. No doubt this is sometimes important, but it is hardly fundamental, since it can occur equally well in a non-sexual friendship. The point one would like to have clarified is the psychological soundness of a sexual relationship between a man and a boy in our kind of society, which is not the same as certain historical, womanless, warrior societies, where such relationships were institutionalised because they had a purpose. Nor is such a relationship the same phenomenon as a sexual bond between two men of more or less the same age, who can assume equal responsibility for their behaviour from the start. A lot of people have expressed approval for Gide's general attitude but would no doubt jib at its particular application. I knew an eminent Parisian literary critic who praised Gide in his articles and yet was careful not to let his son become too friendly with the Master. I understand his practical reservation, because nothing that Gide says, whether he is referring to paid partners or unpaid, illuminates the crucial point. He is not as explicit as John Addington Symonds, who admits in his unpublished autobiography that most of his homosexual relationships with boys and young men were based on money, even though they might ripen into the type of friendship that can exist between client and prostitute, as between master and servant. One would like to know, in the case of Gide, how lyrical the reality actually was. The "Victor" episode, which he describes in the part of his *Journal* dealing with his stay in North Africa during the Second World War, and which was later commented on from a different angle by "Victor" himself, is not reassuring.

A similar ambiguity hangs over his well-known distinction between desire and love. He claims that love was what he felt for his cousin, Madeleine, who later became his wife, and that desire was aroused in him by boys. It is probably true that he never felt any sexual desire for Madeleine and that, as Jean Delay suggests in *La Jeunesse d'André Gide*, he married her through an unconscious urge to give himself a point of anchorage after the death of his domineering mother. In the early work, *Les Cahiers d'André Walter* (1891), he recounts a nightmare in which Madeleine, in the guise of the heroine, Emmanuèle, appears as an image of the Virgin, whose dress is lifted up by a monkey, only to reveal black nothingness beneath; the monkey is presumably his sexual impulse, which realises that it will find no satisfaction in that quarter. He must have been totally unaware of the significance of the passage (which was written, of course, long before the Freudian interpretation of dreams became common knowledge), because he seems to have counted on *Les Cahiers d'André Walter* as a literary achievement that would influence Madeleine in his favour as a prospective husband. Whether he ever intended, or attempted, to consummate the marriage is left unexplained in *Si le grain ne meurt* and the other autobiographical writings. However, since he indicates that he consorted with boys even on his "honeymoon", we must suppose that the possibility of physical relations with his wife was soon abandoned, and perhaps had never been seriously entertained.

This would not be strange, if he and Madeleine had discussed the matter frankly and decided on a *mariage blanc*, like George Bernard Shaw and Charlotte, or had come to some arrangement after marriage, as happened in the case of John Addington Symonds and his wife. But Gide reveals that he never once broached the subject with Madeleine. He became world famous as an apostle of sexual liberation, yet never talked things over with her or even asked her opinion before exposing her, along with himself, to the danger of public embarrassment. However deep a love for her he may profess, it seems impossible to avoid the conclusion that he was utterly self-centred, to the point of never fully realising that he had a moral responsibility towards her. Perhaps they were both paralysed by a puritanical shyness. Or perhaps he was unconsciously revenging himself on her as mother-substitute, for the restrictions his real mother had imposed upon him during childhood and adolescence. Whatever the explanation, the facts are such that one cannot but have doubts about the quality of the psychological relationship between Gide and his wife, although he constantly asserts how intimate and perfect it was. It cannot have been as intimate as all that if one of his major preoccupations—perhaps the essential one—remained unmentioned. And, unless I have misread him, he never gave a thought to what Madeleine should do with her sexual life; it is just tacitly assumed that she will not have any. Such an attitude betrays a very limited view of sexual liberation.*

Eventually, there was a real break between them when, against her expressed wish, he went off to England with Marc Allégret. She took her revenge by burning all the letters he had ever written to her, thus wounding him in his most sensitive spot, his literary vanity. He expresses reproachful bewilderment, but seems blind to the fact, which is obvious from his *Journal*, that he had actually fallen in love with Marc Allégret and was flatly contradicting his theory about the distinction between love and desire. Clearly, he had always preferred his own pleasure to his wife's convenience or feelings; but she must have sensed that her importance even as a psychological sheet-anchor was now in jeopardy, or had actually disappeared. As far as one can tell, no degree of confidence was ever restored between them again; and Madeleine withered away at Cuverville, while Gide continued to lead his roving life and to publish his confessional literature.

A further ambiguous point remains to be mentioned. In 1924, Gide had an illegitimate daughter by Elizabeth, the

* Towards the end of his life, Gide told Denis de Rougemont that he had been ignorant of the possibility of sexual desire in women and added: "*C'est ainsi que je me suis blousé* (That is how I went wrong)." Such ignorance is hard to credit in a Frenchman, since French popular lore is so full of references to female desire.

daughter of his old friend, Mme Théo van Rysselberghe. Given the disgust with heterosexual experience he expresses in *Si le grain ne meurt*, one cannot help wondering how this came about, especially since he himself left no explanation in any of his published writings. It is true that the story, *Geneviève*, contains an episode which seems as if it might have some bearing on the matter. The young heroine tells an older man, whom she admires, that she would like to have a child by him, but he replies that he cannot accede to her wish for fear of hurting an older woman whom he loves, and who loves him. Elizabeth (later Mme Herbart) has never told the story from her point of view, so we do not know how far Geneviève's behaviour corresponds to what actually happened. However, it is interesting that, whereas in real life a child was born and is now the mother of a family and Présidente of the *Association André Gide*, in the novel the man refrains from having a child through moral delicacy. I have gathered from two of Gide's friends, who have been kind enough to answer questions I have put to them on this point, that Gide went to some pains to conceal the existence of the child from Madeleine at least for a few years; in the end she got to know about it. Also, it seems to be agreed that Madeleine was passionately fond of children and would have liked to have some of her own. This being so, I wonder if there may not have been some unconscious, or half-conscious, element of revenge in Gide's fathering of the child. Madeleine had destroyed his letters, the quintessence of his life, he says, and therefore his dearest spiritual offspring. He could retaliate by having a real child with someone else. If this seems an unworthy suspicion, it should be remembered that, in his *Journal*, he often writes about his wicked impulses without specifying what they were, and the strangely cynical tone of *Ainsi soit-il* leads one to believe that he could behave very badly with a certain amount of bravado. Such behaviour could have been followed by a mood of repentance, which led him to adopt a policy of secrecy, at least for a time, until he tired of it. The more one listens to the accounts given by the people who knew him, the more complicated, devious and ruthlessly egotistical he appears, in spite of the charm and unpredictability that everyone also stresses.

At any rate, the evidence, when looked at in this light, tends to contradict the initial picture of a totally successful life of personal liberation, based on the gradual application of a coherent philosophy. His apology for paederasty is not altogether convincing. Even if we accept the reality, in his case, of the distinction between sex as a spiritual emotion and sex as physical desire (it can be looked upon as a formulation of courtly love or of the Beatrix-complex, which occurs in different varieties in some other modern writers, and notably in Claudel), we may wonder whether it is anything more than a rationalisation of his peculiar personal position. He needed a woman in his life, at the same time as he wanted physical satisfaction with little boys; but he was not vitally concerned about the happiness of the woman or the psychological soundness of the arrangement from the point of view of the boys. In any case, his distinction broke down at the crucial point when he showed that he was more devoted to Marc Allégret than to Madeleine. His wife, whatever her own limitations may have been, inevitably appears as a victim of his self-realisation.

I have assumed so far that we are entitled to expect Gide, as a sexual liberator, to put forward valid arguments in favour of his opinions and behaviour. He often adopts an argumentative attitude and writes as if he were defending an enlightened form of humanism. But there are other contexts, in which he adopts an amoral, neo-Nietzschean stance: morality is pettifogging; the important thing is to obey one's impulses, without worrying about whether they are "right" or "wrong"; in the struggle for life, the weak must go to the wall; it is better to sin by commission than by omission; and so on. There is some doubt about the date at which he became acquainted with Nietzsche and about the extent of his debt to the German philosopher. However, as early as 1898, in the *Lettres à Angèle*, we find him quoting Nietzsche's precepts with approval, and in particular the specific rejection of morality:

Voyez enfin quelle naïveté il y a à dire: l'homme devrait être tel ou tel. La réalité nous montre une richesse exubérante de types . . . .

(Let us admit, in short, how naïve it is to say: man should be such and such. Reality offers us a luxuriant richness of types . . . .)

This is a frank acceptance of a philosophy of nature rather different from Rousseau's, which was expressed even more forcibly in the 18th century by the Marquis de Sade than by Nietzsche in the 19th. It admits of no meaningful distinction between the animal and the human worlds; the individual is entitled to do what he likes, provided he can get away with it.

The uncertainties of Gide's writings, and particularly of his fiction, arise to a large extent from the fact that he oscillates between two contrary points of view or tries to express them simultaneously. Bourgeois morality should be discarded in favour of an emancipated, enlightened new morality; bourgeois morality should be discarded and impulse allowed full rein since it alone leads to total living. The contradiction lies behind three of his fictional works which deal, in a transposed form, with the clash between his homosexuality and his conjugal situation—*L'Immoraliste* (1902), *La Porte Etroite* (1907) and *La Symphonie Pastorale* (1919)—and behind one which refers to homosexuality but is really more concerned with self-assertion in the general sense—*Les Caves du Vatican* (1914).

The hero of *L'Immoraliste*, Michel, is a studious, well-balanced young man, who marries his childhood sweetheart, Marceline, in circumstances comparable to those of Gide's own marriage. Michel comes under the influence of a Nietzschean liberator, Ménalque, and feels an urge to escape from his over-intellectualised existence. At the same time he has to travel south to Africa, because he is discovered to have tuberculosis. His wife accompanies him and looks after him devotedly during his illness and convalescence. His recovery is the kind of awakening to a new life which provided the lyricism expressed in *Les Nourritures Terrestres*. He exults in the companionship of amoral Arab boys and, when he gets back to his country estate in Normandy, enjoys a similar relationship with the poachers who snare his game. Gide gives a brilliant, but probably unconsciously comic, picture of the bourgeois *rentier* getting a thrill out of violating the conventions which protect his property, without realising at all that his income depends on the smooth functioning of the society he is flouting. His hero speaks fervently of the need to get rid of possessions to achieve spiritual nudity; but in the context this means disencumbering oneself of houses, furniture and responsibilities to live a roving life, based on the income from one's capital in the bank. The second phase of the story tells how Marceline contracts tuberculosis and the couple move south again. But this time Michel is so obsessed with this thirst for sensual enjoyment and in particular for Arab boys that he involves Marceline in journeys which overtax her strength, and she dies, killed in a sense by him. In a theatrical gesture, Michel summons his best friends to join him on the edge of the Sahara, where he tells them the tale and asks them if he has done wrong. Again there is an unconsciously comic touch. We do not hear their verdict. Gide merely puts the question without allowing them to answer it, and, although he entitles the book *L'Immoraliste*, the overall tone suggests that Michel is not really guilty; the life-force has compelled him to be ruthless.

The book contains two admirably written passages—the convalescence and the poaching episode in Normandy—but it seems to me to be mainly a transparent piece of special pleading disguised as fiction. Gide is both expressing his sense of guilt and giving himself absolution.

In *La Porte Etroite*, Madeleine Gide is symbolically killed again, although in this instance her death appears at first sight to be a semi-suicide. Many of the events in the life of the heroine of this book, Alissa, directly follow the known facts of Madeleine's biography. Alissa is loved by Jérôme, and the assumption is that they will eventually be married. However, through a kind of puritanical masochism, she repeatedly rejects marriage on various pretexts. In the end she dies, leaving behind a private diary which shows that she has tried to replace her human love of Jérôme by the love of God and has failed; she cannot really believe in God and she has wrecked the relationship with Jérôme.

The two books are obviously complementary, as Gide himself said they were. Michel satisfies his "natural" instincts and wonders whether he should feel guilt at his wife's death. Alissa systematically thwarts her "natural" instincts and, to all intents and purposes, commits suicide. However, the style of *La Porte Etroite* is so suave and pious that some readers have taken it to be a genuinely religious book, which it cannot be, since Alissa's sacrifice is shown to be a tragic waste.* But the puzzling aspect of the novel, for any perspicacious reader not acquainted with the real-life situation, must be Jérôme's passivity in face of Alissa's prevarications. If he were passionately in love with her as he claims to be, he would lose his temper and break through her objections. His limpness can only be explained by the fact that he reflects Gide's own lack of physical desire for Madeleine, *i.e.* his homosexuality. *La Porte Etroite* is, of course, the strait gate of the Bible, as well as the little garden-gate in the story; I suggest that it may also be an unconscious symbol of Alissa-Madeleine's unbroken virginity, the tragedy of which Gide senses but about which he can do nothing. On this reading, the theme of the book is the misguided martyrdom of a woman involved with a homosexual who is incapable of playing the normal, aggressive male role in order to save her. Gide had pressed Madeleine into marrying him, but Delay is no doubt right in suggesting that his keenness was due to his desire to find a mother-substitute. If so, his "marriage" was not an adult act. It was a recreation of a childhood pattern of relationships in an innocuous form, since Madeleine could both be used to play the part of mother and be defied with impunity.

La Porte Etroite is a much less self-indulgent piece of writing than *L'Immoraliste*, yet it too hardly stands on its own as an independent work of art, and the religiosity of tone is partly at variance with the theme. I would say that Gide only got his problem fully into perspective ten years later in *La Symphonie Pastorale*. This is a beautifully ironical book, in which the tension between his lust for amoral completeness of experience and the inevitability of moral consequences is held in a satisfactory aesthetic balance.

* I have been assured by students that it is presented as a Catholic novel in convent schools in England.

The narrator is a Swiss pastor, who sounds so like the Vicar of Wakefield that I suspect a direct influence. He rescues a blind and uneducated girl from being sent to an institution and, in spite of his wife's complaints, lavishes more care upon her than on his own children. The girl, Gertrude, grows up to be charming and sensitive, and the pastor rediscovers the beauty of creation with her and through her, and unconsciously falls in love with her, much to his wife's chagrin. Gertrude's sight is restored through an operation, with disastrous results. She falls in love with the pastor's fresh young son, and he with her, but the pastor cannot control his jealousy. The family is disrupted and Gertrude commits suicide, thus revealing to the pastor for the first time the full extent of his self-deception.

It is perhaps significant that Gide expressed irritation with the success of this book and said he preferred *L'Immoraliste* and *La Porte Etroite*. Yet it is surely a much more successful allegory of his sexual complications. The blind girl, to whom the pastor stands in an affectionate, educative relationship, could be any of the boys in whom Gide took an interest, and in particular his beloved Marc Allégret. The destruction of the pastor's family could be an echo of the break-down of his own relationship with Madeleine. If so, Gide, with great acuteness, is in this instance accusing himself of moral blindness and showing that his pursuit of the "fruits of the earth" had a cruel and irresponsible aspect, as well as a lyrical one.

Meanwhile, in the intervening work, *Les Caves du Vatican*, he had carried the Nietzschean assertiveness of the individual as far as he could by presenting a dashing young hero, Lafcadio, who commits a murder as an *acte gratuit*, *i.e.* as a would-be pure expression of personal impulse. This is not the place to go into the philosophical complexities of the *acte gratuit*, and the book is really outside my subject, since it does not deal with sex, except to imply indirectly that homosexuality is an acceptable feature in the hero. The point I wish to mention is that, here again, as in *L'Immoraliste*, Gide presents the totally amoral view favourably, and then seems to panic. He shifts the blame for the murder partly from Lafcadio on to a devil-figure, Protos, and also brings the book to an end in a very unsatisfactory chapter, in which Lafcadio wonders inconclusively whether or not he should accept the social consequences of his "crime". From the moral and artistic point of view, the conclusion of *Les Caves du Vatican* is just as irritating a piece of chicanery as the pathetic let-down at the end of *L'Immoraliste*. In so far as the *acte gratuit* can be taken as an image of any self-expressive behaviour, such as a debatable sexual initiative, the book simply repeats the oscillation between non-morality and morality that I have already emphasised.

In the last resort, then, Gide gives no real guidance. He is an amoral liberator with a nagging conscience—as he himself said, "*Je ne suis qu'un petit garçon qui s'amuse, doublé d'un pasteur protestant qui l'ennuie*" (I am just a little boy having fun, with a Protestant Minister nagging away inside him)—who occasionally made literature out of his internal struggle, but the literature itself is to some extent distorted by the struggle. It cannot be said that he ever transcended his situation to produce a valid philosophy of liberation. The serenity of his later years must have been due to the fact that he got his problem off his chest by writing about it and expressing it, and so could move into the future with forgetfulness and indifference.

There remains the question: has his influence been for the good or not? It could only be answered properly by means of statistics which, of course, are not available. Judging from personal observation, I would say that he may be responsible for the fact that some young Frenchmen, dazzled by his prestige, found themselves involved in sexual complications in which they were morally at sea, and which they later regretted. But, by and large, the evils of commission seem less harmful and stultifying than the evils of repression and so I believe that, in spite of the serious reservations I have indicated, the effect of his writings has probably been beneficial.

6. *The Solar Revolution*

One should always begin by trying to justify the title of a lecture. Why have I chosen to talk about the place of the sun in modern French literature? First of all, because the Westfield Festival is, in its modest way, an act of sun-worship, since it is timed to coincide with the summer solstice; therefore any homage one can pay the sun is relevant to the total operation. Secondly, because the sun is a great, newly discovered force in the modern world. Sun-worship as a thorough-going religion is, of course, as old as recorded history, and two outstanding examples of it occurred in Ancient Egypt and Ancient Peru. But I think we can say that, in Europe, the sun is by way of being a very recent invention. I notice that the present generation of students here take it for granted that, on any fine day, they should lie about on the college lawns wearing as few garments as possible and exposing themselves to the rays of the sun, partly because sunlight is supposed to be health-promoting but partly also for a deeper metaphysical reason that I shall try to elucidate as I go along. I am fairly certain that, possibly up to 1939, it had still not occurred to any of the successive generations of young ladies of Westfield to do this, and I would guess that, before 1914, far from taking their clothes off, they must actually have walked about with parasols, to shield themselves from the sun. These changes are symptomatic of what we might call the solar revolution which has taken place in Europe during rather less than a hundred years. It has been particularly striking in France and has penetrated to a quite important extent into French literature.

Where this solar revolution began exactly, and how it spread from one country to another, I am not sure and—so far as I know—there has been no thorough study of the question.* It seems, in the first place, to have caught on more quickly in Sweden and Germany, perhaps because certain pagan traditions were more deeply entrenched in those countries than elsewhere. It was certainly helped, around the beginning of the century, by the discovery that exposure to sunlight was good for patients suffering from bone tuberculosis. In 1903, a Swiss doctor, Auguste Rollier, opened a sunshine clinic in Leysins in the Swiss Alps, and he seems to have become almost as famous in his day as Dr Christiaan Barnard is in ours. When he published an English version of his book, *Heliotherapy*, in 1923, he was hailed here as "the high priest of modern sun-worshippers," and he was no doubt the person largely responsible for the now almost universal belief that sunshine is good for one, and is, in fact, an elixir of youth, like the flames that the heroine of Rider Haggard's *She* stepped into every time she needed to renew her lease on life. This belief, which is only fifty or seventy-five years old, is a modern commonplace, and has only recently been called into question because certain rich American women who have devoted their lives to following the sun throughout the year, so as to be always sun-bathing in high summer, have found that the effects are not always beneficial. But it is perhaps significant that the musical *Hair*, which is a compendium of fashionable attitudes, ends with a religious chant in honour of the sun: "Let the sunshine in!" The young may have a stronger belief in the sun than the middle-aged.

However, I don't think the new popularity of the sun is due simply to the discovery of its therapeutic properties, although this has been an important factor. I see the change as being rather part of the general return to the idea of nature which began, let us say, at the Renaissance, and has gathered momentum, more especially since the 18th century. However, it is rather curious that Rousseau, the great 18th-century apostle of the idea of Nature, who did more than anyone else to generalise the concept throughout Europe, did not discover the

* I broached the subject in an article in *Encounter*, "A View of the Côte d'Azur", October 1959.

sun as such. He refers, of course, occasionally to the sun, but for him external nature meant primarily the open air, mountains, woods with birds singing in them, moonlight at times, and water—not the sea, which for some reason he doesn't mention, although he crossed the English Channel—water in the form of Alpine waterfalls and Swiss lakes.

The more one thinks about the matter the stranger it seems that Rousseau, who did so much to make the so-called natural landscape fashionable, should not have isolated the sun as being the centre of external nature. Perhaps his failure to do so is connected with his mistrust of science; he prided himself on being a botanist, but his botany was really a kind of practical naturism, a reverent naming of parts. Perhaps it has something to do with his hostility towards Voltaire, which tended to give him a negative attitude to anything that Voltaire was enthusiastic about. Voltaire believed more or less in the advantages of scientific knowledge and, above all, he was a keen student of the dominant science of the time, Newtonian cosmography. Rousseau, unlike the majority of his educated contemporaries, paid little or no attention to Newtonianism. The idea of the solar system did not fire his imagination, and so he remained obsessed with discrete, subsidiary or more immediate and concrete natural phenomena, such as mountains and plants. If he had connected up his naturism with Newtonianism, the intellectual history of the 19th century might have been very different, because it was Sir Isaac Newton who had finally put the sun in its proper place at the centre of our solar system, showed how the planets are dependent on it and therefore, by extension, implied that all forms of terrestrial life are regulated by it. However, Rousseau wasn't interested in this view of things and his naturism remains untouched by it.

It must be added, of course, that he was a believer, a kind of deist, and so God was the centre of his universe, and a divine presence behind all natural phenomena. Nature, for him led the individual to God. A man contemplating a mountain or listening to the song of the nightingale had feelings of sublimity which put him directly into contact with the invisible transcendent. In other words, although Rousseau rejected the divinity of Christ, he was still very much within the Christian tradition of Western Europe, and his naturism did not cause him to fall back on to paganism.

Nor can it be said that the majority of poets or prose-writers of the 19th century were thorough-going pagans; they can practically all be put into the category of neo-Christian deists. They may have been heretics in respect of the official religions of their countries but, for the most part, in their various ways, they found evidence of the transcendent in the immediate phenomena of nature. Wordsworth contemplating the daffodils or the lesser celandine, Baudelaire describing Nature as a temple with living pillars, were continuing the Rousseauistic attitude. They were supposing the existence of the transcendent behind appearances. The same remark might even be made about Byron, who almost certainly wasn't a believer. Some of his most famous lines, such as *"There is a rapture on the lonely shore"* or *"She walks in beauty like the night"* owe their quality to their religious resonance. And I think that what is true of the bulk of the literature of the 19th century is reflected in the living habits of the people of the time. In so far as they returned to nature, they were concerned with the incidental phenomena of mountains, landscape, and sea, rather than with the central phenomenon of the sun.

The 19th century was the great period of mountain-climbing, a sport which had the advantage of combining healthy exercise and an element of danger with an upward movement towards the sublime. It was also, in England rather more than in France, a period when people went for walks through the countryside in order to experience Rousseauistic or Wordsworthian emotions, and the Lake District in particular became a sort of national park for the enjoyment of lyrical naturism. Sea-bathing gradually developed in both countries from the end of the 18th century onwards, but, as is quite clear from pictures and photographs, there was little or no exposure to sunlight. People went to the sea for momentary contact with the water and for the inhaling of sea-breezes, and they sat fully clothed on the beach. As for the poets, they continued, as poets always have done, to write more about the moon than about the sun, and I think one can suggest an obvious reason for this. Sunlight, or daylight, can pass unnoticed as an accompaniment to the multifarious business of living, which absorbs the attention. Moreover, we can look directly at the sun only when it is in its weakest state; when it is fully present, it has to be contemplated through a smoked glass. The moon, on the contrary, appears in the night sky, when the business of the day is over, and the more brilliant it is, the more it attracts attention. It is therefore intensely visible as an isolated and dramatic object to which emotions can be attached—the emotions which have survived the business of the day and more especially the tender emotion of love. This, I submit, is why the moon has traditionally occupied a privileged position in literature, although, as we know, its light is only reflected sunlight.

Towards the end of the 19th century and at the beginning of the 20th, there was a change of emphasis, but I am not sure by what stages it occurred, or whether it originated in life, science, literature or the fine arts, I can only point to a number of more or less contemporary happenings, without being able to say exactly how they were interlinked. In painting, for example, the Impressionists made sunlight the most important element in external nature, in a manner that had never been equalled by any previous school of painters. Their cult of external nature, which they went out to explore physically, may have had something Rousseauistic about it in the first instance, but they move far beyond his brand of naturism by reducing the objects in the external world from the status of things in themselves, with metaphysical implications—a tree, a water-lily, a cathedral, etc.—to the different role of being mere reflectors or supports for sunlight. The tree, the water-lily, or the cathedral, instead of being separate entities pointing beyond nature to God, became part of the pagan décor of the world to be appreciated for its own sake in its relationship to sunlight. One has only to walk into a room devoted to the Impressionists in any picture gallery to get an immediate feeling of the dominance of sunlight as a pantheistic presence. By pantheistic, I mean that the lyrical emotion remains embedded, as it were, in the physical experience, and does not point to any transcendence which might be different from, or superior to, the actual sensation.

Now this pantheistic celebration of the sun, which I see as being clearly distinct from the average, traditional Rousseau-istic nature-feeling, is also found in certain writers who rebelled against 19th-century social conventions and were very influential in bringing about the change-over from the moral high-mindedness of Victorianism, whether in England or in France, to the present atmosphere of permissiveness. I am thinking particularly of André Gide and D. H. Lawrence, who can be considered as having carried Rousseauistic naturism several stages further than it was usually taken in the 19th century. Lawrence is outside my subject, but I can perhaps recall that both he and Gide were tubercular, and thus travelled south towards the sun, and ended by incorporating the sun to some extent into their philosophies. Gide, in his famous pagan testa-ment of "this-worldliness", *Les Nourritures terrestres,* which was first published in 1897 but much later (in the 1920s and '30s) became the bible of French youth, preached a doctrine of pantheistic sensationalism, which included appreciation of sunlight. He has one or two very fine descriptive passages expressive of the sheer pleasure of exposure to the sun, such as one could not find, I think, in any previous French writing. Then, in *L'Immoraliste,* which came out in 1902, his hero actually takes off all his clothes and lies down naked in the sunshine. So far as I know, this is the very first mention of sun-bathing in French literature, and it seems to have preceded the general practice of sun-bathing in France by at least twenty-five years, because, as late as 1920, French journalists were still writing articles about sunbathing in Austria and elsewhere and saying that, of course, such naïve pagan behaviour would never catch on in a sophisticated country like France. But, of course, it did catch on to a quite extraordinary extent and, as I shall try to show in a moment, one can make certain definite statements about the spread of the habit.

However, a point I would like to emphasise while I am still speaking of Gide, is that this first instance of sun-bathing occurs in a book, *L'Immoraliste,* which links up naturism with uncer-tainty about moral values. Rousseauistic naturism had been extremely moralistic, and had believed in definite moral values which were derived, more or less obviously, from Christianity. The new naturism tends to go beyond good and evil. This is tantamount to placing good in the self-development of the individual, either because the individual has become an end in himself since there is no longer any transcendence, or because the self-development of the better or stronger individuals will help the evolution of mankind. To put it in Nietzschean terms, which Gide does not use, although he probably owed something to Nietzsche, in this new naturism, self-realisation—achieved if necessary at the expense of ordinary moral values—is a duty for exceptional individuals, because they are bridges leading to the Superman. Gide isn't a thorough-going Nietzschean; he has no real concept of *die Brücke zum Übermenschen;* but he does at times accept the principle that self-realisation is more important than respecting moral rules.

When Michel, the hero of *L'Immoraliste*, takes off his clothes and bathes naked in the sun, he is not simply performing a physical action. The gesture is also, I think, a symbolic recognition of the truth that all life depends ultimately on the sun, and incidentally an assertion that life should, in the first place, be accepted as an undifferentiated explosion of energy, before one tries to categorise that energy as good or bad. I may seem to be reading a lot into the episode, but these implications are present throughout the book, and in various other parts of Gide's work. I don't think it matters at all whether Gide got this attitude from Nietzsche, or whether he invented it independently. But I think it is probably the case that, in both Nietzsche and Gide, it stems from the new view of Nature which became current from the middle of the 19th century onwards, as a consequence of Darwinism.

As I said before, Rousseau's nature still has behind it a transcendent God; Rousseau saw the moral law as being inherent in nature, since nature, being properly understood, is an expression of God; Darwin, on the contrary, saw nature as a totally amoral process, evolving for reasons unknown in some incomprehensible direction. Nietzsche and Gide try to combine the two conceptions: they get rid of Rousseau's transcendent

God; they reject the idea that any social moral law can be inherent in nature; but at the same time they would like, as it were, to adhere emotionally, even pantheistically, to the natural process, in a way which would have been very puzzling to Darwin and still more so to Rousseau, or at least to Rousseau in his ordinary moods. And it so happens that Gide, in particular, singles out the sun to identify with it—perhaps through sheer accident, perhaps because he was tubercular, or perhaps because he happened to go to North Africa at an early stage. At any rate, what we have in Gide seems to be a mixture of Newton, Rousseau, and Darwin. The sun is the centre of our fragment of the universe, *i.e.*, of nature as we know it, and the source of life and energy on this planet; we should follow nature, because nature is good and lyrically true; but the goodness of nature for the individual is above the average laws of good and evil as they are found in traditional society. I would not go so far as to say that all sun-bathers are pantheistic immoralists in communion with the centre of the universe and temporarily indifferent to the requirements of society, but I think it is just as likely that they may be that as imitators of the Rousseauistic noble savage. And, from what I am told, institutions founded on sun-bathing, such as the Club Méditerranée, appear to be patronised in about equal proportions by pantheistic immoralists and would-be noble savages.

Mention of the Club Méditerranée takes me back to the actual history of the spread of sun-bathing which, in France, is connected with the spectacular development of the Riviera, which the French call the *Côte d'Azur*, a development which has been helped in certain ways by literature.

It is well known that the Mediterranean coast between Menton and Cannes was, during the whole of the 19th century, a preserve first of the English aristocracy and then, more generally, of the various European royal houses and aristocracies connected with Queen Victoria. The Riviera was used then as a winter resort, because of the mildness of the climate, but no one stayed there during the summer, because the hot summer sun was thought to be unhealthy. Only a few French people ventured to go to the Mediterranean in those days, in spite of the efforts of one or two publicists, such as Stéphen Liégeard, the man who seems to have invented the term, *Côte d'Azur*. The French middle classes, as they gradually discovered sea-bathing and summer walks, went to Normandy, Brittany, and the Atlantic coast, but not to the South of France, and (as I said before) in Normandy and Brittany there was no question of sun-bathing. These Northern holidays are enshrined for all time in Proust's *A la recherche du temps perdu*, and there is no sun-bathing in that novel, although it shows an Impressionist feeling for light. However, the first major change came after the First World War which, to all intents and purposes, swept away the royal houses and aristocracies, so that the cosmopolitan winter season on the *Côte d'Azur* was never re-established in its former glory.

From about 1920 onwards, for the first time people began to stay along the Mediterranean coast in the summer. They were still not French; they were a second cosmopolitan wave, composed not of aristocrats but of artists, writers, bohemians and drop-outs of all kinds, predominantly American, English, German and Scandinavian. This was the period of Isadora Duncan, Scott Fitzgerald, D. H. Lawrence, Aldous Huxley and Somerset Maugham, and it was of course very different from the previous aristocratic dispensation, because it combined the attributes of immoralism, naturism, and non-conformism, that I have mentioned as being characteristic of André Gide. The winter sun had been quite decorous and reserved, and consonant with Victorianism, since Queen Victoria herself had visited the Riviera. It may have become slightly more racy with Edward VII, but only marginally so. But, in the aftermath of the First World War, the summer sun became synonymous with freedom and revolt, as can be seen from Cyril Connolly's excellent short novel, *The Rock Pool*.

Then, very gradually, the French themselves began to discover the Riviera and to go there in summer. André Gide's literary celebration of the sun was mainly associated with North Africa, but he went occasionally to the South of France. Colette, another great naturist and amoralist, took a house in St Tropez and used the *Côte d'Azur* background in many of her stories, and her works were being read at the same time as Gide's *Nourritures terrestres* was turning into a best seller. The flood gates were finally opened in 1936, when the *Front Populaire* government introduced annual paid holidays. The mass of the French population then discovered for the first time that their country possessed a Mediterranean coastline where sunshine could be almost permanently guaranteed.

The rush to the south was interrupted, of course, by the Second World War, but it began again with renewed vigour after 1945, and it has been one of the most extraordinary social phenomena in France during the last twenty-five years. The Riviera has become, as it were, the Florida or the California of France, the sunshine area where people want to have a house or flat during their working lives, and where they hope to spend their retirement. In other words, the French attitude towards the sun has been transformed, in the space of thirty-five or forty years, from one of negativity or relative indifference to one of positive enthusiasm. There is now a double annual migration towards the sun: towards the beaches and the sea for sun-bathing in the summer, and towards the Alpine slopes in the winter. This is a very dramatic change in French habits; it is, in itself, indicative of a philosophic shift, and it is bound to breed further changes of attitude in the future.

Incidentally, I am struck by a curious interaction between literature and life in the course of this development. I said before that Gide's *Nourritures terrestres*, although written in the 1890s, became the great naturist text of the 1920s and '30s. I think Gide was just as important in France as D. H. Lawrence in England, and that both were extremely influential, whatever one may think of their literary or intellectual value. Now Gide's concept of the sun, based primarily on North Africa, was quite easily transferable to the *Côte d'Azur*. And the transfer was helped, in the years after the Second World War, by the emergence of a new female ideal in France, the most famous French feminine symbol since Mistinguett, and indeed for a time a world figure. This was, of course, Brigitte Bardot, and what is particularly interesting about her is that her creator, Roger Vadim, conceived of her not as the traditional vamp or classical French seductress like Mistinguett, but as a child of nature, equally devoid of clothes, make-up, and sophistication, almost a female Tarzan, indifferent to bourgeois morality. Edgar Rice Burroughs' Tarzan had been, of course, a late male version of the noble savage, combining—in a very Rousseauistic way—morality, nature and impeccable descent from the English aristocracy. Mme Bardot was the female of the species but, belonging to the next generation or so, she was able to drop both morality and blue blood and retain only nature, thus representing the new ideal of the amoral savage. The film which made her famous, *Et Dieu créa la femme*, was shot in the south of France; it contained no reference to God except in the title and included what was, as far as I know, the first nude sun-bathing scene ever recorded in the French cinema. Moreover, Mme Bardot actually bought a house at St Tropez and, for a number of years, was the tutelary spirit of that village in the sun. It may be that Vadim had absorbed the concept of the child of nature from the general atmosphere and that the sun-bathing scene in *Et Dieu créa la femme* was an unconscious echo, some fifty years later, of the similar scene in *L'Immoraliste*.

So far, I have dealt mainly with the solar revolution as it has taken place in French life during the last fifty years, and the probable influence upon it of Gide's neo-Rousseauistic and neo-Nietzschean or neo-Darwinian naturism. I have also mentioned Colette, whose importance should not be under-estimated. I might also have quoted Henry de Montherlant, a pagan with Catholic overtones, who helped to popularise the notion of action in the sun by writing about his experiences as a bull-fighter in Spain and as a hedonistic individualist in various Mediterranean countries. In all three writers, the sun is a positive force, and their treatment of it contrasts neatly with the way the sun is referred to, for instance, in the works of a non-permissive Catholic writer like François Mauriac who, with monotonous insistence, equates sultry summer afternoons in the Bordeaux area with sensations of sexual guilt. I could also refer to a number of younger, minor writers who take the new solar naturism for granted and send their heroes to the south of France or to North Africa. The sun-consciousness they describe does not go much beyond the kind of philosophy inherent in a great many modern French films, such as *Plein Soleil, La Piscine, Les Biches*, and so on.

But there are three more important contemporary writers, who deal more directly and more philosophically with the subject of the sun, and it is these three whom I would like briefly to discuss. They are, in chronological sequence, Paul Valéry, Francis Ponge, and Albert Camus. They have little or none of the didactic naturism of André Gide; they are not primarily concerned with the fight against 19th-century convention, but all three belong to the same post-Enlightenment tradition as Gide. They are non-believers looking at the universe in the modern way which has only been fully possible since the final development of the scientific view of nature in the mid-19th century, and they use the sun both as a point of reference and as a symbol, in a manner which is quite unprecedented in French literature, although one can perhaps see intimations of their points of view in some late 19th-century writers such as Leconte de Lisle, Rimbaud and Mallarmé. They have no parallels that I can think of in English literature. I might add that, although none of the three is specifically an Existentialist, they can all be brought under the general heading of Existentialism, and I would also say that this is very characteristic, since there is a strong Existentialist element in the general sociological phenomenon of the solar revolution. It is perhaps significant, too, that all three are Southerners, people in a situation where they could not fail to notice the sun, if their emergent philosophy prepared them to be sensitive to it. Valéry was born in Sète, on the Mediterranean coast, and brought up in Sète and Montpellier; Ponge was born in Nîmes and brought up in Avignon; and Camus was, of course, an Algerian. All three, however, lived the major part of their creative lives in Paris (Ponge, the sole survivor, is still there), and Paris is an ideal place for putting a metaphysical construction on to an individual perception. In all three cases, as we shall see, the metaphysical constructions are remarkably similar.

Valéry is famous as a poet, but his major poetry-writing phase was a relatively short period in middle life, when he was between forty and fifty-five. His life-long concern from adolescence to his death at the age of seventy-four was self-analysis or (to be more accurate) the analysis of consciousness, that is— to put it in Existentialist terms—the attempt to achieve coincidence with being through the use of language. All the year round, wherever he happened to be, he rose every morning at dawn—and in winter even before day-break—to pursue this task in his notebooks. It was of course, a hopeless endeavour, because the self has no internal shape; it lives from moment to moment in time and it can only know itself retrospectively to some extent through the imprint it has made on the external world and on other people. Jean-Paul Sartre was to express this dilemma of the consciousness very clearly in the generation which followed Valéry's; but Valéry himself lived the dilemma concretely, and never got the better of it, as indeed no one can, and it forms the subject-matter of all his writing. He was perpetually trying to define the essence of life, and since, by definition, he couldn't relate it to any transcendent absolute, his final philosophy is a sort of nihilism. All that the consciousness can say is that it tries perpetually to understand the process of life, and just as perpetually fails. To use an image that recurs all through Valéry's work, it is like a serpent trying to swallow its own tail. And then, in the end, it is defeated by death.

Now the sun is important in all this, because it is the source and regulator of life and consciousness, and therefore the exact opposite of death. It is no accident, for instance, that Valéry rose every morning at dawn to try to catch his consciousness, as it were, at the initial point of the daily solar circle, when it might be supposed to be at its freshest and purest. His notebooks are full of lyrical passages which are really prose poems to early morning light. Nor is it an accident, I think, that his best known poem, *Le Cimetière Marin*, which is a meditation on the three major external realities: the earth, the sea and the sun, as they stand in relationship to the consciousness, should be situated at midday, in midsummer, *midi le juste*, as he calls it, the point in time when the sun is exactly above the cemetery, that is above the earth containing the human life-cycle, and above the sea which intensifies the sunlight, so that the consciousness is caught in a momentary and perfect balance between the three basic and essential elements, fire, earth, and water:

> *L'âme exposée aux torches du solstice*
> *Je te soutiens, admirable justice*
> *De la lumière aux armes sans pitié!*
> *Je te rends pure à ta place première*
> *Regarde-toi . . . .*

> (With my soul exposed to the torches of the solstice
> I uphold you, admirable justice
> Of light so pitilessly armed!
> I return you pure to your place of origin,
> Look at yourself. . . .)

That is, the highest function of the consciousness at its most acute is simply to be aware of the sun in its relationship to the earth. This manifestation of the contemplative faculty, which is a pantheistic parallel to religious contemplation, might be termed spiritual sun-bathing, and it may enter to some extent into physical sun-bathing. After all, when people take off their clothes to sun-bathe, we cannot be sure that the action is to be understood only literally. It may also be a symbolic baring of their non-transcendental souls to the principle of life.

Valéry's *Cimetière Marin* has justifiably become a modern classic, but there is an even finer, if less well-known poem, entitled *Ebauche d'un serpent*, which contains a magnificent invocation to the sun, on the part of the Devil in the Garden of Eden. The paradox of this passage, and indeed of the whole poem, is that it combines total nihilism—the sun is seen as "God's" great mistake: "He" should never have said, *Let there be light*, but should have allowed the dark void to continue eternally—with intense appreciation of the beauty of the sunlit world:

Soleil, soleil! . . . Faute éclatante!
Toi qui masques la mort, soleil,
Sous l'azur et l'or d'une tente
Où les fleurs tiennent leur conseil;
Par d'impénétrables délices,
Toi, le plus fier de mes complices
Et de mes pièges le plus haut,
Tu gardes les coeurs de connaître
Que l'univers n'est qu'un défaut
Dans la pureté du Non-être.

Grand soleil qui sonnes l'éveil
A l'être, et de feux l'accompagnes,
Toi qui l'enfermes d'un sommeil
Trompeusement peint de campagnes,
Fauteur des fantômes joyeux
Qui rendent sujette des yeux
La présence obscure de l'âme,
Toujours le mensonge m'a plu
Que tu répands sur l'absolu,
O roi des ombres fait de flamme!

(Sun, sun! . . . Brilliant error!
You, sun, who mask death
Beneath the azure and gold of a tent
Where flowers hold their council;
By impenetrable delights,
You, the proudest of my accomplices
And the highest of my snares,
You prevent hearts from knowing
That the universe is only a defect
In the purity of Non-Being.

Great sun, you who sound the awakening
To being, and accompany it with fire,
You who enclose it in a sleep
Deceptively painted with landscapes.
Creator of the joyous phantoms
Which make the obscure presence of the soul
Subject to the eyes.
Always has that falsehood pleased me
With which you overlay the absolute,
O king of shadows made of flame!)

Francis Ponge, compared to Valéry, is a minor poet, but a very charming one, who has made it his business for the last fifty years to compose prose poems about objects, any objects— a glass of water, an open door, a wasp, a piece of soap, etc. The point about this, of course, is that for someone with what we might call an Existentialist sensibility, there are no privileged objects, as there were in traditional poetry. Shelley wrote an *Ode to the West Wind*, Keats an *Ode to a Nightingale*, because the wind and the nightingale are sublime romantic objects; Ponge has written an *Unfinished Ode to Mud*. This is because everything outside the consciousness is object, and the lyrical emotion can be engendered by establishing a sufficiently subtle linguistic web between the sense-perceptions relating to any particular object and the rest of the consciousness. However, in our corner of the universe, there is one object which takes precedence over all others, and this is the sun, of which the earth is presumably only a cooling fragment. Also, by a process of what we might call narcissistic parthenogenesis, the sun has evoked life on the earth, but all that this life can do in the last resort is contemplate its source, that is look back at the sun. Now man thinks he is a subject, because he can look at the central object, the sun, but in fact what appears to be object is subject. The sun is subject and man is object; the human consciousness, which thinks it is subject, is really an unconscious object with regard to the sun, and so on. Ponge develops this parody of a creation myth in one of his longer works, *Le soleil placé en abîme*, in Volume III of *Le Grand Recueil*. *Placé en abîme* is a heraldic term, which means placed in the centre of the escutcheon. The sun is in the centre of our escutcheon, *i.e.* our universe, but *abîme* also has the meaning of abyss, limitless depths, and the sun is of course suspended in the infinity of space. Ponge's poem, which is in several parts, consists of a series of variations on the idea that the sun is an intangible pseudo-object operating as supreme subject at the centre of the universe. Let me quote one or two extracts:

> *Qu'est ce que le soleil comme objet? C'est le plus brillant des objets du monde. . . .*
> *Le soleil ne peut être remplacé par aucune formule logique,*
> CAR *le soleil n'est pas un objet.*

LE PLUS BRILLANT *des objets du monde n'est—de ce fait—*
NON—*n'est pas un objet ; c'est un trou, c'est l'abîme métaphysique :*
la condition formelle et indispensable de tout au monde.
La condition de tous les autres objets.
La condition même du regard.

(What is the sun as object? It is the most brilliant of the objects in the
  world. . . .
The sun cannot be replaced by any logical formula,
FOR the sun is not an object.
THE MOST BRILLIANT of objects is not—for that very reason—
NO—it is not an object: it is a void, the metaphysical abyss:
the formal and indispensible condition of everything in the world.
The condition of all the other objects.
The condition even of our seeing.)

Then follows a definition of the relationship between the sun
and the planetary life dependent upon it:

Voici en quelques mots ce qui s'est passé.
Le soleil, qui n'est pas la Vie, qui est peut-être la Mort
. . . qui est sans doute en deça de la Vie et de la Mort,—
a expulsé de lui certaines de ses parties, les a exilées,
envoyées à une certaine distance pour s'en faire contempler. . . .
Ainsi elles refroidissent, car il les a vouées à la mort,
mais d'abord—et c'est bien pire—à cette maladie,
à cette tiédeur que l'on nomme la vie.

(Here, in few words, is what happened.
The sun, which is not Life, which is perhaps Death,
. . . which is doubtless on the hither side of Life and Death,—
expelled certain of its parts from within itself, sent them into exile,
dispatched them a certain distance away so that they should look back
  upon it. . . .
Thus they cool down, because it has doomed them to death,
but first—and this is much worse—to that illness,
that tepidness which is called life.)

This is an obvious parody of the relationship between God and
the creature in Christianity. Ponge expands it by attributing
to the sun all the ambiguities possessed by God in the traditional
religions:

Ainsi les corps et la vie même ne sont qu'une dégradation de l'énergie solaire, vouée à
la contemplation et au regret de celle-ci, et—presque aussitôt—à la mort.
Ainsi le soleil est un fléau. Voyez, comme les fléaux, il fait éclater les épis, les cosses.
Mais c'est un fléau sadique, un fléau médecin. Un fléau qui fait se reproduire et qui
entretient ses victimes ; qui les recrée et s'en fait désirer.

Car—cet objet éblouissant—un nuage, un écran, le moindre volet, la moindre paupière qu'il forme suffit à le cacher, et donc à le faire désirer. Et il ne manque pas d'en former. Et ainsi la moitié de la vie se passe-t-elle dans l'ombre, à souhaiter la chaleur et la lumière, c'est à dire les travaux forcés dans la prison de l'azur.

(Thus bodies and life itself are only a degeneration of solar energy, doomed to regretful contemplation of that energy and—almost immediately—to death.

Thus the sun is a scourge or flail. See, like a flail it bursts open heads of grain and pods. But it is a sadistic, therapeutical flail or scourge. It causes its victims to reproduce themselves and it supports them; it *recreates* them and causes them to desire it.

For dazzling object though it be—a cloud, a screen, the smallest shutter, the smallest eyelid formed by it is enough to hide it and therefore to cause it to be desired. And it is not backward in forming such things. And so half of life is spent in shadow, wishing for warmth and light, that is for hard labour in the azure prison.)

N.B. There is an untranslatable half-pun in the French; *dans l'ombre* "in shadow" suggests *à l'ombre*="in jug."

This very nice expression *"les travaux forcés dans la prison de l'azur"* could be taken from Ponge and used as a sub-title for the whole of Albert Camus' work, and more especially for *Le Mythe de Sisyphe*, because it corresponds fairly accurately to Camus' concept of the Absurd in its relationship to sunlight. His attitude towards the sun is even more markedly dualistic than that of Valéry or Ponge. Whereas they see the sun as being primarily the creative God, with its diabolical and destructive aspects in a subordinate position, for Camus the sun is at once God and the Devil. This point may seem rather difficult to disentangle at first, because Camus may appear to be more of a sun-worshipper than the other two writers. In one sense, he is rather like a traditional Manichean who equates good with sunlight and evil with darkness. His early poetic prose in *Noces* and *L'Envers et l'Endroit* uses sunshine as a source of lyrical joy, and all through his work he tends to have recourse to the symbolism of the light and the dark. Northern towns—or towns that he considers as Northern—*e.g.* Paris, Prague, and Amsterdam—are associated with feelings of sorrow and guilt, whereas he repeatedly suggests that one can never be completely unhappy in the Mediterranean, because there is always the consolation of sunshine, which may be tragic, but at least is bracingly so.

However, beneath this light and dark symbolism, there is a deeper perception, which is very close to what I said about Gide's view of the sun as being an undifferentiated source of energy. In any case, Camus can't have the average, modern European view of the sun as being simply healthy, because although he was brought up in the sun, he was tubercular. Therefore, it is not surprising that, in spite of the concept of the light and the dark, he should set the action of his book, *La Peste*, which is a parable about the problem of evil, in North Africa, and should make the plague increase in intensity with the heat and decline again in the cooler weather. After all, the plague germs are just as much a part of nature as man is; therefore it is quite logical that they should flourish in sunlight, if sunlight is a source of life.

But what Camus senses much more definitely, I think, than either Valéry or Ponge is that it is difficult, if not impossible, for man to achieve an optimum relationship with the sun. This is an aspect of the Absurd; if many were not contingent, the weather—in the last analysis, the solar cycle—would be related to him in a necessary way. However, we know only too well that this is not so. We are usually either too hot or too cold. We are creatures of the sun, but it is difficult to get just the right amount of it. In some places there is not enough, and in others too much, and people have been known to grow weary of it even on the Riviera. This is beautifully expressed in *L'Etranger* in two important passages: first in the funeral scene, where there is a discrepancy between the brilliance of the weather, which causes the tar to melt and the people to perspire —*i.e.*, produces a superfluity of effect—and the deadness of the hero's mother, who is being buried. And secondly, in the famous episode of the shooting of the Arab, which takes place in the early afternoon after lunch, when the light is at its most intense, and the heat most oppressive. This, curiously enough, is just a little later than midday, which Valéry saw as a point of balance; for Camus, this is a moment of imbalance, when the killing is committed. We are clearly meant to understand that it is not the hero, Meursault, who is really responsible for the death of the Arab; he is just the person who happens to pull the trigger, and he is just as much an absurd victim of the universe as the Arab is. In a sense, the murderer is the sun, which brings too great a pressure to bear on the moment. In other words, the sun creates life and destroys life, with absolute indifference, as if the power behind the universe, or inherent in it, had no inkling of the human distinction between good and evil. Only a slight shift in emphasis is needed to move from this point of view to the more despairing attitude that the power behind the universe is predominantly evil; Camus makes this shift at least once in the late short story, *Le Renégat*, which is about a Christian missionary being converted to devil-worship in the Sahara. Here the blinding glare of the sun becomes a totally evil force to be adored, as it were, for its own sake as an aggressive manifestation of the Absurd.

I am not sure that Camus himself fully realised the implications of this. Perhaps his creative instinct sometimes carried him further than his conscious thought was prepared to go. At any rate, in his major theoretical work, *L'Homme révolté*, he tries to maintain a very different philosophical standpoint. There he seeks to build up a humanistic philosophy on a kind of average relationship to the sun; it is almost as if he wished to humanise the sun itself. He argues that wisdom lies in what he calls *la pensée de midi* or *la pensée solaire*, which is distinguished by *la mesure*, *i.e.*, the Greek sense of measure, and is characteristic of the Mediterranean. He even falls back on to a pseudo-Rousseau-istic conception of the goodness of Nature, which he transposes to the Mediterranean, and sees as being a permanent and valuable feature of that area, to be contrasted with the harm-fully rampant ideologies of the Northern countries, which are unnatural through being divorced from the Mediterranean. All this, I am afraid, is just a lot of wishful thinking that Camus is yielding to in a mood of weakness. No doubt we have to respect the Mediterranean as the cradle of European civilisation, but it certainly has no monopoly of sanity, and its intermediate solar position, between the equator on the one hand and the Arctic circle on the other, is only a geographical fact which can be turned into innumerable different psychological realities, as the historical record shows.

In the house of the sun there are many mansions, and we can perhaps say that some (such as the Riviera) are more desirable than others, but in the last resort—to revert to Ponge's expression—they are all equally contained within *la prison de l'azur*.

7. Surrealism and Super-realism

As a movement, Surrealism had fallen apart well before 1939, yet even today it is remarkable how many of its features survive, sporadically, in the life around us, particularly in advertising and show-business. While I was reading this English translation of Maurice Nadeau's book,* I went to see the Beatles film, *Help!*, a very unsatisfactory concoction, I thought, but interesting in that it was obviously made by people who have assimilated something of the Surrealist principles that Nadeau describes.

The film is conceived as a dream in which no explanations are given. The location changes irrationally. The story, such as it is, is based on the magic significance of a ring, *i.e.* it combines a pun—ring/Ringo—with the mystic quest theme. A gas-pipe comes through the navel of an Elizabethan portrait, as it might in a canvas by Dali. The heroes are pursued simultaneously by Oriental priests (the Occult) and scatty scientists *(cf.* Jarry's *Dr Faustroll)*. One Beatle shrinks like Alice in Wonderland, a great favourite of the Surrealists. All four Beatles have the edgy, jeering attitudes and uncouth expression of minor Ubus, and form a sort of quadripartite Id. Although none of this rises above the level of commercial gimmickry, it is all Surrealist paraphernalia, whether it has been taken directly and consciously from the Surrealists themselves or has been relayed to the makers of the film through the Marx Brothers, the Goon Show, and other sources.

Traces of Surrealism can also be seen on all sides among various social and aesthetic rebels, such as the Beats (the Surrealists rejected the indignity of earning a living), drug-

* Maurice Nadeau, *The History of Surrealism*, translated by Richard Howard, with an Introduction by Roger Shattuck (1965).

addicts (drink, drugs, and any other artificial paradises are better than the acceptance of the humdrum), and Pop artists (the irrational collocation of found objects can be a creative act). Two or three years ago, I noticed a strong neo-Surrealist feeling at the Writers' Conference of the Edinburgh Festival. We were treated to a "happening", very like the *spectacles-provocations* organised by Tristan Tzara nearly fifty years earlier; William Burroughs described his "cut-up" method of composition which seemed reminiscent of the Surrealist cult of chance; Alexander Trocchi, an admitted drug-addict, talked about the "exploration of inner space" almost in Occult terms. I may add that the Scottish poets on the platform, perhaps unnerved by these outbreaks of weirdness, drank themselves into such a state of incoherence that the atmosphere, on one occasion, became almost as rowdy as that of the famous first night of *Ubu Roi* in 1896.

It is difficult to decide what exactly these various manifestations mean. Are parts of the *avant-garde* still soldiering on, fifty years behind the times? Did Surrealism, before it disintegrated, inject some inexhaustibly fruitful ideas into society? Or did it open a sort of Pandora's Box that has never been closed again? Was it, in other words, a marvellous upsurge of hidden truths or merely the establishment, on a more or less permanent basis, of age-old, anarchistic saturnalia?

In stating the problem in this way, I am, of course, asking a rational question and this—from the Surrealist point of view—may be an inadmissible thing to do. I am struck by the fact that even expository books about Surrealism tend to be written in a non-rationalistic way. Nadeau's history, for instance, is couched in a highly emotional tone, and another well-known study, Michel Carrouges' *André Breton ou les données fonda-mentales du surréalisme* (1950), is even more passionate. I am not suggesting that partisan feeling is wrong. The point is that reading Nadeau and Carrouges on Surrealism is like reading an explanation of Christianity by a Christian apologist who is not going to raise any serious doubts about fundamental points of dogma. Surrealism presents itself as a system of belief requiring an act of faith before it can even be understood.

Something of this attitude has even rubbed off on to English and American academics who are interested in the subject, or perhaps these academics have become interested because they were potential converts. Professor J. H. Matthews, an Englishman now at the University of Minnesota, recently produced a lucid, useful, but avowedly uncritical *Introduction to Surrealism* in which he declares: "No one who has not viewed it from within can hope to fully comprehend Surrealism." Professor Shattuck, in his Introduction to a volume of translations from Jarry,* refers to *Dr Faustroll* as "an exasperating and haunting work" and adds that "terms in which to judge its success or failure scarcely exist outside its own pages". Both these statements seem strange, coming from academics, because academic discourse is by definition rational and its function, in dealing with the irrational, is to define it and judge it in detail, from the point of view of reason. There is a difference between a normal university and the Collège de Pataphysique. Although Professor Shattuck is a member of the latter, I am willing to bet that he does not lecture pataphysically at the University of Texas, just as I do not expect Professor Matthews to punctuate his lectures at Minnesota with Ubu-like cries of *Merdre*. We don't need propaganda for Surrealism from academics *qua* academics, and I think Professor Shattuck is writing as a believer and not as an academic when he states, in his Introduction to Jarry:

> All his writings circle about the moment of authentic enactment that can make the unreal real and vice versa. . . .

Or, again, when he says of Surrealism in general, in his Introduction to Nadeau:

> We had best be attentive to this intense catharsis-sublimation of the Twenties and Thirties. More urgently than ever our children face the challenge of liberating their desire, and here for their scrutiny lies one of the great corporate case-histories of that search.

"Moment of authentic enactment" and "liberating their desire" I recognise as Surrealist phrases, but Professor Shattuck

---

* Alfred Jarry, *Selected Works*, edited by Roger Shattuck and Simon Warson-Taylor (1965).

does not explain them, and I cannot give them any rational meaning. Of course, "reason" too is opaque, but I feel I know, on the level of academic discourse, what is meant by a rational explanation.

Looked at from the outside, the history of the "catharsis-sublimation," as described by Nadeau, is fairly easy to follow in broad outline, although it is as chequered with quarrels and splinter-movements as the history of the Communist Party or of Psycho-analysis.

The starting-point was the First World War, which came as a traumatic shock to so many intellectuals. Since rational, civilised governments could perpetrate such horrors, it was felt that there must be something wrong with reason. One can quibble straight away about the logic of this; perhaps it is the irrationalism of governments, disguised as rationalism, that starts wars and wages them systematically; if so, what is wanted is more reason, not less. However, the first reaction was Dada, invented by Tzara in Zurich. The name is a nonsense term, signifying presumably that since language, the primary instrument of reason, has broken down, any combination of syllables is as good as any other. Tzara moved to Paris where, we are told, a number of young men were waiting for him "as if he were the Messiah". By 1922, Dada had given way to Surrealism under the aegis of André Breton, who asserted himself almost at once as a stronger leader than Tzara. The theoretical difference between the movements was that Dada remained purely destructive and anarchistic whereas Surrealism claimed to have a positive content. It was "a mode of life," an attempt "to change life," "to transform the world," not merely a literary school. Its adherents carried the traditional anti-bourgeois, anti-Catholic revolt to the last extreme, denounced patriotism, attacked the pillars of the Establishment, and were openly scandalous in behaviour. For many of them, bliss was it in that dawn to be alive; others expressed their negative exasperation, or their positive thirst for the super-real, by committing suicide.

What exactly Breton, Soupault, Aragon, Eluard, Desnos, *et al.* lived on is not explained in Nadeau's book. We may suppose that they led a bohemian, hand-to-mouth existence, while they were evolving their Surrealist techniques of automatic writing and dream-association, and reconnoitring their spiritual ancestry: Apollinaire, Jarry, Lautréamont, Rimbaud, Baudelaire, Lewis Carroll, Gérard de Nerval, the Marquis de Sade, Rabelais, the alchemists, the Kabbala, etc. Freud confirmed their belief in the unconscious, although they did not emphasise that Freud's work was meant as a rationalistic exploration of the unconscious. Like some Christian believers who assume that what belies common sense also refutes rationalism, they took Einstein's Theory of Relativity and Heisenberg's Indeterminacy Principle to indicate that science had transcended reason. Simultaneously, the painters and sculptors were being inspired by the pre-rational features of primitive art and the absurd nature of random objects picked up in the flea-market.

In its initial phase, Surrealism was both anti-political and anti-literary, although writing and the founding of reviews was an important, and indeed the most tangible, feature of the Surrealists' activity. After being as hostile to the Russian Revolution as they were to Western bourgeois society, some of them went over to Communism and, in the end, almost all had a pro-Communist bias. How they managed to reconcile a belief in materialism with their emphasis on the mystical is not easy to understand from Nadeau's book, and of course Surrealism as such could never be acceptable to Soviet orthodoxy. Possibly, they came to feel the need to attach their rebelliousness to some concrete political symbol and this was supplied for a time at least by the Soviet Union. Another concession was their gradual admission of the fact that they were writers and artists, rather than men of action, and it is notorious that some of the artists became extremely rich. Perhaps they were led to stress their aesthetic role, because the cult of the folk-unconscious and of anti-rationalism was being embarrassingly successful in Nazi Germany.

When Breton left for America at the beginning of the Second World War, Surrealism as a movement had come to an end. By the Liberation, Existentialism had taken over in France and it is interesting to see that both Sartre and Camus, while they borrow quite a lot from Surrealism, are at pains to indicate their rejection of it.

If we take a general view and try to see this whole cultural phase in perspective, it appears as an intellectual and aesthetic explosion comparable to the Romantic Movement, and in fact the analogy has often been drawn. Just as the Romantics were in revolt against neo-classical convention and Enlightenment rationalism after the cataclysm of the French Revolution and the Napoleonic Wars, so the Surrealists attacked bourgeois conventions and nineteenth-century positivism after the cataclysm of the First World War.

A point that has not been made, so far as I can discover, is that a contemporary intellectual movement in the twentieth century was Logical Positivism, which can be defined as an attempt on the part of rationalism to bring itself up to date by a close scrutiny of language. Its puritanical mistrust of loose language was the exact counterpart of the Surrealist cult of automatism. While neo-primitives in Paris were surf-riding on the artificially stimulated waves of the unconscious, neurotic young men in Oxford and Cambridge were writhing in agonies of precision.

I think the people in Paris perhaps had more fun, but on neither side did language yield up its secret. Logical Positivism was not a science of language, and it was ultimately desiccating, if allowed to invade the emotional life. Surrealism was marked by a strong vein of religiosity and oscillated between destructiveness and mystic affirmation. The destructiveness was logical enough. Man has not been let into the secret of creation and so, through pique, he may wish to smash what he can of it, as a child breaks an incomprehensible toy. This attitude is quite clearly indicated in Sade, Lautréamont, and Jarry. Breton presumably meant something similar when he wrote that the simplest Surrealist act is to go down into the street and fire at random into the crowd. Those Surrealists who committed suicide were no doubt also consistent on this score. But the positive professions of Surrealist faith are much less convincing and, in particular, Breton's oft-quoted statement, made in 1929 in the *Second Manifeste du Surréalisme*:

> Everything suggests that there exists a certain point of the mind at which life and death, the real and the imaginary, the past and the future, the communicable and the incommunicable, the heights and the depths, cease to be perceived contradictorily. Now it is in vain that one would seek any other motive for surrealist activity than the hope of determining this point. . . .

Nothing, surely, suggests the existence of such a point except the recurrent human feeling, thwarted daily in the experience of living, that everything must in the end somehow make sense. (It should be noted incidentally that this feeling is also the fundamental emotion behind rationalism.) The Surrealist does not want to formulate the sense in a fully articulate form; he wants to enter into mystic contact with it, or even to enter into it, as if it were some accessible state outside time, *l'Eternel surréel*, as Artaud called it. Therefore, in spite of frequent denials and a noisy hostility to revealed religion, he is really a transcendentalist. He locates the transcendent in the unconscious, which is at once individual and collective, and his channels of communication with it are automatic writing, dreams, drugged or hypnotic conditions, the acceptance of chance objects or events as signs, and the utterances of the mentally deranged.

In the *Premier Manifeste du Surréalisme*, Breton blandly assumes that *le fonctionnement réel* of the mind is everything *except* the exercise of reason. This act of faith has certainly produced interesting results, especially in painting and sculpture, where inarticulate promptings can be concretely rendered and where technical questions of composition and draughtsmanship can engage the conscious mind, leaving the unconscious to supply the content. In literature, whose medium is language, it is much more difficult to set out consciously to be unconscious, and for this reason Surrealism must have a greater proportion of sheer rubbish to its credit than most other movements. Breton himself is a gifted writer, but he is not a natural translator of the unconscious, like Lewis Carroll, or Blake, or Baudelaire in certain moods, or Ionesco perhaps in his early plays. His literary theme is not the Beyond, but nostalgia for the Beyond, which is quite a different matter. *Nadja*, the account of his association with a mad woman, owes its charm and its naïve contradictions to the unhappy rationalist's wistful longing to enter into communion with the crazy, just as Michel Leiris's *L'Afrique fantôme* is a fascinating description of a civilised, Surrealist ethnologist trying hard to be at one with the uncivilised.

To refer to Breton as a kind of *rationaliste qui s'ignore* may seem like addressing a terrible insult to that pontificating figure, but he strikes one as being radically different from the genuinely unbalanced characters, such as Jarry, Artaud, and Raymond Roussel who, conversely, at times give the pathetic impression of trying to be sane. Breton and some of the others, in exclaiming about the marvels of the unconscious, are rather like people pressing their fingers on their eyeballs and raving about the beauty of the stars they see. The stars are visible to them all right, and they are pretty in a random, given way; but they are neither works of art nor philosophical systems. Breton wrote in the *Premier Manifeste* of tapping the strange forces of the unconscious and then "submitting them subsequently, if need be, to the scrutiny of reason". Yet there is little or no discussion of the "higher rationalism" in any of the Surrealist writing I have come across. There is much talk of "desire" which, like Existentialist "freedom", appears to be man's spiritual autonomy, his proclaimed ability to assert his will against the forces of the universe. It would be difficult to quarrel with this as an initial conception because we are all pitchforked into the world as a bundle of appetites and are kept going by the instinctive unfolding of vitality and the illusion, or reality, of choice. But "choice", or "desire", or "freedom" can only be made more real by an ever greater conscious, *i.e.* rational, knowledge of what we are and of the conditions in which we operate. Such knowledge has always been infinitesimal in quantity compared to the welter of the irrational, and this may be because deeply rational statements are more difficult to achieve than irrational ones, because more organically complex. And what danger is there of rational knowledge ever destroying the marvellous, since the marvellous is all around us and gleams only too obviously through the fabric of rational discourse?

It is perhaps easy enough to see this now, when so much has happened in the last half-century to teach us that common sense covers only a very limited area of experience and that the rationalistic study of the universe, far from diminishing wonder, increases it. The situation was probably different in the oppressively prosaic atmosphere of 19th-century France, when the revolt against common sense had to be flamboyant and suicidal in order to exist at all.

II

THEATRE AND CINEMA

8. Saint Artaud

In the argument about *Marat-Sade* and the Theatre of Cruelty some people have thought fit to take a stand against what they consider to be an outburst of sensationalism. A stage covered with lunatics, a pink-fleshed, sinisterly soft-spoken Marquis de Sade being whipped into orgasm by the strands of Charlotte Corday's hair, jigging movements directly suggestive of copulation, a general atmosphere of madly controlled frenzy always ready to flare up into anarchistic violence—can Aunt Edna be expected to take this? She has strained to accept the kitchen-sink, provincial accents, the Absurd and homosexuality in national heroes. Can she go still farther in her concessions to modern culture? The answer seems to be that she who can tolerate a Birmingham whine will not jib at a phallic ritual. It was Uncle who objected, and Uncle does not appear to have done his homework.

The concept of the Theatre of Cruelty, which inspired Peter Weiss, the author, and Peter Brook, the producer, of *Marat-Sade*, is not a strikingly novel feature of the European theatrical movement. It was formulated as long ago as 1933 by the Frenchman, Antonin Artaud, and he was harking back to Alfred Jarry's *Ubu Roi*, first performed in 1896, and to the English Elizabethan theatre of violence, for which he had a great liking. The recent happenings at the Aldwych Theatre are just another incident in the vast revolt against rationalistic humanism, which has been in progress now for almost a century, has relaunched Sade, and has thrown up in France two such typical figures of anguish as Rimbaud and Artaud. Incidentally, those anti-rationalists interested in the mysterious implications of names have not failed to point out that *Art (hur Rimb)aud* equals *Artaud*. If this sign produces in the reader

K

a religious shudder transcending all the feeble joys of rationalistic etymology, he will know at once where he stands with regard to the movement.

There has, as yet, been no systematic biographical or critical study of Artaud and, while he is referred to in histories of Surrealism, he does not rate a mention either in *L'Encyclopédie Larousse* or in the *Oxford Companion to French Literature*. The details of his life are not easy to piece together with any certainty, but Gallimard are in process of publishing his *Oeuvres Complètes*.* The edition itself is rather puzzling, as if it had been put together without any firm guiding principle. The writings are classified partly according to chronology and partly according to subject-matter, so that the reader has to move backwards and forwards in order to follow Artaud's development. These uncertainties were perhaps inevitable in the case of a writer who had so chequered a career and whose literary remains seem to have been so widely scattered.

He was born in 1896 in Marseilles and came to Paris in 1920. He gives no details about his family in his works and appears to have prided himself on being a self-invented man. It is said that he spent some time in a mental home even before he left Marseilles, although it is uncertain whether or not he was already an opium-addict at this early stage. The first autobiographical details are contained in a series of letters he wrote to Jacques Rivière in 1923 when Rivière, as editor of the *Nouvelle Revue Française*, turned down some poems Artaud had submitted. Rivière, rightly enough, saw more talent in the letters than in the poems and eventually published the former. This is possibly a unique instance in literary history of an editor rejecting a creative work and then treating the subsequent correspondence between the author and himself as a valid creation. The letters describe a state of stress verging on mental breakdown:

> Je souffre d'une effroyable maladie de l'esprit. Ma pensée m'abandonne à tous les degrés. Depuis le fait simple de la pensée jusqu'au fait extérieur de sa matérialisation dans les mots. Mots, formes de phrases, directions intérieures de la pensée, réactions simples de l'esprit, je suis à la poursuite

* Antonin Artaud, *Oeuvres Complètes*, (Gallimard, Vol. I, 1956).

constante de mon être intellectuel. Lors donc que *je peux saisir une forme*, si imparfaite soit-elle, je la fixe dans la crainte de perdre toute la pensée. Je suis au-dessous de moi-même, je le sais, j'en souffre, mais j'y consens dans la peur de ne pas mourir tout à fait.

(I am afflicted with an appalling sickness of the mind. My thought deserts me at all levels, from the mere fact of thought to the external fact of its materialisation in words. Words, sentence-forms, inner directions of thought, simple reactions of the mind . . . I am constantly in pursuit of my intellectual being. On those occasions when *I can grasp a form*, however imperfect it may be, I note it down for fear of losing the whole of my thought. I am below my true level, I know, and this makes me suffer, but I accept the fact for fear of not entirely dying.)

The negative in the last sentence seems to be a mistake but, on the whole, the letters give a vivid picture of the pressure of the inarticulate within a mind that cannot adequately handle language, or is dissatisfied with it. Other letters indicate that this anguish was often a physical pain or paralysis, and the drug-taking may have begun in the first place as a way of relieving suffering. Perhaps this initial trouble with language also explains why Artaud was later to spend so much of his time advocating a form of theatre that would not depend mainly for its effect on the use of language.

His first volumes of "poems" or prose fragments, *L'Ombilic des limbes* and *Le Pèse-nerfs* are both in the Surrealist vein and give a less explicit reflection than his letters to Rivière of the mental anguish to which he was subject. To earn his living, and also in accordance with his active vocation, he worked as an actor both on the stage and in the cinema, and his major achievement in this field was probably his performance as a saintly young monk in Carl Dreyer's *Joan of Arc*. His presence on the Parisian scene appears to have been intermittent, because he was constantly in and out of mental homes and nursing homes. But, through thick and thin, he persisted in one idea, which was to create a new form of "total" dramatic art. He expressed this ideal to some extent in connection with the cinema, and the better part of Volume III of his *Oeuvres* is devoted to writings related to that art.

However, he was primarily a man of the theatre, and he made frequent attempts to establish himself in the Parisian theatrical world. With Roger Vitrac, the author of *Victor ou les Enfants au Pouvoir* (another work which recently caused a mild scandal in London, although its date of composition, 1927, makes it as venerable as the early Coward), he founded the Théâtre Alfred Jarry, which never had any building of its own and put on only a few, ill-rehearsed performances, with indifferent results. Later, he badgered Paulhan, Gide, Jean-Richard Bloch and others to help him to found a *Théâtre de la Nouvelle Revue Française*, and at various times he approached established *metteurs-en-scène* such as Charles Dullin and Louis Jouvet with requests for work in their theatres. He did eventually succeed in being responsible for a few productions. Some, such as his version of the Cenci story, were rather badly received; others, in particular a performance of a Strindberg play, enjoyed a modest *succès d'estime*. But he never managed to do what he wanted to do in the theatre and his correspondence is a pathetic record of failure, not unlike Baudelaire's. "*Je ne suis pas aussi fou qu'on le dit* (I am not as mad as they say I am)," he cries despairingly at one point. Even Paulhan, who was well disposed towards him, apparently found him trying and was not as keen to publish his writings as Artaud would have liked.

After 1936, when he went for a few months to Mexico and was delighted with the direct and primitive nature of Mexican everyday life, it becomes difficult to follow his career by means of the volumes of the *Oeuvres* so far published. From other sources, it can be learnt that he spent an increasing amount of time in mental homes, and, much to his indignation, was subjected to electro-shock treatment. His mental disturbance is quite clear in the *préambule* already mentioned, which begins rationally enough and ends in delirium. When he re-emerged in postwar Paris, he was convinced, among other things, that evil, occult forces were at work against him. In 1947, a few months before his death, he gave a reading of some of his works at the Vieux Colombier to an audience which included Gide and Breton; several people who were there refer to the session as a remarkable experience. Artaud held the stage for three hours, oscillating, apparently, between genius and madness.

Artaud was, then, an extreme example of the *poète maudit*, and opinions will vary about how far he was a poet and how far he was just *maudit*. His theatrical doctrine is probably his most substantial achievement; he embodied it in a series of articles written from 1932 onwards, which first came out in book form in 1938 under the title of *Le Théâtre et son double*, and have been reissued as Volume IV of the *Oeuvres*. Presumably, it was the 1938 volume which popularised his name among the European theatrical *avant-garde* and is ultimately behind the *Marat-Sade* play. There was also, no doubt, some direct transmission of his ideas by word of mouth, especially through Jean-Louis Barrault, with whom he worked for a time.*

Like so many theatrical reformers, he begins with a fierce condemnation of the commercial, middle-class theatre, with its immediate realism, its discursive psychology and its dependence on a written, linguistic text, for which the actors serve primarily as mouthpieces. Although he declares himself a total enemy of existing society, his attack is not prompted by ordinary political or social motives. He is not just anti-bourgeois; like D. H. Lawrence, he is a critic of western civilisation as a whole, and the burden of his complaint is that "living" and "culture" have split off from each other.

> . . . un civilisé cultivé est un homme renseigné sur des systèmes, et qui pense en systèmes, en formes, en signes, en représentations.
>
> C'est un monstre chez qui s'est développée jusqu'à l'absurde cette faculté que nous avons de tirer des pensées de nos actes au lieu d'identifier nos actes à nos pensées.
>
> Si notre vie manque de soufre, c'est-à-dire d'une certaine magie, c'est qu'il nous plaît de regarder nos actes et de nous perdre en considérations sur les formes rêvées de nos actes au lieu d'être poussés par eux. . . .
>
> Toutes nos idées sur la vie sont à reprendre à une époque ou rien n'adhère plus à la vie. . . .
>
> Protestation contre l'idée séparée que l'on se fait de la culture, comme s'il y avait la culture d'un côté et la vie de l'autre; et comme si la vraie culture n'était pas un moyen raffiné de comprendre et d'exercer la vie.
>
> (. . . a cultured, civilised man is someone who knows about systems, and who thinks by means of systems, forms, signs and representations.
>
> He is a monster in whom there has been developed *ad absurdum* our

---

* See Barrault's memoirs, *Souvenirs pour demain* (1972).

---

capacity to deduce thoughts from our actions instead of identifying our actions with our thoughts.

If our lives are lacking in sulphur, that is in a certain kind of magic, this is because we prefer to contemplate our actions and lose ourselves in daydreams about the imaginary forms of our actions, instead of being prompted by our actions. . . .

All our ideas about life need to be revised now that nothing is in contact with life any longer. . . .

I protest against the idea that culture is something separate, as if culture were on one side and life on another; and as if true culture were not a refined means of understanding and exercising life.)

Since Artaud looks to the theatre to remedy the evils of civilisation, he is trying to raise it to the level of a religious ritual. Both in the ancient and in the modern world, the theatre emerged from religion. Artaud would like to reverse the process of secularisation, without returning to any specific religious doctrine. He hopes to find a group of men *"capables d'imposer cette notion supérieure du théâtre, qui nous rendra à tous l'équivalent naturel et magique des dogmes auxquels nous ne croyons plus* (capable of imposing that superior concept of the theatre, which will restore to all of us the magic and natural equivalent of the dogmas in which we no longer believe)". He was enthusiastic about the Balinese Theatre, which he saw perform in Paris, and he also claimed that everyday life in Mexico was conducted in a state of "constant exaltation". Both experiences confirmed him in his oft-repeated beliefs, first of all, that rationalistic language, and indeed verbal expression of any kind, is, in the theatre, often harmful, and of secondary importance at best, since any clear idea is dead and useless; and, secondly, that the public must be brought into contact with the real nature of existence, which is "cruel". His ambition was to affect the whole public, not just an élite.

The expression "Theatre of Cruelty" has caused some confusion, not only in the public mind but also perhaps among certain theatrical practitioners. Artaud, in his two *Manifestes du théâtre de la cruauté*, does not intend it in a sadistic sense, and, in spite of his connection with the Surrealists who had a fondness for the Marquis de Sade, he does not appear to mention the divine name at all in the works so far published. His meaning is that the theatre should be fully cognisant of the problem of evil, of the terrible mystery of life. It should be, in his striking phrase, *"de la métaphysique en activité"*. Without being a believer, he was reacting against the tendency, common since the Enlightenment, to play down the strength of evil in creation. There is, of course, a connection here with the Marquis de Sade. Mr Philip Toynbee, who recently deplored the present modish interest in cruelty, has said that no one nowadays would think of inventing a Theatre of Kindness. Perhaps not, but such a theatre existed in the 18th century; it was the bourgeois drama, which preached do-goodism and dripped with virtuous tears. The Marquis de Sade, however muddled he may have been in his philosophical statements and however woefully untalented as a writer, did at least proclaim the essential amorality of nature, and the power of instinctual drives; and he did so precisely when the Theatre of Kindness was at its height. Part of his fame is due not to his sexual specialisation but to his dogged emphasis on the intractability of evil. For this reason, Artaud might well have used Sade as an example, had it occurred to him to do so. He would also probably have approved of the *Marat-Sade* spectacle at the Aldwych, because the sexual episodes in it, far from being naughtily stimulating, produce a shudder of horror at the grotesque mystery of sex, and Artaud was obviously a sex-hater. This is the dividing line between him and D. H. Lawrence (as well as between Sade and Lawrence), since Lawrence's *metaphysique en activité* involved joyous sexual functioning.

To say that Artaud wished to restore the problem of evil to a central place in the theatre and to express it by means of concrete stage action rather than by words is to reduce him to a clear idea, and this he would have loathed. It should therefore be added that a number of things about his theory are not clear.

For instance, his use of the concept of the "double" is not immediately comprehensible. He begins his manifesto with a long and brilliant description of a plague, and seems to be suggesting that the epidemic, by bringing people into over-whelming contact with evil, is fulfilling a purpose comparable to that of the theatre, when properly understood. Then he draws a parallel between the kind of theatre he wants and certain forms of metaphysical painting, in which truths are stated by means of the quality of colour and paint, rather than by the story. Again he suggests that the "double" is a metaphysical dimension of reality, which is represented on the stage by "hieroglyphic" actions. These conceptions are not unconnected with each other, but from the rationalistic point of view they betoken a loose treatment of the term "double", and one may wonder if Artaud's mental disturbance did not involve that obsession with reduplication which leads to the notion of the *Doppelgänger*. Still more obscure to the commonsensical student is his apparently firm belief in fortune-telling through cards and his attempt to evolve a technique of acting based on male, female and neuter breathings, according to the doctrines of the Kabbala. When, in his later writings, he proclaims that he is a male principle penetrating the universal matrix of the cosmos, it can only be hoped that he is in possession of some mystical truth, since his use of words is vacuous.

In studying him, the reader is constantly reminded not only of the *Marat-Sade* production but also of many other manifestations of the modern theatre: Barrault's performances of Claudel, which depend so much on stage movement and cosmic symbolism; Planchon's playing down of language in favour of stage-business; Ionesco's continuous emphasis on the fragility of the commonsense world; Beckett's use of symbols to refer to what might be called an inarticulate or intractable metaphysics, that is, a suggestion of perspective and depth without understanding; and Genet's elaborate theatre of ritual. The bourgeois theatre still survives no doubt, and has even scored new successes. But perhaps we can say that there now exists, alongside it, the theatre as secular church, mostly without dogma, and rational only in its more or less careful organisation of the irrational. In so far as Artaud contributed to this theatre, he is undoubtedly an important historical figure. He is, in fact, one of the saints of the new church and, like many saints, he leaves the ordinary mortal rather embarrassed to decide what, in his vision, is craziness and what is true insight.

9. The Play as Fable

For several months now I have been struggling with the translation of a book by Claude Lévi-Strauss, *Le Cru et le Cuit*, which is a structuralist interpretation of some of the myths of the South American Indians. The eminent French anthropologist is so good at proving that different folk-tales are variations on basic themes involving polar opposites—the hard and the soft, the fresh and the rotten, the mortal and the immortal, etc.—and that the same material is being endlessly rehandled by various tribes or groups of tribes, that I am beginning to be obsessed by his way of thinking and to see the whole of life and literature, even in Western Europe, in these terms. Two things which appear to be different are often the inverted images of each other. Something that strikes one at first sight as being very individual may turn out to be the nth variation on an ancient theme. The power of the collective imagination is so strong that particular artists, like particular folk-tales, often seem to exist, not for an intrinsic reason, but to complete the general pattern of possibilities at a given time. If a theme is "strong" in one quarter, it tends to be "weak" in another; an omission may be as significant as an inclusion; what is coded in oral or tactile terms in one context may be given a colour-coding or a taste-coding in another.

The theatre especially may lend itself to this kind of interpretation, since it is a half-spontaneous, half-synthetic folk-product, and a much more gregarious and primitive medium than most forms of art. I do not simply mean that there are tribes in the theatre, clans to the North of the river and clans to the South, with much painting of faces and flaunting of penis-sheaths. The plays themselves, for the most part, are hardly more individualised than fables. This is more immediately obvious when we are dealing with the past. I spent a lot of time last year reading 19th-century French bourgeois drama, and I must say that most of the plays seemed to have been written by the same faceless author, who was ringing the changes on the average sensibility of his class and his period and, in particular, combining the contradictions of his social context in such a way as to make them reassuringly acceptable for the duration of the play. A play may be actually composed by one man, but it often has a collective air about it, as if that man were a medium transmitting the pattern of conventions of a limited society. No doubt the same thing is observable during certain periods of the English theatre. The butler heaves to through the French windows, the maid answers the telephone, and "Who's for tennis?" rings out the merry cry.

To use Lévi-Strauss' terms, plays exist in series, and what one has to try to understand is the basic impulse behind each series and its direct and indirect manifestations. There may be interference between one series and another. Since we live in progressive time rather than cyclical time like the savages, succeeding series may overlap, with strange, anachronistic effects. But the most curious thing, perhaps, is that a good play practically never occurs on its own; it seems to be an optimum arrangement of elements that are already in the public domain. It may come at the beginning, the middle or the end of a series and, as in the case of native myths, there may be no means of deciding whether we can single out a parent work or whether we are dealing with several spontaneous expressions of the same tendency. To quote two further French examples: Racine was near the beginning of his series and all that came after him for a century was null and void; Beaumarchais occurred at the end of a long phase of the *picaro*-clever-valet-harlequin series and carried it to perfection.

Recently, I have noticed two themes that some disciple of Lévi-Strauss might set to work on. One is homosexuality, which seems to be comparatively new in the English theatre, although it has occurred from time to time in contemporary French drama. The other is alienation, which has been with us on the present-day French and English stages since Caligula and

Jimmy Porter began insulting God as Father-Image and bullying their women.

It is rather surprising that homosexuality, after being such a popular theme in novels, films and public discussion, should have taken so long to reach the English theatre, where it is in fact endemic. In the last few months, there have been three plays specifically on the subject: *The Killing of Sister George* by Frank Marcus, *Staircase* by Charles Dyer, and *When Did You Last See My Mother?* by Christopher Hampton. The first two are "well-made" plays, in which the mixture of genuine perceptiveness with theatrical convention is skilfully managed; the third is a very honest work, I should say, but technically uncertain towards the end. There have also been two plays that skirt around the subject: Noël Coward's *A Song At Twilight*, on which I animadverted at length in *Encounter*,* and *The Odd Couple*, which deals with divorcés living together and falling into a parody of the husband-and-wife relationship; it is not much more than a collection of gags, and is only half redeemed by the excellence of Victor Spinetti's performance as the neurotic, and therefore female, male. For good measure, we should perhaps add Danny La Rue's transvestite frolic, *Come Spy With Me* (written by Bryan Blackburn), about which I can imagine Lévi-Strauss waxing very subtle. Danny La Rue is a sort of inverted pantomime dame, *i.e.* a man is playing a woman, as in traditional pantomime, but instead of being comically ugly, he is comically alluring in the style of a rather old-fashioned glamour-girl. He is a kind of prettier Mae West, firing off smutty jokes so broad as to be almost innocent. I suppose that this androgynous brassiness, which combines a caricature of sex-appeal with the immediate male response to it, is meant to satisfy male narcissism or self-applauding phallicism; it is cheery stuff for the tumescent troops, in other words a semi-homosexual holiday for heterosexuals. My wife loathed it, but I found it fascinating in some unfathomable way. Perhaps the fact that Danny La Rue looks and sounds more like a large ventriloquist's doll than a real person is part of the explanation.

* July 1966

Come Spy With Me, The Odd Couple, and *A Song At Twilight* refer modishly to homosexuality, but do not deal with it and so are marginal or "weak". The other three are the "strong" central works, and they are uncannily alike. They are sour comedies which allow three actors—Paul Scofield, Beryl Reid, and Victor Henry—to give virtuoso performances of a subtly nasty quality, on the verge of tragedy but never quite settling into it. In each, there is one character, the "male", who does most of the talking, is always striking postures and is constantly abusing the "female." If this is a realistic feature taken from life, one has to conclude that nagging is much more consistent and violent in homosexual relationships than it is normally in heterosexual ones. Possibly it has to be, through the need to create that polarity which is present by definition when the partners belong to different sexes. The suspicion may then cross our structuralist minds that an ostensibly heterosexual play, in which nagging seems to have exceptional importance—there is one obvious example—may be a transposed expression of a homosexual sensibility.

The basic message of these three plays, as regards the quality of homosexual love, is very bleak. The relationship is, in each case, profoundly unsatisfactory. The middle-aged men in *Staircase* detest each other and are bound together only by the fact that they have no one else to turn to. The two women in *The Killing of Sister George* enjoy moments of fun, but their partnership is also on the rocks. The young man in *When Did You?* does not actually start his relationship because of a complicated system of repressions, but the end of the play seems to suggest that if it does now begin, it is doomed to failure. In each instance, the "male" character wilfully destroys the marriage and is morally unreliable. Nor is there any indication that the unreliability is due to the social stigma attaching to homosexuality; it is inherent in the erotic relationship itself. It would be interesting to know if this is actually the case, or whether the three authors have respected some unwritten rule that homosexuality may now be talked about, but that it should not be shown to be happy, just as adultery was dealt with endlessly in 19th-century drama and usually shown to be punished. It seems to me, from observation, that there are happy and durable homosexual relationships, yet these three English playwrights reproduce, in their slightly different ways, the unstable subject/object antagonism which is such a feature of the psychological pattern of Jean Genet's plays and novels. However, Genet's lack of adaptation to "normal" life goes much further than mere homosexuality.

Genet is, in fact, the supreme example of alienation, and this leads me on to the second theme. The aggressive young homosexual monologuist in *When Did You?* talks part of the time like the Osborne/Amis *révolté*, of whom Osborne and Amis have produced several versions, and who joins hands across the Channel with the Existentialist Outsider. This has probably been the most widespread of all recent dramatic characters. For a time he turned up regularly in every other television play. We saw him, for instance, on the stage in *A Bond Honoured* (Anglo-Spanish) and in *Tango* (Polish). He has had an undoubted success in the cinema as natural man driven mad by civilisation in *Morgan*, and he occurs once again as the slightly deranged bastard in David Mercer's play, *Belcher's Luck*.

However, in spite of his contemporary prevalence, I don't think he is a modern invention; he is a recent variation on a permanent Western character. He is the isolated consciousness who has fallen foul of existence, and there is no more universal type, from classical antiquity down to modern times. His basic feature is that he cannot understand why things are as they are, and his complaint may stem from a number of causes that are not clearly distinguished and that he himself confuses with each other. Sometimes, he is, or thinks himself to be, a social misfit (bastard, servant, slave, provincial, scholarship boy). He may have father-trouble, mother-trouble, uncle-trouble, sex-trouble, God-trouble.* I confess I am getting a little weary of

---

* Job, Prometheus, and Hamlet come in here, and the attitudes and imagery connected with them have been used again and again by the more modern exponents. Job has sat on many middens, a lot of them located, it would seem, in the Midlands; Prometheus has been gnawed at by different vultures, but homosexual guilt has recently been one of the most voracious; Hamlet has declaimed "To be or not to be" in excellent French prose.

listening to him railing against human Daddy and divine Daddy, as if nobody had ever done it before, but I suppose there has to be a first time for everyone. And it may be, of course, that this is the basic literary subject.

Belcher's Luck is a weird mixture, as if the young, alienated, sexually ambiguous monologuist had wandered out of *When Did You?* on to the set of some abandoned production of *The Cherry Orchard* or of a dramatisation of *Lady Chatterley's Lover.* In the declining great house is an ineffectual Christian gentleman who, all his life, has been little more than an appendage to his hard-drinking, much-copulating man-servant, Belcher. Belcher's bastard son is really burdened with two fathers: Belcher himself, unredeemed, witless natural man, and the Christian gentleman, whose religion and scruples represent civilisation at its most negative. Who will inherit the estate? The bastard doesn't want it, because he has opted out of society. Along comes a cool-as-ice upper-class niece who tricks Belcher into murdering his master, then drives him out and lives on in the great house with the bastard, keeping him beside her as a kind of impotent caricature of manhood, a blatherer without sex, a pet, a deranged fool.

The only telling parts of all this, I think—*i.e.* the only bits that don't sound borrowed but actually felt—are the speeches by the young bastard in which he complains, Job-like or Hamlet-like, about the absurdity of existence. He has one especially brilliant outburst in which he meditates on the absurdity of spermatozoon meeting ovum. As I listened to this, I was reminded of something else. Where recently had I heard a similar note of total rejection, of nihilistic rhetoric, of utter, gleeful alienation?

In Genet's *Les Paravents*, of course, where, under the guise of dealing with relationships between the French and the Algerians during the Algerian War, Genet expounds his view of the ultimate worthlessness of everybody, in a blend of sumptuous eloquence and violent obscenity. Whereas extreme alienation in Mercer's hero takes the form of ridiculing the process of conception, in Genet it leads to a preoccupation with death. One condemns the movement out of non-being into life, the other is obsessed with the exit back from life into non-being.

The difference is, that Genet, being alienation personified, is far more systematic in his symbolic destructiveness, so that the Comédie Française, that citadel of organised culture, resounded with maniacal cries and outrageous statement. One of Genet's beautiful young soldiers is killed while defecating, and describes the process in exquisite detail on his arrival in the world of shadows. Another, after dying, is saluted by a chorus of wind-breaking from his patriotic companions, who thus claim to give him a final taste of truly French air.

These scatological extremes are, incidentally, not unlike some of the episodes in the South American myths described by Lévi-Strauss. The deliberate and poetic obscenity of the *avant-garde* seems to have come full circle back to the neutral obscenity of the pre-historic. The savages invented myths of origin to explain how things came into being, and very unexpected some of those myths are. Since our sensory language is limited, it is no doubt inevitable that the modern myths of refusal should use elements of the same code.

10. A Pad in Paddington

The film which has been chosen to inaugurate the cinema in the new premises of the Institute of Contemporary Arts in Nash House is yet another—and immense—variation on the theme of the alienated individual. In the hand-outs concerning Don Levy's *Herostratus* there is no mention of Jean-Paul Sartre's *Erostrate*, but the resemblance between the film and the short story can hardly be accidental.

Sartre's hero, who was created some thirty years ago, is a Parisian so disgusted with the absurdity of life that he determines to go down into the street with a loaded revolver, fire five shots into the crowd as a flamboyant gesture, and kill himself with the sixth. In the event, he cannot commit suicide and we leave him cowering in a lavatory with the public clamouring outside. Mr Levy's hero, who is now four years old but has had to wait that time to get a showing in England, is a young Beatnik living in a picturesquely filthy room in the Harrow Road, who decides to have his suicide handled by a publicity firm but, in the event, cannot bring himself to jump, as arranged, from an office block next to St Paul's. A stranger who happens to be taking photographs on the roof at the same time tries to pull him back from the edge, and such are life's little ironies that it is the stranger who falls to his death, while our hero is left distraught and uncatharsised, running wildly once again through the asphalt jungle.

Now I cannot help thinking that this is a monumentally bad film—overblown, muddled, and incoherently imitative—but it is worth discussing because, clearly, a lot of loving effort has been put into the making of it, and if it is the sort of thing the ICA approves of, it has a symptomatic value which is more important than the film itself. It seems to me to prove that the

A Pad in Paddington

time has perhaps come to declare a closed season for the
absurdist hero, who is by now almost as big a bore as the
romantic hero ever was. The Absurd is part of the modern
consciousness: agreed. But the obvious points about it have
been made so many hundreds of times that one has difficulty in
sitting patiently in one's seat as the absurdist hero rants and
raves once more and the camera moves slowly—oh God, how
slowly—over the mute surface of the world.

The co-producer, Mr James Quinn, who presented the film
on its preliminary showing at the National Film Theatre,
invited the audience to look upon it as "an Abstract," "an
Event," which should be received outside the categories of
traditional cinema. This statement is itself a new commonplace, if we can apply the term "new" to something which goes
as far back as the early Surrealists. A more immediate pre-
decessor is, of course, Robbe-Grillet, with his enigmatic
sequences of recurring images. But Robbe-Grillet creates (or
claims to create) obsessive phantasms which have no relationship to the everyday world of politics and money-earning:
reality is never allowed to break into their dream-like structures.
Mr Don Levy's hero, on the other hand, is at odds with the
real world. We see him eating his heart out in his pad in
Paddington. We hear him confiding to the golden-hearted
Negro prostitute from the floor above that he is short of cash.
From time to time, he takes part in other real-life conversations
(improvised, according to the hand-outs, and sometimes
remarkably feeble). We gather, from the slogans on the walls
and the newsreel extracts that are interpolated into the film,
that the state of the modern world has a lot to do with his
misery; he says at length that he wants to die because he
cannot stand "all this crap". It follows that he is in a story, not
in a phantasm and, this being so, it is difficult to understand
why the story-line should be broken up by so many apparently
irrelevant images.

For instance, there is a fateful-looking lady in black leather
and carrying a black umbrella who keeps walking towards us
along the same glass-and-concrete modern street. When she
had occurred about a dozen times, it struck me that she must

161

L

be Death, like Maria Casarès in Cocteau's *Orphée*. She does not seem to be in the hero's mind. She must therefore be a comment by the director in the form of a semi-quotation. But what is the psychological or aesthetic point of repeating such a quotation *ad libitum*? Similarly, why keep flashing back to earlier glimpses of the story—a doll dangling from the ceiling of the pad or the hero running along by the canal—if they have no cumulative bearing on the episode that has been reached? Again, why the cross-cutting between a strip-tease act and the arms of a slaughter-house worker dripping with blood? We can hardly be meant to think that strip-tease is a revolting manifestation of the sensuality of the modern world, because the camera lingers lovingly on naked flesh all through the film. The hero has his shirt off more often that he has it on and, after two hours twenty minutes, one feels intimately acquainted with every inch of his cherished body. Nor can we be meant to think that slaughter-houses should be abolished, because the hero, in his one moment of boyish enthusiasm *post coitum*, says how much he likes sausages. No, these are just dramatic images which are added more or less indiscriminately to the visual broth. And for good measure, every now and again the photography is distorted so that the characters have the twisted shapes and prettiness in horror of paintings by Francis Bacon.

In spite of all the experimental films I have seen and experimental novels I have read, I am still of the opinion that if one begins telling a story, it should be told convincingly either on the imaginative or the realistic level. The author can be as oblique and allusive as he likes, provided that what he presents hangs together according to the mode he has chosen. But this film doesn't make sense. We are expected to believe that the publicity men—the bloated, efficient, empty profiteers of the modern world—turn the hero's projected suicide into a campaign. This seems utterly improbable, because there is never any indication of what they might get out of it. Then, on the eve of the suicide, they send their glamour girl along to sleep with him, so that he is "softened up" for the morrow. He, poor naïve soul, thinks he has been reconciled to life by the love of a good woman, and the girl herself is so touched by his "authenticity" that she has a genuine and noisy orgasm (head thrown back, threads of saliva, *cf.* Jeanne Moreau in *Les Amants*) and is afterwards furious with her boss. When our hero learns that she has received eighty guineas for her services, he bellows like an animal in pain and describes beautiful, balletic patterns on the floor. Yet if he had a grain of the intelligence he is credited with, he would know that good women do not arrive opportunely at nightfall, swathed in gold lamé, and proceed to run their exquisitely manicured fingers over naked male shoulder-blades. He would know that she has turned up because any modern film, without showing the sex act in its entirety, has to have at least one scene, like the opening sequence of *Hiroshima*, in which a whirl of anonymous arms and legs indicates that copulation is boldly in progress. It will be a great relief to us all when, in a few years' time, film-makers are able to photograph sex from start to finish, as they can already photograph childbirth, so that the public can complete its voyeuristic experience in absolute clarity.

Another principle, too, is involved in this kind of film. All absurdist heroes are in a state of "revolt," which is a very understandable phase that practically all young people now get into and that some never emerge from. Since no one has yet found a method of transcending the Absurd except by an act of faith, the absurdist heroes have every right, intellectually, to go on being as negative and suicidal as they wish, however tedious and repetitive we may find them. The trouble is that so many of them rail against society when, in fact, they are really annoyed with God. It is not at all clear how far the hero of *Herostratus*, or the film as a whole, is critical of society as such, in the name of an ideal that might be achieved, and how far he, or it, is expressing disgust with life in general. The confusion is natural enough, and I dare say that none of us manage to avoid it all the time; but it is not a sign of intelligence. For instance, the news-reel interpolations set some very uninspired and pious remarks by Churchill, Attlee, and Herbert Morrison alongside a much more exciting and diabolical bellow from Hitler. In the context, whether the effect is intentional or not, Hitler may seem more attractive than the "democratic" politicians. At any rate, one cannot help feeling that the hero is nearer to Hitler than to the other three, and this is not surprising since Hitlerism was, to some extent, a response to awareness of the Absurd. When the film juxtaposes these political figures without comment (this is perhaps what is meant by an "abstract" or "an event"), it appears to be equating them; but there is no doubt about the fact that, Absurd or no Absurd, in real life one has to decide whether one is going to accept the moral categories of Attlee, Morrison and Churchill, however inadequate, or the amoral category of Hitler. There is a very important difference. When the hero shouts insults at his landlady and smashes his room to pieces with an axe, he may be protesting against God and/or society, but it is the landlady who bears the brunt of the protest. When the film dwells on the gory arms of the slaughter-house worker, it is presumably expressing revulsion at the fact that human life preys on animal life; this is a universal phenomenon of nature, which has nothing to do with politics or advertising or the other evils of the modern world. To run all these issues together is just to wallow in an emotional muddle. It is this that makes the film so unsatisfactory; if the emotions were in an aesthetic pattern, the necessary intellectual distinctions would be implied.

It seems to me that one can salvage only two things from this long, and alas pretentious film. Michael Gothard, in the lead part, manages to retain sympathy in spite of all, which is no mean achievement; the photography, by Keith Allams, is often superb, and gives visual beauty to scenes that are, dramatically, quite ill-conceived.

11. Bald Remarks on Hair

When we went into the theatre, slightly grubby and hirsute boys and girls, dotted around the auditorium and the stage, were making those slowly convulsive movements that young people also seem to go in for at advanced poetry readings. They gyrate with raised arms and closed eyes, undulate like seaweed, follow the contours of some invisible mystic vortex, as if they were so many sibyls or sorcerers drunk on sacred fumes. Since this drifting self-absorption is common in American underground films, I suppose it represents the state of being "sent" or "high". If this is what marijuana does, it is quite pretty to watch, not bleak and grisly like the fumblings of the hard drug addicts I have seen around midnight in Montparnasse.

As we took our seats, a radiantly smiling girl, got up like an unorthodox squaw, handed my companion a slightly *passé* yellow chrysanthemum. At first I took her to be part of the audience, because there were so many people around us dressed in lace curtains or remnants of furnishing brocade that the distinction between performer and spectator was difficult to establish. However, I later decided that she must be a member of the cast welcoming us with love, love, love. It may not be all we need, but we can always do with a little more, even if it is slightly professional. Or perhaps she was saluting my companion's hair, which hangs down in an ample shower and almost meets the hem of her rising skirt. In either event, I was able to settle back happily with a receptive mind.

But to be quite honest, if one was expecting to be startled, *Hair* comes rather as an anticlimax. The actual performance did not seem to contain any features that have not already been present in other *avant-garde* productions. *Marat-Sade* was much dottier, *US* more passionately political, some American underground

165

films more positively erotic, and Arrabal's *Le Cimetière des voitures* more gleefully barbaric. I don't know how long *Hair* has been running in New York, but I suspect that certain of its peculiarities must have seeped across to Europe during the Lord Chamberlain's unconscionable agony, and we have got used to them. At any rate, although I kept waiting for the shock, none occurred. The young people woke up suddenly from their poetic driftings, the orchestra maintained an almost constant barrage of good, thumping music, the story-line wobbled uncertainly into motion as it usually does in musicals and, as usual, was interspersed with weak jokes, stilted bits of dialogue and a sprinkling of sentimental ditties, some quaintly poised between parody and seriousness. Although moon was never made to rhyme with June, xxxx did not rhyme with xxxx as often as one might have expected. Nevertheless, I have to report that the audience went wild. They whistled and shouted *bravo* and, at the end, many of them leapt up on to the stage and disappeared into the dusty pandemonium. I wondered if they were not responding more to the myth of *Hair* than to the show itself. Perhaps we should have stayed to see whether saturnalia really developed in the wings, but this thought did not occur to me until we were on our way home.

In spite of the din and the flashing lights, the one surprising thing about the performance, in comparison with other *avant-garde* shows, was its lack of aggressiveness.

The theme, basically, is another protest against the Viet Nam War. A boy belonging to a drifting herd-like mass of drop-outs receives his call-up papers and, after trying ineffectually to escape his fate, has to submit and is shorn of his anarchistic locks. But these events are commented on wrily, rather than pugnaciously; it is as if the pet lamb of the flock had been snatched from the pastoral bliss of the hippie world and rudely clipped by Them, the grown-ups, the incomprehensible people who run society on the strange assumption that it is a serious, going concern. The flock itself, which keeps scattering and reforming in a manner more animal than human, is a micro-society within society, dressed in oddments, living presumably at subsistence level, copulating in heaps and composed of members who are all vaguely interchangeable, although they are still slightly bothered at times about the fact that A may prefer B who prefers C. What the music seems to suggest is that they are at their happiest when twitching and stamping in chorus. Each jerks and jangles separately, like a puppet on an invisible string, but they are all held together by the rhythm, which irons out uncertainty and solitude and beats on steadily to a collective climax. I suppose this is the dance as sublimated group orgasm, which would perhaps explain why the audience got so excited. The actors gave the impression—whether deliberately or not I cannot say—of performing for themselves rather than for the public, and this too was refreshing.

The term "tribal musical", which is used in the programme, is perfectly justified. For one thing, the performers are a crowd, not a chorus-plus-stars. They are physically nondescript, only one of them—Oliver Tobias, who does not have the central role—being conventionally beautiful in the theatrical manner. None of the women appear to have been chosen for their looks, and the most forceful of them was a pinched-faced little person bulging below with pregnancy padding. It is curious that "beautiful" people should be presented as lacking in beauty, or should be at pains to disguise such beauty as they have under odds and ends of indifferent clothing. In the nude scene, which was chastely limited to a fleeting glimpse, I spied a girl with a splendid body, but nothing was made of it outside this one, thirty-second vision. Had she been in a traditional chorus, she would have jigged from left to right and from right to left at intervals, and her naked limbs would have earned their keep by working like pistons. I am not saying that this would have been better; I am not arguing in favour of the traditional chorus, which I have always thought rather comic and non-erotic; I am only trying to define an impression of puritanism at one remove, of deliberate scruffiness, of rejection of romantic prettiness or obvious physical appeal in a show that one ex-pected to be sensual.

It *is* sensual, collectively rather than individually, if such a distinction can be given a meaning. And it is this collectiveness without a hierarchy that the elderly spectator senses as foreign. I found myself looking for the star and watching Tobias, because he was particularly shapely and agile, yet feeling at the same time that he wasn't meant to be more prominent than the rest. He just happened to be noticeable, in the way that one African dancer, thanks to his superior physique, may stand out to some extent from an anonymous tribal mass. It would take me some time to get used to this direct democracy on the stage, because it blurs the aesthetic effect. I realise that I like to know, in watching any performance, exactly what the pattern of importance of the actors or dancers is meant to be, and the show is imperfect if some secondary part is much better played than a primary one. But I imagine that, in the hippie world, such definiteness is anathema, and that *Hair* explicitly set out to reject it. However, in that case, why did only two or three of them take their clothes off in the nude scene? And did they stand motionless with genuine poetic intent, or in ironical deference to the Lord Chamberlain's old rule about nudes having to look like statues? I would have expected the whole cast to throw their garments into the wings and to romp porkily, like Cézanne's *Baigneuses*. Standing still for thirty seconds in a dim light was effective enough in its own way, but strangely solemn, as if they were saying: "Here is that sacred object, the naked body. Look upon it with awe," whereas the rest of the performance would seem to imply that only squares could have such feelings, the true hippie taking all the natural manifestations of the flesh in his stride.

In the last resort, the dominant impression was one of bracing vitality and slightly muddled innocence. The young men said fucking this and fucking that, and made jokes about penises. From what my grandchildren tell me about their play-group, I gather that tiny tots now chortle about this sort of thing over their morning cocoa. Perhaps they always did, and the adult world is just recapturing publicly the Heaven that lies about us in our infancy. My billy is bigger than yours, plus cocoa, later becomes my billy is bigger than yours, plus pot. If so, the linguistic and intellectual gain is imperceptible, and indeed there was practically nothing in *Hair* on the level of

articulated implications or convincing lyrics, except the charming song made up of the learned words for sexual perversions,
which owed its effect precisely to the fact that it was sung as
children sing hymns, mouthing the words with no regard to
the meaning. It seemed to me that the songs hardly counted,
and were only put in to provide pauses between the vigorous,
mindless, tribal stampings into which each of them eventually
merged. What mattered was the pulse-beat of blind nature,
hammering through these young limbs, raising clouds of dust
and threatening to bring down the antiquated theatre which
no doubt once vibrated in time to those milder intimations of
nature, the can-can and the Charleston.

12. Plays or Psycho-dramas?

The theatre at the moment is enjoying a period of saturnalia. Obscenity, scatology, nudity, transvestism, perversions and hysteria are the order of the day. The same mild, middle-aged people seem to be sitting in the stalls, eating chocolates and imbibing alcohol and coffee in the intervals, but what they see and hear must be quite unprecedented in the history of the English drama; even Restoration comedy did not go so far. And since they accept it all without a qualm, we must conclude that it comes well within their experience or imagination. What is happening, I suppose, is that the theatre, like the cinema and some other art forms, is now belching up all those things that have always existed but were formerly suppressed because they were thought to be inimical to civilisation. The Id is having a holiday—an indefinite one, maybe—at the expense of the Super-Ego, because the Super-Ego itself now believes that the Id is entitled to its fling. Perhaps we could call this the ultimate democratisation of the human personality. The Super-Ego has abdicated its central position of authority and the different parts of our make-up are clamouring with separate voices, so much so, indeed, that incipient schizophrenia is almost as widespread as the common cold.

I am prompted to make this remark by the fact that, of the various plays I have seen during the last few weeks, only one— Mart Crowley's *The Boys in the Band*, imported from New York —could be called "normal", although all nine characters in it are homosexual. I mean that it is an enjoyable, old-fashioned play, governed by a single, presiding view-point and with a beginning, a middle, and an end. Its only peculiarity or boldness is that it deals with the emotional entanglements of male homosexuals, as the traditional "well-made" play dealt with

heterosexual love and the family. Since by definition homosexuals cannot create a family, they tend to live to some extent
in groups, which reproduce an echo-pattern of the polarities
and emotional tensions of the family. In this play, the "boys,"
each confessing his dilemma in turn, even express themselves
in rather elaborate, theatrical prose, and the obscene phrases
with which their conversation is peppered appear to be no
more than conventional signs of intimacy. How honest this
play really is I cannot say. I heard the author declare on television that it is not about homosexuality but about the human
condition, which is manifestly untrue. At times, I suspected
that it was perhaps slightly arranged for the heterosexual public,
as a Jewish play might be for Gentiles, or a Negro play for
Whites. In spite of the in-jokes and *mots d'auteur* (*e.g.* "There's
one thing to be said for masturbation, one doesn't need to look
one's best"), the message is reassuringly "normal": homosexuals are hopelessly anguished, insubstantial, twilit figures,
always at a tangent to reality, and thus, we may assume, rightly
called fairies.

The other plays I am thinking of hardly recognise the concept of reality, even when they purport to have some application
to the modern world. Alan Bennett's *Forty Years On* is a bitter-
sweet cavalcade of English memories; Peter Barnes' *The Ruling
Class* centres on the old theme of the decline and fall of the
aristocracy; Joe Orton's *What The Butler Saw* is a farce about
sex and the ludicrousness of psychiatry, and Edward Albee's
A Delicate Balance is presumably a comment on the decadence
of American middle-class society. Yet although they appear to
be based on value-judgments about modern civilisation or the
lack of it, and indeed to be strongly critical of contemporary
life, they deal with it neither literally nor figuratively. In other
words, they are neither naturalistic nor symbolic, but range
from apparently direct statement to the wildest and most
gratuitous fantasy. This puzzles me, because the literal statements sometimes contradict the fantasy, and the fantasy itself
may have internal contradictions. For this reason, I am tempted
to call them psycho-dramas rather than plays. They enact
various odd perceptions or impulses dramatically, without

bothering to maintain any line of development or consistency of point of view. They are collocations of bits and pieces, intellectual and emotional flotsam and jetsam. Perhaps, in the contemporary situation, this is what plays have to be, but if so, it is a pity.

All four works have received rapturous notices from some critics, so presumably the good bits in each of them help to put over the rest. All I can say is that I got little satisfaction from any of them, even from *Forty Years On*, although I am as prejudiced in Alan Bennett's favour as I am instinctively mistrustful of Edward Albee's rhetoric. I go on being obtusely convinced that there are different modes of apprehension, and that they cannot be mixed just any old how. For instance, one can either be naturalistic or symbolic, but if one wants to be both at the same time, then the relationships between the two modes need to be properly managed.

In the programme note introducing *The Ruling Class*, Mr Peter Barnes condemns "the deadly servitude of naturalism" and advocates "the dramatic reality" of "a comic theatre of conflicting moods and opposites where everything is simultaneously tragic and ridiculous". I can see how the Theatre of the Absurd, if misunderstood, may lead to the belief that naturalism should be replaced by irrational juxtapositions, but I cannot quite understand what Mr Barnes is up to. He sets his action in a stately home, where the 13th earl, who is also a judge (has there ever been a hereditary peer who was also a judge?) takes his pleasure of an evening by hanging himself from the canopy of his bed, while wearing a *tutu*. He is about to remarry in order to replace his dead sons, who have perished in outposts of Empire. However, instead of giving himself a pleasurable erection, to be followed by a restorative whisky and soda, he slips off his step-ladder and hangs himself *pour de bon*. His loony surviving son inherits and arrives from a mental home in a Franciscan habit and convinced he is the God of Love. Whereupon many old jokes about madmen who think they are God. The family gangs up against him and, having married him off to a compliant chorus-girl so that he can have a son to carry on the line, propose to lock him up for good. He

turns into the God of Vengeance or Jack the Ripper, and slits
the bellies of his wife and sister-in-law.

A lot of the scenes depend on the convention that aristocrats
are decadent, ruthless, and still in charge of England. At the
same time, we are clearly meant to sympathise with the dotty
14th earl, whose schizophrenia has connections with the contingency sickness of so many Absurd heroes. But the whole
thing is just a farrago of nonsense which falls between several
stools. Judging by fragments of the dialogue, I should say that
Mr Barnes could write quite a good play on the tragi-comedy
of schizophrenia, but why he mixes up the theme with all the
anti-feudal stuff is a mystery. His skit on the House of Lords as
a mouldering collection of corpses is as wide of the mark as if
it had been written by a hack propagandist in Moscow. Almost
the only thing I remember with pleasure from the show was a
charming little review sketch about a courtship by means of
bird-calls.

Forty Years On is a series of review-sketches, purporting to be
the annual dramatic performance at a symbolic public school
called Albion House, whose worried traditionalist headmaster
is retiring and will be replaced by a faceless new man. It is a
strangely mild and muddled view of England's recent past,
interspersed with some baffling lapses in taste. I am not referring to the fact that the smooth-faced schoolboys sing what
appears to be a traditional song about arseholes. This is part of
the valid process of showing that public schools breed essentially
the same kind of obscene collective attitudes as borstal institutions
or prisons (*cf.* Lindsay Anderson's really excellent film, *If*). I
recently had the opportunity of reading John Addington
Symonds' unpublished autobiography and I was startled to
find that Harrow in the 1850s, in respect of tyrannical bar-
barism and sexual enslavement, was scarcely distinguishable
from the penal institutions described by Jean Genet. Perhaps,
after all, it was a quality of the old English public schools that
they introduced their pupils to all forms of sordidness and evil
at an early age, so that they were as well educated in the
horrors of life as slum children, delinquents, and prostitutes. I
am thinking rather of a totally unjustified skit on Virginia

Woolf, which made me wince with embarrassment, and of a puzzling satire on T. E. Lawrence, delivered by the retiring headmaster, who would have been the very person to have a great admiration for the repressed and mixed-up hero. I couldn't see what Alan Bennett, any more than Peter Barnes was up to. I gathered that he has a love/hatred of England and that this show is a sort of dirge, but where his centre of gravity is, and what relationship he really sees between the past, the present, and the future, I again couldn't guess.

Here is another puzzle: Frank Marcus, whose *Sister George* I much admired, has declared in the press that Joe Orton's *What The Butler Saw* is a new classic. Now my opinion is that Orton wrote one good play—*Entertaining Mr Sloane*—which was given a superlative performance on television by Sheila Hancock and Edward Woodward. *Loot* (which won him the *Evening Standard* Award) was much less good, and *What The Butler Saw* is still more inferior. It is a laborious farce, in which any device is used to get a momentary laugh, and it has no structure at all. Sir Ralph Richardson plays the part of an asinine psychiatrist, who misinterprets everything that happens in accordance with psycho-analytical theory and in a way that might have appeared funny twenty-five years ago, but is now quite threadbare. Morever, a farce is normally built on the assumption that the characters have a conventional reason for concealing their behaviour from one another. Stanley Baxter, as the randy (yet impotent?) husband, goes to great lengths to hide his peccadilloes from his wife—but what need is there to do so, when she is a self-confessed nymphomaniac, alcoholic, and Lesbian, who proclaims the failure of their marriage? There is surely no point in maintaining the paraphernalia of farce, if you don't accept the conventions of bourgeois respectability on which it is based. Towards the end, there is a slight suggestion that Orton may have started from, or incidentally conceived, the idea of producing a play that would be a derisive illustration of the Freudian pattern of father/daughter, mother/son incest, but, if so, he doesn't work out the theme properly, because one cannot tell whether he is accepting Freudianism or making fun of it. Again we are faced with a jumble, not a work of art, and many of the obscene jokes are not knitted into the fabric at all.

A Delicate Balance is a very different case, since Albee pays great attention to what one might call the external patterning of his dialogue, which even has a Jamesian elaboration. The problem is to know what, if anything, he is saying about American society or about life in general. There is a predatory mother and an ineffectual father, a maladjusted daughter who has left her third husband, a loud-mouthed alcoholic sister sponging on the household, and a married couple who come to stay, having been driven out of their own home by a nameless fear. Is this fear caused by the prospect of death, the nausea of the Absurd, or the emptiness of their relationship? The episode is not naturalistically motivated, although it is treated as a naturalistic problem: are the couple to be accepted into the household as old friends, or not? Father writhes in an agony of doubt, trying to do the virtuous thing; daughter screams her head off because the couple have been given her room; sister (played in Lesbian style but with no admitted Lesbian characteristics) acts as chorus and comic relief, commenting on the action with the cynical wisdom of one who has known the lower depths. But surely, the whole thing is just saying fee-fi-fo-fum about life in a *chichi* way, without ever coming openly to grips with any problem. Marriage is a failure, some girls never grow up, others take to drink, anonymous fears haunt the prosperous suburbs—these are modern clichés, which are being juxtaposed in a falsely knowing manner without being freshly perceived or rethought.

I recently heard Mr Albee say that his plays are written by his subconscious, but I wonder if this too is not a fashionable concession to the view that the Super-Ego is out, or even a more-unconscious-than-thou kind of boast. The Super-Ego wants to have its productive team of hidden monsters, just as saints used to have their voices. Frankly, I prefer the genuine philistinism of *The Boys in the Band*.

13. God's Bodikins!

In the play by Peter Barnes, *The Ruling Class*, about which I said some rude things last month, there is an English earl who thinks he is Jesus Christ. When someone remarks: "Show us your Godhead," he begins unbuttoning his trouser-flap. This month, in Pier Paolo Pasolini's film, *Theorem*, we are actually shown Christ's Godhead (in effect, Mr Terence Stamp's), and —like Ionesco who dreamed he was in Heaven surrounded by people speaking Italian and concluded, when he woke up, that, since dreams never lie, he had at least learned that Italian is the heavenly language—we can conclude that Christ has black pubic hair, which, when you come to think of it, was always fairly likely. The lighting is not clear enough for us to see whether he is well and truly circumcised. Precision on this point might have introduced a regrettable racial note into a film that has, apparently, won the approval of part of the Catholic Church. It was safer to dwell on the fair prospect of Christ's various pairs of natty trousers, whether empty or slightly bulging (Christ appears to wear esteemed nature, *die werte Natur*, on the right), and this Signor Pasolini's camera does very lovingly. In fact, Signor Pasolini is obviously well qualified to do an *étude de braguettes* or codpiece symphony, which would be a worthy pendant to Miss Yoko Ono's *Bottoms*. His study of the flies of the Lord certainly makes him lord of the flies.

Pasolini, like Fellini, has a rich, treacly Italian talent, and *Theorem* is one of the most marvellously preposterous films I have seen for a long time, almost every moment of it being deeply enjoyable. I hope he made it with tongue in cheek; if he didn't, the imagination boggles at what goes on inside his head. Let us suppose, at any rate, that it is a conscious work of

art and a brilliantly poetic joke about the mixture of homosexual feeling and religious fervour which is so often found in
the more artistic areas of the Catholic Church.

The theme is, of course, "The Passing of the Third Floor
Back." I have just read, or re-read, Jerome K. Jerome's short
story, which was published in 1907, and a very genteel and
old-fashioned little thing it appears by comparison. Christ, in
a long raincoat and an old felt hat, turns up unexpectedly in a
boarding-house at 48 Bloomsbury Square and, by the exquisite
graciousness of his presence, brings out the better self in each of
the inmates. When he moves on, the landlady has become a
real lady, the distressed gentlewoman has ceased to be a snob,
the middle-aged spinster has agreed to grow old, the flighty
girl has decided not to sell herself for money, and the men have
given up being various types of bounder. These moderate
conversions were all no doubt in keeping with average, English,
middle-class feeling before 1914.

Signor Pasolini's mysterious stranger is very different. He is
a dazzlingly beautiful youth who, for no apparent reason, comes
to stay in a splendid Italian villa on the outskirts of Milan. He
says nothing; he just sits or moves about, exuding an intense
sexual aura. He looks, indeed, like a placid and slightly soulful
gigolo, or perhaps a Billy Budd on dry land, perfectly at home
in the luxurious setting. The camera shifts occasionally from
the house to the town, and to the huge and hygienic factory
from which the family draws its wealth. Then, every now and
again, the modern world disappears, to be replaced by a bleak
and rolling landscape of grey-green dust, half-hidden by
restless clouds; this, presumably, is the earth just after creation,
"without form and void". The image seems to occur every time
sexual union is about to take place, as if copulation always
went back to the beginning of time or had a prehistoric echo,
as in a poem I remember once reading somewhere:

> *Three smart floors above old earth,*
> *On rubber beds with springs of steel,*
> *They tied the knot that links the birth*
> *Of future soul with ancient eel. . . .*

M

Since this is 1969 and not 1907, Signor Pasolini's Christ operates directly through the genitals. The peasant maid, mowing the lawn, is driven to distraction by the beauty of his trousered legs and tries to commit suicide. He saves her and lies down with her on her bed. The son of the house, having glimpsed his Godhead when they undress together, sobs with desire and is suitably consoled. The mother, after adoring Christ's underpants, which he has shed to go bathing, lies down naked to intercept him on his return and is duly rewarded. The daughter leads him into her virginal bedroom and bares her breasts. The father and Christ take a drive into the countryside and stretch out among the ferns. Each episode is left slightly ambiguous, in the sense that Christ wears an intensely wise and noble look as the crisis approaches, so that one cannot be quite sure whether he is doing the obvious thing, which normally involves a degree of facial contraction, or administering some peculiar form of physiotherapy, The equivocalness is beautifully calculated, with the result that these highly suggestive scenes have the awful fascination of bad religious pictures. Theological language, at least in pre-Enlightenment days, used often to borrow the terminology of human love in an attempt, so it was said, to translate the ineffable. Here, the reverse process is in operation. The explicit fleshiness of the body fills the large screen and has a parody of spiritual meaning oozing from it like sweat. One could imagine no more damning satire on the dubieties of popular, idolatrous religion. This is faith as a phallic fantasy.

The fun continues when Christ is summoned away, as he had been announced, by a telegraph boy who dances with bliss, like a holy idiot. It then appears that *Christus fornicator* is also *Christus redemptor*; he has planted seeds of spiritual rebirth, and gestation ensues.

The maid returns to her village to become a miracle-working saint. She lives entirely on nettle-soup, and sits motionless on a bench or levitates above the chimney-pots. Then she has herself buried up to the eye-balls, so that the tears she sheds for the world will form a living spring. This episode, which is wonderfully photographed, has a kind of absurd poetry. The saint is both ludicrous and touching when she points dramatically to the nettles, as in a medieval painting, or hangs splayed out in the sky, like a suddenly solidified television image. What was the point of saints levitating, one wonders, if they just looked like cosmonauts who have forgotten their space-suits? Also, with the sublime thoughtlessness of saints, she has herself buried on a building-site, just under a vast mechanical excavator, which will no doubt uproot her in one movement next day.

Signor Pasolini's inspiration falters a little, I think, with the other characters. The son is a budding artist and we have seen him looking appraisingly at reproductions of Francis Bacon's ghoulish figures. Now that he has been divinely sodomised, he has to find something better to express the terrible, yet joyful, meaning of life. Unfortunately, he just repeats some well-known stages of modern art: he invents a form of action painting, then a plain, blue square (Klein?), on which he piddles to express his disgust, and finally a haphazard, blue blot, which must represent the abandonment of art and the acceptance of chance. Perhaps the joke is that a lot of modern pictorial art, when it tries to be consciously metaphysical, ends up as a non-significant happening. But if so, the effect is somehow muffled.

During Christ's stay, the daughter has taken a photograph of him lolling in a deck-chair, in the slack and broken attitude he has in so many pictures of the descent from the Cross. After his departure, she is rummaging through the chest containing her childhood treasures, which include the photographic album, and we think she is about to put away childish things by burying the chest in the garden. However, she runs her finger over the pattern of Christ's limbs in the photograph and falls into a cataleptic trance, with her right hand tightly clasped. Perhaps the divine afflatus passing upwards from those wonder-working trousers has paralysed her arm and propelled her directly into mystic union with the Beyond. Her departure on a stretcher carried by two white-coated attendants is in the nature of an Assumption.

The mother roams about in her little car, picking up handsome youths who whip off their clothes and do what they can for her. It seems to be exactly what Christ did, and in fact one of the youths is approvingly and lingeringly photographed in the nude, in the classic pagan attitude of repose after love. But obviously an Ineffable Something is missing; not all Godheads are equal, since the mother retains her anxious look and finally disappears into a church, as if it were a telephone booth for communication with the divine lover.

The most painful change occurs in the father. He turns his factory over to the workers and wanders off, looking hungrily into the faces of romantic young men with a resemblance to Christ. In the middle of a crowded railway-station, he takes off all his clothes and we see his naked feet padding through the streets and then out into the formless void, which now invades the screen for good. The last sequence shows the nude, hairy, middle-aged body staggering over the wastes and uttering a piercing cry of desolation. If he is Adam, he can clearly do without Eve. It is Christ, in the shape of Michelangelo's David or Leonardo's John the Baptist that he is howling for.

The splendid Italian villa has thus been emptied of its five inhabitants by pentecostal fire, in the form of heavenly lust. Such goings-on would have startled the inmates of 48 Bloomsbury Square, where Christ always kept his long raincoat "tightly buttoned" and, far from being sexy, had a slight hump, presumably through carrying the Cross. But in this day and age, as they say, we can enjoy *Theorem* as an exercise in black humour,* an extraordinarily lush and grotesque illustration of the possible weirdnesses of the human temperament.

* Since writing this appreciation I have seen Signor Pasolini on television, and am forced to the conclusion that there is no humour in his make-up. So what I took to be an elaborate joke is, on the contrary, neurotic self-revelation.

14. Rites at the Round House

According to an article I read somewhere recently, Julian Beck's *Living Theatre* would now appear out-of-date in America, where the liveliest minds have progressed to the Theatre of Total Copulation and Public Masturbation. It is very interesting to see how the drama, which presumably emerged as a simulated ceremony from real ceremony, is straining so hard to return to the religious immediacy of its origins.

One of the great problems in the modern industrialised world is that our official ceremonies lack conviction; even the investiture of the Prince of Wales, which in one sense has been a public relations triumph, has at the same time been written about and commented upon, as if it were an elaborate non-event. But since official ceremonies are obviously decadent, and religious seriousness has largely deserted the churches, there has been —and there is—a persistent attempt to de-commercialise the theatre and turn it into total rite or substitute church. I would say that the impulse which makes people want to copulate or masturbate publicly and ceremoniously, or to watch such spectacles, is fundamentally religious. They want experiences which they feel to be genuine to assume a social and cosmic significance. In some ancient tribes, the king had, at intervals, to demonstrate the principle of potency by covering a mare in full view of his assembled people. It will be some time, no doubt, before the President of the United States is required to do this, but meanwhile a pop-singer or a group of actors can turn a theatrical occasion into a real priapic holy-day. The next step, logically, should be the Theatre of Genuine Bloody Sacrifice and Authentic Hara-Kiri. It was perhaps, after all, a mistake to abolish public executions, whippings and scourgings, the pillory and the stocks; perhaps they were necessary as a permanent, real-life Theatre of Cruelty. It was certainly a mistake to abolish them while hoping to keep alive the symbol of the Cross. Needless to say, Christianity itself has a most elaborate sado-masochistic structure, possibly the most perfect in existence, but for a variety of reasons it has gone dead on us and the most we can expect is that it will be rediscovered in the 21st century by the Chinese or Lunar *avant-garde*.

Mr Julian Beck, as I understand him from his television interviews and the performance of *Frankenstein* I saw at the Round House, is squarely in the middle of the theatrico-revivalist tradition, slightly senior to, and more intense than, Mr Peter Brook, slightly junior to, and much more intense than M. Jean-Louis Barrault. He is definitely not yet *passé* in London, because the Round House, normally the Albert Hall of the way-out, was filled with a very fashionable and intellectual audience of pop-personalities, actors, and writers, most of them in bright plumage and as pretty as if they had just stepped out of a Persian miniature.

Facing the hemisphere which they decorated so gaily and filled with the marvellous buzz of up-to-the-minute chatter was a three-tier construction in scaffolding, against a dull grey backcloth; and, on the floor beneath, the Living Theatre company, all hirsute, threadbare, and dedicated, squatting in the Oriental posture of meditation with their *guru*, Mr Beck. Mr Beck's physique is, as the French say, a whole programme in itself. I always admire bald men who make a go of it, and Mr Beck combines baldness with a fringe of long hair and the cadaverous, unsmiling countenance of a relentless, medieval monk. Is he consciously trying to resemble the last photographs of Antonin Artaud, I wondered, or has a similar passion produced a similar pattern of skin, bone, and eyes? At any rate, here was a common modern situation: the successful, the wealthy, and the worldly about to watch a performance by the devoted, the self-sacrificing, the utterly convinced. It was, in fact, not unlike Mass in a fashionable Parisian church.

Mr Beck seems to me to derive directly from two French sources. His concept of the company as an egalitarian guild, with everyone doing a bit of everything and all working together in a spirit of austerity, comes from Jacques Copeau. This is acting as a way of life or spiritual travelling circus. In the intervals, the performers did not disappear but set about tinkering with their scaffolding in preparation for the next episode, just like the people on the roundabouts and aerial wheels at the Hampstead Fair. Mr Beck moved about with the rest, hieratically adjusting an electric bulb or majestically tightening a screw. Then, the spirit of the performance derives from Artaud, because the action is not conceived at all as a play in the sense that has been traditional since the 16th century but as a sequence of theatrical images in which bodily movements, inarticulate noises, and rhythmical patterns of sound are much more important than the spoken word; it is symphonic ritual rather than cathartic statement. It is also Artaud-like in that the emphasis is on extreme situations and unbearable suffering. Although I heard Mr Beck talk a lot about love, one cannot imagine him, any more than Artaud, conveying a sense of lyrical tenderness or spiritual happiness. He comes to flay and to scourge, to tell us we are damned if we do not change, to rub our noses in the rottenness of civilisation. He is a hell-fire preacher.

About *Frankenstein*, let me say at once that it is a lot more impressive than I had supposed from the fragments given on television. As one might expect from the title, it is a kind of panoramic vision of human history, superior in theatrical impact to that strangely overrated play by Thornton Wilder, *The Skin of Our Teeth*, which was revived last year at Chichester, and reminiscent in tone of William Winwood Read's *The Martyrdom of Man*. The message is, apparently, that man has recreated himself as a monster, although it is not quite clear whether this process began a long time ago, or whether it has been particularly acute since the advent of the capitalist and scientific phase of Western civilisation. Possibly the latter implication is taken for granted, but I feel that the ambiguity is regrettable.

In the last resort, I think, we have the choice between only two philosophies of life: the tragic view and the tragico-progressive view. The latter admits the idea of progress as a good working hypothesis, while at the same time recognising that tragedy will keep breaking in. I am not sure that Mr Beck has thought the matter through to its intellectual foundations. Like so many indignant moralists, he appears to assume that "they" (*i.e.*, various groups or individuals) are responsible for the evil in the world, and that we should rise up and fight them because the task is obvious. "How can we end human suffering?", he cries just after the beginning of the performance. The answer obviously is that, in the absolute, we cannot, and the question is profoundly naïve. We can only mitigate human suffering here and there, and hope that the improvements will not cause a new evil. On any showing, human beings are only partly responsible for evil, and it is no use getting annoyed with them beyond a certain point, as if they had created themselves and the universe. Artaud—at least if I have grasped his meaning—had a less political view than Mr Beck; he felt that life was permanently and inherently tragic, and he wanted to evolve a ritual that would give mystic expression to the tragedy. It would not have occurred to him, as it has done to Mr Beck, to give any theatrical performance the programmatic title of *Paradise Now*. I suspect that Mr Beck wants to be as intense as Artaud, and at bottom he is perhaps just as tragic, but he has overlaid the tragedy with a partly unassimilated politicism.

Frankenstein opens with the company meditating for three minutes, with the proclaimed object of inducing the levitation of the actress in the middle of the group, whose name, according to the programme, is Mary Mary. Not surprisingly, she is contrary and fails to levitate, whereupon bedlam breaks loose; half the company sets about torturing and killing the other half. Mary Mary is caught in a net and carried off behind a transparent screen, where, in beautiful shadow outline, Mr Beck-Frankenstein performs nameless operations on her luscious body. The only effect of this on me, alas, was to inspire sadistic nostalgia. What a pity it is, I suddenly realised, that we cannot go about the streets with a net, catching pretty, long-legged creatures as if they were butterflies, and taking them covetously home for private games. But this, I suppose, was a subjective irrelevance; we are no doubt meant to understand that, levitation not having taken place, *i.e.* no relationship with the transcendent having been established, humanity tears itself apart.

The dead are used by Dr Frankenstein, who at this stage appears to be a demonic figure, to create a new artificial and horrible creature. The body of the monster is put together, part by part, while the company marches and counter-marches along the different levels of the scaffolding, imitating the rhythm of industrial society and chanting fragments of various creeds and psychologies. All this is jolly good teamwork, but the intellectual content is hardly equal to the vigour of movement.

What importance have we to attach to the various slogans? Are they sincere or derisory? Is the guying of the heart-transplant operation meant to suggest that science is creating horrors? But any forward-looking mind is bound to approve of science when it is used for good, as in medicine. I was puzzled. However, in the end, the monster is complete on the operating table, while at the same time the company, hanging on the scaffolding like a swarm of bees, form the silhouette of a gangling figure with two red eyes, half man half dinosaur. Very effective, in a Grand Guignol way.

I thought Act II contained the most telling theatrical image. A tube of electric lights, set against the scaffolding, formed an enormous human head in profile—the head of the creature on whom Frankenstein was still working at the operating table. (The white actor representing the creature had now been replaced by a negro, but I couldn't guess the significance, if any, of the change.) While Frankenstein carried on his experiments, the company moved up and down inside the head, over the three levels of the scaffolding, like a visual translation of Descartes' animal spirits circulating from the body to the brain. As the half-naked men and women slithered up and down the poles like aesthetic monkeys, they formed many beautiful patterns and groupings, which were, in fact, old-fashioned *tableaux vivants* put to a new symbolic use. It was not all successful; some episodes taken from Greek myth were like clumsy charades—and in any case, why should an artificial creature relive Greek myth?—but the representations of sleep and dreaming were very fine. At this point, I think, Mr Beck had forgotten that the creature was an artificial monster and was just treating him as an incarnation of Everyman.

Act III turned the scaffolding into a prison and Dr Frankenstein, surprisingly enough, into a hero. Half the company, skulking in the back of the auditorium, was arrested by the other half, finger-printed and encaged, with much barking and blowing of whistles. Each prisoner gibbered and writhed in his cell, presumably to convey the anguish of man in a totalitarian society. However, good Dr Frankenstein instigated a revolt, the warders were knocked unconscious, and the rebellious prisoners set fire to their jail, which was soon enveloped in smoke. As the murk cleared, the company could be seen clinging to the girders once more, in the shape of the gangling monster with two red eyes. The phoenix had risen again from the flames, but perhaps we were meant to think that he is no more assured of survival than the dinosaur was.

That is the most I can make of the performance. As usual, in my niggling way, I have looked for a meaning and have found conflicting ambiguities. Who is Dr Frankenstein: the devil, the perverse instinct in man, or the active impulse which may create or destroy? Is the creation of the artificial man good or bad? As one doesn't know, the piece has little coherence. Act III, a simple affair of goodies and baddies, has hardly any connection with Acts I and II, and all three have internal contradictions. I am left with the memory of one or two independently impressive moments, of an athletic company with a good rhythm producing great splodges of emotion not attached to anything in particular. They are convinced, or appear to be; Mr Beck is their high-priest; but what, in the last resort, is the precise content of their religion? Perhaps just emotion for emotion's sake.

15. The Outsider Rides Again

One of my favourite bedside books is Lance Robson's *Varieties of the Picaresque*,* in which that rather eccentric critic demonstrates, to his own satisfaction at least, that the outsider, far from being a specifically modern phenomenon, has always been the commonest type of hero, both in real life and in art.

The Existentialist *étranger*, of whom "the angry young men", the hippies and the drop-outs are Anglo-American versions, was preceded (says Robson) by a long series of alienated types. To name only a few: the late 19th-century aesthete, the *poète maudit*, the Romantic hero, the 18th-century picaresque adventurer, the Renaissance individualist or Don Juan figure, the medieval knight-errant, bastard or rogue, and the clever slave or recalcitrant plebeian of classical antiquity. He even carries the theme back into mythology. What are Prometheus, Oedipus, Orestes and Ulysses but variations on the outsider? Jesus of Nazareth was a sacred bastard, just as T. E. Lawrence was a puritanical one and Jean Genet is a profane one. And he adds that he places them all under the heading of the "picaresque" (a term that was not invented until the late 15th century), because it combines the idea of the uncertain or hostile attitude of an individual to existing society with the concept of movement. The outsider tends to be peripatetic, because he is *fleeing from, looking for*, or *passing through*. However—and this is perhaps where Robson strains his thesis into paradox—he invents the category of the "stationary picaresque". This includes both those people who never move from one spot yet act out their alienation imaginatively or rhetorically (*cf.* Jimmy Porter in *Look Back in Anger*) and the hordes of motorists in all countries

---

* I must possess the only copy of this work, since it appears to be unobtainable from booksellers or in libraries.

who move to and fro simply for the sake of moving and whose encapsulated oscillation is at once equivalent to immobility and a strange collective expression of their dim awareness of contingency.

But the most interesting part of Robson's thesis is the assertion that "society" is, and always has been, much more of an illusion than people usually think. The surprising thing, he argues, is not that there should be so many outsiders, but that disparate individuals can ever agree with each other sufficiently to create an "inside". By what miracle, he asks, do men establish an Establishment? He finds it astonishing that trains should run on time, hospitals function more or less adequately, and people be willing to respect each other's property or pay income tax. It is clear that Robson is basically a Hobbesian and has little confidence in the natural benevolence or collective efficiency of man. He seems to think that everybody is ultimately an outsider trying, more or less effectively according to his talents, to impose his own view of what society should be on his fellows, and the ideal more often than not is an extension of his own ego. Robson makes some stimulating, if debatable remarks, about "the adventurer from the periphery"— Napoleon, Stalin, Hitler, *et al.*—the picaresque significance of the Jewish diaspora and the complexities of the "upstart-downstart" relationship. (He sees Churchill, for instance, as a downstart conditioned by his non-inheriting position in the aristocracy and the traumatic effect of a doomed, syphilitic father, whereas de Gaulle is an upstart inhabiting a magnificent, synthetic persona.)

I mention all this because the Robsonian analysis, exaggerated though it may be, kept coming into my head again and again as I watched two recent and enjoyable American films about the alienated individual: *Easy Rider*, the much publicised hippie work associated with the name of the producer, Peter Fonda, but actually directed by Dennis Hopper, and *Good-bye Columbus*, directed by Larry Peerce and based on a short story by Philip Roth.

Good-bye Columbus is the simpler of the two, and is immediately comprehensible as an instance of what Robson would call the stationary, Jewish picaresque. The story was published as long ago as 1957 and since then, as we all know, Roth has gone on to write *Portnoy's Complaint*, which is an aggressive, and much more highly developed, version of the same theme. The background in both is not so much society in general as the New York Jewish community. It is a commonplace that Jewish family and social life is still close-knit even today, because the Jews have had to compensate for their historical alienation as a group. Much of the humour of *Good-bye Columbus* comes from the fact that the film centres around a Jewish family that has made good and is therefore super-American in a conventional way. The old furniture "from when we were poor" is kept in an attic, but the new house bristles with gilt and gadgets. Poppa showers benefits upon his children; the son is a baseball champion at Columbus (Ohio), and so neurotically intent on integration that his favourite record is the college anthem (hence the title); the elder daughter is the beauty of the country club, and the younger one an impossibly spoiled American child. When the son marries, the wedding—the major sequence of the film—is a riot of American materialism and Jewish community feeling, covering the essential isolation of the individuals concerned.

All this is seen with quizzical detachment by the hero, Neil, a Jewish opter-out, who is having an affair with Brenda, the elder daughter. Neil has several reasons to be alienated; he is a metaphorical orphan/bastard, his parents having left him at an early stage in the care of an oppressively affectionate aunt. He has also been affected by military service, and has given up various lucrative jobs because he found them soul-destroying. He is now earning a bare living as an assistant in the public library, and has no ambition: "I am not a doer, I am a liver." In short, he is exactly like the original modern outsider, Meursault in Camus' *L'Etranger*, except that he is more humorous. Richard Benjamin acts the part beautifully, equalling the subtlety of Dustin Hoffman's performance in the similar role in *The Graduate*.

The limitation of the film is that the psychology remains undeveloped and the tragedy is not completely focused. Neil is a quietist, who does not want to get married, does not want children, does not want to get on, etc. The anti-ambitious outsider is, of course, just a reversal of the ambitious *pícaro*, and the crunch usually comes when sexual attachment or love obliges him to take responsibility for someone else and so come to terms with society. However, Neil just gives up Brenda without a struggle, as if he were egotistically unfeeling, and the film peters out, with his character or temperament sadly diminished. This is not the fault of the director, who does wonders with the details of the scenario, but a weakness of the short story form which can accept a trick ending.

The superiority of *Portnoy's Complaint*—if I may digress for a moment—lies in the greater intensity of the central character. Portnoy is a Jew with a mythic concept of Gentile society, which he wishes to enter by going to bed with blonde Gentile girls; hence his picaresque adventures. The repeated joke is that everything which makes him a recalcitrant insider in Jewish society makes him an outsider in Gentile society, until he gets to Israel, where his non-Israeli Jewishness makes him an outsider in the Promised Land. But a more profound and universal perception in the book is that the sexual impulse, even without a specific object, can create alienation within the male. Portnoy is whisked along helter-skelter by his penis, as if it were a runaway horse, or a spirit that had got possession of him, and he is trying to deflect it significantly on to Gentile girls, away from auto-eroticism which is a sterile polarity or division within the self. Perhaps, if the permissive wave continues, some film director will find a way of expressing this on the screen. He might, incidentally, get some useful ideas from *Varieties of the Picaresque*, which has an amusing chapter on "The Phallus as Picaresque Familiar,"* running the whole gamut from Pan, Mercury, and Harlequin to Don Juan/ Leporello, Scapin, and Figaro.

Easy Rider is, technically, not so accomplished a film as *Good-bye Columbus*, because it is self-indulgent and rather empty in places,

---

* Alberto Moravia has now (1972) published a novel on precisely this theme.

but it is absolutely up-to-date in mode and theoretically more complex. It is the first full-scale commercial hippie film I have seen, and the first open presentation of marijuana-smoking as a way of life, or anaesthetised prelude to death. There have been many underground films with a similar flavour, but they are for the most part disjointed, often repulsive, and totally un-commercial. With *Easy Rider*, the hippie exercises charm, exudes pathos, and breaks into the big money; that is, the outsider mentality, at least in a weak form, has become so general that it is now an immense market ready to be tapped. The phenomenon is the same as the hippie gathering in the Isle of Wight, at which (according to the newspapers) Bob Dylan earned £35,000 by an hour's singing. He later com-plained—whether cynically, wryly or naïvely, it is impossible to say—that singers like himself are taken too seriously by the press; but the press, being a function of the consumer-society, naturally pays most attention to those people who make the biggest killing.

In a long and revealing interview published in *Rolling Stone*, Peter Fonda says it has taken him some time to convince Hollywood that an absolutely sincere movie could be a success. I think I see what he means; this film is presumably meant to be a genuine expression of the outsider-philosophy of its makers, Fonda and Hopper, neither of whom is very young any more (twenty-nine and thirty-five?), and who at times must both have lived marginally and precariously. There are also signs that Fonda has a famous-father complex, which is often a contributory cause of alienation. But I suspect that sincerity has many false bottoms. One can be sincere in one's *mauvaise foi*, especially if it is rather different from what one takes to be the prevailing *mauvaise foi* around one. In other words, alienation can be genuine, without leading to total honesty of thought. Fascinating as I found *Easy Rider*, I think it represents just such a case.

The press hand-out says: ". . . 'freedom' is . . . the subject of the picture—the freedom longed for by so many people all over the world today." The two heroes, one tall, lean and rather spiritual (Fonda), the other round, clumsy and fleshy (Hopper)

—*i.e.* a variation on the typically picaresque pair, Don Quixote and Sancho Panza—set out on a pilgrimage across America from Los Angeles to New Orleans in search of freedom. They finance their expedition by smuggling some unspecified hard drug across the Mexican border, thus collecting a fat wad of notes all in one go. Technically, this is a criminal act, if one believes in the official law, but presumably hippies do not. Morally, it is reprehensible, if one thinks that drugs are harmful and drug-profiteering disgusting. The film is undecided on this point; the heroes accept marijuana as a necessary concomitant of life, but stall on the vital question of the relationship between marijuana and the hard drugs. Intellectually, it is a contradiction; money, which is by definition a medium of exchange, can only retain its value if society is a going concern and the majority accept the unwritten social contract. Individuals who steal money or get it by immoral means are counting on other people remaining more moral than they are. They can only be consistent with themselves if they are cynical anarchists, who despise humanity in the mass. But in the very first episode of the film, which is an encounter with an honest rancher who feeds the travellers according to the old traditions of hospitality and says grace before meat, Peter Fonda looks around, nods his head sagely and opines with apparent seriousness: "You ought to be proud. . . ." Well, if the rancher ought to be proud, the hero played by Fonda ought to be deeply ashamed of himself, but there is no indication that he is. His implied morality is not at all in line with his initial misdemeanour. Possibly we are meant to suppose that, society being imperfect, the freedom-living individual is entitled to use egotistical means to win his freedom. Common sense surely tells us that this has always been the philosophy of the crook and the speculator.

However, let us accept the fact that two characters have "made their pile" immorally, like any early capitalist adventurers. This is a first picaresque act. They then use the money to go on a spiritual quest or odyssey, in search of "freedom", that is, of pure experience outside the normal obligations of society. This is a second, and quite common, form of the picaresque: the hero, instead of being ambitious to win his way to the inside of the existing Establishment—supposing there is one—is looking for satisfaction elsewhere. He wants to find the Holy Grail, or Shangri La, or El Dorado, or the Land of Eternal Innocence. In this case, the heroes do not set their sights very high; they aim at the Mardi Gras festival in New Orleans, which must be pretty commercialised by now. But I suppose New Orleans is still exotically French, and Mardi Gras, however debased, still has an echo of the Roman Saturnalia, which was a ritual reversal of the social norms. As it happens, the heroes ultimately aim for a brothel in New Orleans; this is a very old-fashioned twist, positively Baudelairean in fact, because one would expect only a muddled, recalcitrant, 19th-century bourgeois to imagine that a brothel is outside established society. Perhaps Fonda and Hopper sense this, because they refrain from actually copulating in the brothel, which would be to accept it for what it is, a flesh-shop on the same level as a fish-and-chip shop. They take the girls out into the festival and then have what is objectively a very unpleasant *LSD* trip with them among the urns and crypts of a cemetery. In the barbaric 18th century, the Marquis de Sade was prosecuted for giving Spanish fly to a prostitute. I don't know what the appropriate penalty would be in the 20th century for someone who gives *LSD* to a prostitute, thus causing her to sob dementedly as she rubs her naked breasts and pubis against a marble tombstone. I would say that there ought to be a penalty for degrading the already degraded; but then I cannot see *LSD* as it is presented in this and other films, as being an agent of liberation. The cemetery sequence must be intended as a highlight, since it is the most elaborate in the film; but to me, and no doubt to most people of my generation, it is just a sickening nightmare. Then the scene changes suddenly, the prostitutes have disappeared without trace, and our two heroes are on their way again, rushing lyrically through the morning landscape on their motor-cycles, as if the nightmare had never occurred.

I am not sure that I can make sense of this. The *LSD* had been given to them by a Christ-like hippie, to be shared with two other people in some exceptional moment of communion. The religious parody seems obvious: the drug is like the bread

N

and wine to be shared ritually "whenever two or three are gathered together"; but in fact the drug separates the four people into slobbering imbeciles. Perhaps we have to understand the "trip" as an individual mental blow-out, orgasm, or temporary suicide, which relieves nervous tension like the detumescence consequent on the sexual act. If so, the term "trip" is fully significant. Just as the heroes travel literally on their motor-cycles, because physical movement gives a potent illusion of freedom, so, on the drug, they travel metaphorically "anywhere out of the world" (to use Baudelaire's phrase). To be accurate, they combine the two kinds of travel in a weaker form all the way through, since they smoke marijuana every day before starting off. Their bodies are travelling on one level and their heads on another. Surprisingly enough, they can still steer; I wonder if this is an honest detail.

I have not yet summarised the story in sequence, and I should perhaps now do so to make my final comments intelligible. The heroes have the following encounters: *1.* with the honest rancher already referred to (pastoral simplicity); *2.* with a hippie commune, who are trying to scratch a living on dry, hilly ground and who pray collectively for rain to an unnamed God (they too represent pastoral simplicity, and Fonda declares sententiously that their efforts will be rewarded, even though there seems to be no hope of such a possibility); *3.* with two of the hippie girls, with whom they bathe in a mountain pool (the pastoral innocence of nudity); *4.* a small-town parade that they make fun of, with the result that they are put into jail (the parade represents average conformity, which they see as comic); *5.* a drunken young lawyer, the son of the local big-wig, who gets them out of jail, joins them on their pilgrimage and is murdered by local roughs, presumably because of this (the character, marvellously played by Jack Nicholson, is a traditional alcoholic drop-out, whom the heroes convert to marijuana); *6.* a bunch of conformist provincials who prevent them being served in a café; *7.* the prostitutes (traditional social outcasts); *8.* two truck-drivers, who shoot at longhaired Hopper to give him a fright but accidentally kill him, and so have to murder Fonda as well to cover up their tracks. The film ends with a vision of the second motor-cycle bouncing off the road and bursting into flames. Death of the outsider, killed by the philistine incomprehension of the mass of insiders, who murder him not for the colour, but for the length, of his hair.

If we stick to the Robsonian analysis, I think we have to say that the two picaresque heroes of *Easy Rider* are doomed from the outset. Their journey is very similar to the drive from Marseilles to Paris in Godard's *A bout de souffle*, which is another example of the outsider, a frankly criminal one, riding to his death. The crime which finances their journey is, in a sense, justified, or at least explicable, by the fact that the freedom they are looking for is unobtainable in this life. Their thirst for it is a concealed death-wish, and indeed their round-the-clock reliance on marijuana, a drug which may be harmless but has the effect of making the initiates giggle happily at everything and anything—*i.e.* provides permanent anaesthetisation—is more ominous than the usual philistine reliance on a cup of cawfee or a nice cuppa tea. They are not really looking for freedom in modern America, which is an advanced industrial civilisation. They move along the margin from drop-out to drop-out, and although they are emotionally in favour of a return to pastoralism and pay lip-service to it, they do not believe in it enough to accept it for themselves. The reason is that even a pastoral society at once raises the problems of community living and imposes the constraints of integration. They are lone riders, appreciating the beauty of mountain and desert scenery, which indeed steals a good part of the picture, but there is no ideal society for them.

However, they can be photographed in their predicament among the lonely hills, and people will flock to see the film when it is shown in the large urban centres. The industrialised philistines will enjoy the pastoral poetry of alienation, and the ex-Outsider can cushion his death-wish with dollar bills as well as marijuana.

There remains one incidental point, about which I am sure Lance Robson will have something to say, if he ever produces the promised sequel to *Varieties of the Picaresque*. Why has the motor-cycle been so often associated with the outsider in recent years? In the existing volume, he waxes eloquent about the relationship between the knight-errant or the highwayman and his horse, from the Middle Ages to the 18th century, and he has a fascinating appendix on the importance of the single- or double-seater aeroplane between 1910 and the Battle of Britain, and the Outsider/Insider philosophy that certain writers (notably St Exupéry) based upon it. Possibly, the motor-cycle seems more personal than a four-seater motor-car. (In *Bonnie and Clyde*, as I remember, the initial car was an open two-seater with a dicky, *i.e.* more of a folk-object than the limousine type.) The rider is *outside* the motor-cycle, not enclosed within it. He is exposed to the air and the weather, and so nearer to nature. He grips the body between his legs and thus simulates the sexual relationship between the rider and his horse, often with precise physical results, as the sociologists investigating the leather-boys have explained.

Nevertheless, the motor-cycle and the petrol which drives it are indissolubly wedded to industrial society, and it is remarkable that the hippie mind can overlook this fact. At the beginning of *Easy Rider*, the heroes throw away their watches in a symbolic gesture and roar off superbly down a metalled road. But without the society that the watches suppose, they could not roar and there would be no road.

Midnight Cowboy, which I have just seen, fits so neatly into the Robsonian pattern and is so obviously the same kind of film as the other two, that I cannot forbear adding a few sentences about it. Technically, it is possibly the best of the three, because of the intelligence of John Schlesinger's direction and two absolutely stunning performances by Jon Voigt and Dustin Hoffman. Of course, like the other films, it is tinged with modishness. Pop songs replace the angel choruses of earlier days; the colour photography has a lush beauty of its own, which gives even would-be drab scenes a sort of tinned-soup vividness; and there is the now obligatory party episode or fiesta, with psychedelic lights and drugged wooziness. Some of these things, I am afraid, will date as quickly and disastrously as the dance sequences and plumed costumes in Hollywood films of the '30s.

The original novel by James Leo Herlihy might well be, but probably isn't, an imitation of the first part of a famous 18th-century, French picaresque tale by Marivaux, *Le Paysan parvenu*, about a handsome peasant boy who comes up to Paris to make his fortune by seducing rich middle-aged women. Joe Buck (Jon Voigt) is a beautiful, blond Texan dish-washer, who dresses up in cowboy kit, jumps on to a bus and goes up to New York where he hopes to get rich quick as a bisexual prostitute. He, too, is a sort of orphan/bastard, and his alienation is increased by his consciously accepted low I.Q., which forces him to trust his only talent ("I'm one helluva stud").

The term "midnight cowboy" would seem to refer to the young men so dressed who hang around certain parts of New York at night looking for trade (*cf.* the similar cowboy in the play, *The Boys in the Band*). Robson touches on the ordinary myth of the cowboy and argues that it is often, as in *Shane* or many TV serials, a modernisation of the knight-errant theme. The cowboy *passes through*, because he is a good or bad man on the run, or because he is an incarnation of supernatural values, which are applied locally through his visitation, but have no permanent residence in this world. He has a horse and a gun, whereas the knight had a horse and a sword or lance. Both heroes symbolise movement plus potency, a two-fold ideal which corresponds perhaps to a deeper male aspiration than the desire to construct in one place (a creative urge involving a female element). The "midnight cowboy" is a strange simulacrum of the normal ideal. He is more or less stationary on the streets at night, instead of galloping across the plains in sunshine; he is waiting to be selected by the cows, in the hope that he may be able to drive them singly; he has no horse, and his only gun is inherent in his person. He is reduced, in fact, to his body and his costume, and the latter is a highly significant symbol both for himself and his clients. This gives great tragi-comic weight to the most sordid scene in the film, a fellatio episode in a cinema lavatory, when the cowboy, still dressed in his hat, jerkin and boots, argues with his pathetic, vomiting client about the price to be paid. The sad little man turns out to be as impoverished as he is, and this shows up the cowboy costume as a tawdry double illusion.

The miracle of the performance is that Jon Voigt conveys the amoral, delinquent zest of the *pícaro*, combined with naïve and fundamental goodness. He has a perfect foil in Dustin Hoffman, as Ratso Rizzo, the crippled, tubercular orphan of an Italian-Jewish shoe-shine man. Ratso is the city urchin with brains, or at least shrewdness, who tries to help the cowboy to make the most of his sexual advantages, for their common benefit. Their relationship is a parody of the Don Juan/ Leporello or Don Juan/Figaro collaboration, in the sense that they always fail but in the process unconsciously become friends, although they bicker comically at every point. Whereas the cowboy dreamed of city lights and his long initial bus ride is a imaginary journey towards easy money, Ratso hopes to set out on the reverse quest; he wants to escape from New York to Florida, where the sun will restore his health and he will recover the dignity of his true name, Enrico Rizzo. By braining and robbing an old queer, the cowboy gets enough money for the trip and they take the bus ride to Florida, where he proposes to give up being a *pícaro* and to look for a job. But, on arrival, Ratso is dead in his seat.

This film is, apparently, just as great a commercial success as *Easy Rider*. It is hilariously funny in parts, especially about sex, but this can hardly explain its popularity because it is also very sad. Robson, I suppose, would say that the Outsider riding to his death, and who makes a Friend on the way, is a universal image.

16. Flesh in the Afternoon

Being curious to discover what the police had thought worth impounding in the present welter of permissiveness, I went along to see Andy Warhol's *Flesh*, after it had been released from imprisonment.

The experience was, in a sense, rather like going to a bawdy-house in the afternoon, at least as my Primitive Methodist imagination conjures up such an expedition. The Open Space Theatre is not a wind-swept, sun-kissed hollow in the mountains of Greece, overlooking the wine-dark sea; it is a moderately sized basement off the Tottenham Court Road, at the bottom of a narrow staircase filled with a queue of apparently sex-starved men in raincoats. There is some fussy business about having to be a member of the club (2s. 6d.) for at least an hour before the performance, and this leads to endless arguments and explanations. Once inside, you find bare brick walls, a small, improvised screen, and a few canvas chairs and wooden benches; the chairs face the screen and cost 17s. 6d., while the benches ranged along either side are priced at 15s. At the 4 p.m. performance, I counted fifty or more men, a few of them in couples, and seven women, one a rather statuesque Negress with a shopping-bag. We all looked like people thoroughly intent on vice; no nonsense about carpets or décor for us; just the real thing. The only anxiety was: would we see everything on such a small screen, which could be half blotted out by any tall and excited spectator in the front row?

In spite of this initial impression, I must report that, to my astonishment, *Flesh* struck me as a good and genuine film of its kind, and not simply as a piece of commercial pornography. Taking it within its terms of reference, I liked it better than some much grander efforts, such as Antonioni's *Zabriskie Point*, or Wexler's *Medium Cool,* or Paul Mazursky's film about group love, *Bob and Carol and Ted and Alice,* all of which have come to us from America in recent weeks and deal, somewhat raucously, with comparable areas of American life. *Flesh* has the charm and directness of some early products of the French New Wave, such as Agnès Varda's *Cléo de cinq à sept* or Jean-Luc Godard's *Une Femme est Une Femme.* And the charm is quite strong, although the content is almost totally obscene from the conventional point of view. A day in the life of a New York male prostitute is not a subject that appears likely to lend itself to poetry, and yet this film is poetic, although it is difficult to tell whether the effect has been achieved by design, accident or self-deception.

One would have liked to have some information about the spirit in which the film was made, but none seems to be available. I saw two previous films by Warhol (or out of the Warhol stable, if his name covers a collective undertaking) at the National Film Theatre's Underground Film Festival, and they were terribly boring, as if they had been made by someone in a drugged state, who was reading deep significance into static scenes totally without interest for the sober eye. There are perhaps traces of drugs in *Flesh,* but they seem to be incidental. The mind controlling the camera does not appear to be drugged, nor is the central character a drug-taker, at least not yet. Things being what they are, he may come to that later. Meanwhile, the film has caught him when he is still handsome and healthy, and in the relatively happy phase of living from day to day in the pure, amoral moment, without the help of stimulants. There are no credits to tell us whether or not he is an actor,* but I guess him to be primarily a prostitute playing his own part. In fact, the fascination of the film, for me, lies partly in its existential treatment of the prostitute mentality, a subject that has been dealt with to some extent in literature, particularly from the female point of view, but usually in terms of sentimental cliché.

* Joe D'Alessandro has since toured Europe and has been interviewed at length. But the point I raise hasn't been cleared up.

Unlike most Underground films, *Flesh* actually tells a story in several episodes. We see the young man being wakened up in the morning by his wife, who seems to be permanently in a giggly, marijuana state. We witness their amorous frolicking, which she initiates and he submits to, rather like a professional chef who, when at home, accepts his wife's cooking with a polite show of interest. Next, he plays meditatively on the carpet with their baby, feeding it scraps from what seems to be a collapsing *vol-au-vent* or a crumbling cup-cake. Then he goes out on his beat—curiously enough, street-walkers still walk, even in America—and picks up two successive clients, a tremulous, well-bred young man, with whom he does something unexplained, and an elderly English homosexual, who photographs him in the nude, in the postures of famous Greek statues, while delivering a lecture on body-worship. Before or after this, there occurs a discussion at a street-corner with two novices about the advantages and disadvantages of being a male prostitute. Not all of this was intelligible to me, because of the crackling of the sound-track and the unfamiliarity of the slang, but I understood our hero to be saying that for someone who had opted out of school at an early age, had no qualifications and was a responsible husband and father, obliging elderly gentlemen at twenty dollars a time was not too painful a way of earning "bread". With a generosity I have never noticed among Parisian female prostitutes, who have a strong sense of territorial boundaries, he even explains to the beginners which are the best street-corners.

After this, there come two episodes which are half professional and half sentimental. In a room, where two transvestites are chattering away with bird-like indifference, as if they were at a tea-party, he submits to fellatio on the part of a third person, some old friend, who looks and sounds exactly like a woman but is possibly an ex-man. Then he moves on to another old friend, the athletic type of homosexual, out of whom he wheedles a promise of fifty dollars, in return for some more amorous by-play.

Finally, he returns home and rejoins his wife on their bed, where she is now frolicking with an apparently Lesbian girl-friend. The women take the young man's clothes off and, after some desultory conversation, all three doze off. The film ends as it had begun, with the camera gazing at the recumbent figure; our little life is rounded with a sleep.

I am rather at a loss to say why this film, the events of which are so unlike the home-life of a good Labour-voter, should appear to me to be fundamentally inoffensive, whereas the other three open-market films mentioned earlier are characterised by uncertainties and bad taste. Perhaps it is because the action of *Flesh* takes place quite outside organised society, and therefore constitutes a form of pastoral. It has a kind of innocence in vice. Sexual activities, I suppose, are neither good nor bad in themselves; they take on moral significance only in relationship to the running of society as a whole. The characters in *Flesh* are all individuals with a low I.Q., who do not think in terms of general society at all. They are content to survive at a certain level, and they form a sub-community, within which there is a certain group solidarity and the various sexual practices are as indifferent as blowing one's nose. Sex is, for them, a source of livelihood and a means of communication, as fishing or carpet-weaving might be in some other accidentally constituted community. Perhaps the film gives too rosy a vision of them. It certainly makes them out to be *nice* people without complexes; they show no sadistic or masochistic tendencies; they have no power-drive, their relationships are casual yet friendly, and although money changes hands, it is not always to the fore. It is as if the real prostitute were always as willing to give as to receive, or as if prostitution depended on the absence of a certain hard frontier to the personality. One is surprised to discover the 19th-century myth of the goldenhearted whore re-emerging, even obliquely, in such a setting. These people may be delinquent in one sense, but in another sense they have all opted for human essentials; they are sensualists rather than materialists; they seem to be living in a form of truth, and even of love.

Contrast the sexual passages in the other films I referred to above. The hero of *Zabriskie Point* is a young Californian ex-student in a state of civil war with society, in a purely anarchistic way. He specifically rejects any political philosophy, yet takes pot shots at policemen, presumably in the name of Existentialist despair. He goes off for a joy-ride in a stolen plane, because that is his impulse of the moment. He woos a girl in a car by swooping down over her like a hawk after a sparrow (a nice touch). Then he lands, and they meet up in a very photogenic desert where, inevitably, because they both reject society, they make love. Their conjunction is reverberated and amplified by a vast imaginary orgy, which peoples the wilderness with similarly writhing couples or trios or quartets. Antonioni is presumably saying that life is a meaningless desert, redeemed only by sex, but sex, as he sees it, is impersonal and mechanical, like a gymnastic display. As a spectacle, it is an entertaining reversal of the old Christian view of the desert as the abode of flesh-fearing hermits. The sequence is brilliant and memorable, because it makes one think of a medieval picture painted by a member of the devil's party: extreme, sophisticated, and inhuman.

Similarly, *Medium Cool* and *Bob and Carol* try to link up sex with general statements about society. In the first, a television cameraman has an affair with a country girl from Virginia, and we are no doubt meant to feel the contrast between the universal indifference of the camera's eye, as it registers the details of the Chicago riots, and the genuineness of the personal relationship. But the director nudges us with such transparent sentimentality and finally kills the couple so gratuitously that he defeats his own purpose. As for *Bob and Carol*, it sets out to be a satire on the longing for hippie permissiveness and group communion among wealthy, middle-class Americans but, after some exquisitely embarrassing scenes, loses its way, as if the director himself no longer knew whether his characters' behaviour was in good or bad taste. Perhaps this film has documentary value as a study of the divorce, in some middle-class American minds, between the direct apprehension of sex and the intellectual concept of permissiveness. If so, it conjures up quite an alarming vision of hysterically aggressive American women and over-sexy, yet in some curious way devirilised, American men. Who would not rather spend a week-end with the perverts of *Flesh* than with any of these?

There remains the question of why *Flesh* seems poetic. At first I thought one might say that the film is unselfconscious about nudity, but that is not quite true; the camera emphasises the callipygian advantages of the young man as carefully as Michelangelo would have done, and presumably for the same reasons. However, apart from that, nudity is brought in casually, instead of being unveiled to a roll of drums, as is usually the case, and the effect is not so much erotic as universally human. Nakedness stresses the vulnerability of human beings, through diminishing the importance of the face—the part expressing the consciousness and the personality—in relationship to the rest of the body, which signifies differently and independently. Curiously enough, the hero has a rather refined and spiritual smile, which flickers strangely above his nudity. I see that Sir Kenneth Clark, in *The Nude*, maintains that, in art, the nature of the face determines the way in which the body will be appreciated, and he instances Manet's *Olympia* as a rare case of a nude full of character, the faces of most nudes being conventionally sublime or anguished. In real life—to which the moving film is of course much closer—the contrast between the human expressiveness of the features and the aesthetic or erotic significance of the body is far more marked. This young man is photographed in the nude, not merely with lascivious intent, it seems to me, but also—whether deliberately or accidentally—in such a way as to suggest something about the tragic ludicrousness of even a beautiful body. The appurtenances of sex, in particular, are at once very serious and profoundly comic, and a sort of permanent reminder of contingency.

Also, the young man cannot really appreciate his own body, although it is the centre of the film; it is an object to be looked at and fondled by others, and his mind—a fairly rudimentary mind, no doubt—is just attached to it with a kind of amused indifference. It is as if he were constantly surprised by, and yet used to, the idea that his body should be an immediate passport to relations with other people. This comes out particularly in the scene with the Englishman, where his eyes glaze over with patient boredom as he strikes the required poses and listens to the aesthetico-sexual discourse. I have never been present at such a scene, but the details strike me as being absolutely true, and very revelatory of a friendly interchange of services, which at the same time amounts to a form of non-communication. Just as true, I imagine, is the episode with the athletic homosexual, where the young man, who is at least partly heterosexual, lends himself to the erotic imaginings of his jovial companion without fully understanding them. This is a very strange passage, with an almost animal simplicity and innocence.

However, the sequence which most impressed me was the remarkable *tableau de genre* of the young man, in his capacity as father, playing solemnly and meditatively with his child on the carpet. In neo-classical pictures of this kind, the child is often nude whereas the adult is fully clothed; here the child was completely dressed and the father stark naked. This reversal, together with the total absence of archness in the relationship between them, produced a very powerful and beautiful effect. Here were two human beings, linked by sex, of course, since one—incomprehensibly, as always—had engendered the other, communing politely and mysteriously without words, through the medium of a crumbling *vol-au-vent*. Is there any real difference between the man and the child? The nakedness of the father seemed to suggest that human beings are children who beget other children and can only look at them with puzzled affection, without understanding what the whole process is about.

17. Flashing the Old Job

A racy, upper-middle-class lady of my acquaintance was once describing to me the sorry plight of a friend who had become an exhibitionist. "There he was," she said, "flashing the old job all over the countryside." This mysterious and poetic expression struck me forcibly at the time, because I had never heard it before, and it popped suddenly out of my memory again at the first night of *Oh! Calcutta!* when, like the rest of the audience, I found myself facing a row of old jobs, interspersed with more familiar triangles. Were these old jobs being flashed at us? Were Mr Kenneth Tynan and his collaborators flashing *par membres interposés* and, when the cry "Author!" went up at the end, would they come forward hand in hand proudly displaying their several virilities? (Mr John Lennon, I understand, has already filmed his for the benefit of world audiences.) Would we be expected to flash back in a surge of audience participation? The experience, new for me (in adult life at least), was rather puzzling. Not since I was in Standard III at the Council School forty-odd years ago had I had the opportunity of being a "thinking *voyeur*", and I didn't quite know what to think.

My first thought, now that I have had time to react, is that *Oh! Calcutta!* was undoubtedly an historic occasion. Total nudity on the stage is something quite novel; it is much more real than nudity in the cinema, and it breaks a taboo which is several hundred years old, if not older. We have been visibly moving in this direction for a generation or two and Mr Tynan, having finally engineered the matter, has made his immortal contribution to the theatre. It causes one to reflect that human nature must be very peculiar if the mere display of *that which is*, and is moreover universally, can cause such a stir. But then taboos, too, are universal, as if human nature always had to forbid something in order to give itself a framework and a feeling of negative certainty. Francis Huxley points out in *Affable Savages* that the naked South American Indians were shocked to see that he did not wear a penis-sheath while bathing; when you look at a photograph of an Indian wearing one of these sheaths, which is for all the world like a little flag, you might think he was flashing the old job with a vengeance, but in fact he is being modest, and his sheath is no more phallic than a top hat (if we can be sure that a top hat was not a transferred symbol of Victorian repression, a displaced erection). What one wonders now is where the taboo will reassert itself in Western civilisation, if it has really been removed from sex. Will one be perfectly in order in showing one's nakedness and yet obscene, for instance, if one develops a rational argument? I sometimes think, in talking or listening to young people, that two or three ideas, strung logically together, are now almost as offensive as indecent exposure would have been some years ago. I have seen young people go red in the face and appear deeply shocked if asked to explain how they reconcile attitude *A* with statement *B*.

However, I imagine that the assertion of nakedness starts from a rational premise. We are all naked underneath our unnatural clothes, and therefore nudity is truer, more genuine, more healthy than the state of being dressed. Clothes are a visible manifestation of *mauvaise foi*, so off with them! Now that the thing has been done, I can see no objection to it in itself. I noticed even that some of the actors and actresses were more impressive in the nude than when they were dressed, as if their talent lay more in the shape and grace of their bodies than in what they were able to do. If, from now on, dancers and pop singers were to perform in the nude, this would be a perfectly acceptable convention since what they are selling is often youth and beauty rather than art, and in so far as they are being artistic, totally naked physical beauty can only enhance the effect.

But this must apply only to a fairly narrow range of performers and performances. A lot of talented people are no doubt cursed with bodies inferior to their artistic ability and are thankful to have clothes to help them to create a temporary illusion. Or, perhaps, clothes serve to cancel out the body, thus allowing the mental presence to be more keenly perceived. I am quite interested in Mr Tynan and Mr Lennon, for instance, as personalities, but I haven't the faintest desire to contemplate them in the nude, and I don't see why they should want to display their nakedness, except to their nearest and dearest. Is there not a distinction to be made between public and private nakedness?

Public nakedness, let us say, has a universal quality and requires a natural gift, like any other profession; private nakedness often needs to be illumined by love or lust, and is only positively significant between the two people concerned. Mr Tynan has struck his blow for truth and freedom, and in one sense at least has carried the day. But although we are all equal in our underlying nudity, here again the universe manifests its terrible unfairness, because some people are more equal than others, even among the performers of *Oh! Calcutta!* There was one of them who, in my opinion, would have done better to keep his light hidden under a bushel.

My second thought is that the blow struck for freedom and truth is still, in spite of all, rather muffled and inconsistent.

The punning title, *Oh quel cul que t'as!*, was apparently invented by an elderly French Surrealist painter, and the backdrop on the stage as well as the front cover of the programme shows an almost nude *belle époque* beauty, presenting the perfect circle of her buttocks, *i.e., une belle croupe*, as the expression was. But why this flavour of Edwardian naughtiness? It refers back essentially to a period when women were marketable objects, and is out of keeping with the modern views on sexuality which have determined the bisexual nakedness of the performance. It also embodies an old-fashioned idea of female beauty, which went with bustles and the can-can. Perhaps the antiquarian note is meant as a joke, like a mahogany *bidet*-stand being used as a drinks table in a modern room, or perhaps it reflects the personal tastes of the elderly Frenchman with the admirably Surrealist name of Claude Trouille. In either case, it is surely rather off-key.

Then, nakedness itself is used both genuinely and conventionally. When the company dance in a lyrical or rhapsodic way, their bodies are operating artistically, and their nakedness is just a sign—although an important one—that they are being true to the natural data. In other words, in all dancing sex is not actual but transposed and therefore the nakedness can be genuine. But in a sketch about copulation, what is the use of two naked bodies simulating the action, if they do not actually perform it? The fact that they are stark naked merely underlines the absence of the essential point, as if they were sexless angels in an old-fashioned Biblical illustration. Clearly, it would be difficult for them to copulate realistically within the framework of a show like this, which is theatre, not ritual. But to go through the motions with complete realism of nudity and almost complete non-realism of action, is to do something which is not a theatrical statement nor, in the circumstances, a valid joke; it merely throws doubt on the heterosexual possibilities of the gentleman concerned.

The problem I am referring to is an aesthetic, rather than a moral, one. The realism of acting is not identical with the realism of mime, and if you mix up poor acting with even worse mime, you are really not doing very much at all. In these scenes, the actors and actresses just looked like adolescent schoolchildren having a naughty romp, and one was surprised at the paradox of so chic a show-business audience being expected to enjoy so crass a display. To do them justice, they didn't sound very enthusiastic in the first half; when drinks during the interval had helped them to respond more easily, their applause became louder and, at the end, they sounded reasonably convinced. But I wasn't. *Oh! Calcutta!* may represent a liberation as far as nudity is concerned, but it doesn't do anything to demonstrate how sex can be acted frankly, if at all, on the stage.

Still less does it show how sex can be talked about, and this, for me, was the greatest surprise. I had expected a revue full of wit and sophistication but, for the most part, it was a collection of old dirty jokes, of the kind that I have always associated with embarrassment about sex, or temporary deprivation. I admit I have no ready definition of the difference between wit and

o

fun about sex and the sort of dirty story that schoolboyish men seem to relate to each other the world over, but I am sure there must be a difference. The last time I heard such talk at any length was during the War, when cosmopolitan types would while away the night watches in the BBC Foreign Service by capping one filthy tale with another; there was a Dane, I remember, with an astonishing command of English obscenity, who was inexhaustible about the goings-on in Shanghai. Again my objection is not one of prudery; it is rather difficult to be prudish if one has been observing the world and oneself for the last fifty years. Besides, it is obvious that obscenity serves a valid purpose from time to time.

The question is: why should one go to the theatre to hear the sort of thing which is ordinary folk-material in schools and pubs? True, it is being trumpeted from the stage, and so there is again a ceremonial breaking of the taboo. Father Ubu said *merdre* in 1896, Eliza Doolittle said *bloody* in 1914, and now the actors can utter any four-letter word. But the mere use of these terms is not of the same order as displaying nudity; nakedness is a pure fact, which is what it is; obscenity is a linguistic phenomenon, that is, an intellectual and emotional manipulation of facts. It is not in itself a datum. It implies an attitude to sex, and the attitude suggested by practically all the sketches in *Oh! Calcutta!* is the coarse, sniggering uneasiness of people who have not assimilated it to any philosophy of life. Perhaps sex is ultimately unassimilable, like the other animal functions, but a lot of artists have got a great deal further with it than the deplorable authors of *Oh! Calcutta!*, who grind away on the level of fifth-rate music-hall, in such a manner as to dishonour sex rather than rehabilitate it.

The programme doesn't specify who wrote what, as if the authors wished to hide behind their collective list, but I have seen it suggested that Joe Orton was responsible for the sketch about sexual complexities in a middle-class family. If so, I am amazed; where is that beautiful sense of genteel innuendo which makes *Entertaining Mr Sloane* so profoundly entertaining? If Joe Orton did write it, he must have done it on an off-day, or as a linguistic exercise in obscenity to prove that obscenity is not enough. I know that Renoir said that he painted with his penis, but the expression needs to be interpreted. Writers can flash the old job directly, if they wish to be in the fashion; but to write with it effectively requires a rather complicated process of mediation.

18. All Flesh is Trash

Because I wrote an "understanding" article on *Flesh* a few months ago, Vaughan Films kindly invited me to a private showing of *Trash*, the next item in the Warhol Factory *oeuvre*. As I write, the question of whether or not it will be put on commercially is undecided,* and so anything I say may be taken as an argument for or against, especially since—I am told—the *Flesh* article was used as an argument in favour of that film, *post facto*.

This is rather inhibiting, because my views on censorship are chaotic. On the one hand, I am opposed to it, on the ground that everything about human nature, either good or bad, should be said, since the only thing that ultimately satisfies the mind and helps development is the truth; on the other hand, I realise that the indiscriminate presentation of the truth can often do a lot of harm, before it begins to do any good, especially in sexual matters, where imitativeness is such a powerful force. Even supposing that *Flesh* is quite a good film, as I think it is, I don't see how one can know whether or not its influence on the young will be good; since the hero is a young prostitute, it may stimulate male prostitution. Who knows whether the influence of *Look Back in Anger* was good or not? Perhaps it encouraged some young men to be more uncouth and caddish to their wives than they might otherwise have been. Even *Hamlet* might promote procrastination and messy solutions, and I have known Biblical illustrations to induce lewd thoughts. So I claim no ability to be definite about the general social effects of a work of art; the best I can do is fumble towards some awareness of whether or not the work seems satisfactory in itself.

* It has only just (1973) been shown commercially in Great Britain.

Nor am I clear about the intentions of the members of the Warhol Factory, even after reading an immensely long but very woolly interview with Paul Morrissey in *Rolling Stone*, that interesting paper which, apart from the swear-words, is as chapel-minded and pompous as *The Times* used to be. I still don't know whether the felicities I thought I saw in *Flesh* were accidental or deliberate. Are these people dedicated to art, or are they cashing in on pornography and having fun with a hysterical market? Perhaps they themselves aren't quite sure. However the films are there, and one can only say how one finds them.

In the publicity handout, *Trash* is termed a comedy, and I must admit that some of the younger members of the audience laughed merrily at several points. But the humour, if humour it is, is so black that I couldn't raise a smile. I give the film full marks for a certain kind of sordid realism, which makes even Buñuel's exercises in cruelty or Fellini's *Satyricon* look quite stagey. This is total abjection, not simply man without God or man alienated from society, but Beckettian man in the dust-bin waiting for death. Whereas *Flesh* seemed to convey a curious marginal happiness existing among perverts and drop-outs, *Trash* takes more or less the same characters and shows the reality of their destitution and sickness. To complete the picture, at the two or three points in the story where they come into contact with "normal" people, the latter turn out to be just as sick, but in a less honest way. Therefore, the drop-outs cannot be judged in relationship to a supposedly healthy society, since by implication there is, or can be, no such thing. All flesh is trash; beauty is non-existent, sex is appallingly ugly and politics cannot possibly be real, since they would suppose a minimum of sense and coherence which is lacking in human nature. To find this sort of thing funny, one would have to be able to laugh at Zola or Breughel. The spectacle of a scarecrow of a woman (but is she a woman or a female impersonator?), all writhing arms and legs like an infuriated octopus, masturbating with a beer-bottle because her lover is impotent, would have turned even Zola's stomach. As cinema, the scene was successful in the sense that it didn't produce that feeling of rhetorical phoneyness which is the usual weakness of horror sequences, but I can't say that I enjoyed it, especially in the queasy state that follows gastric 'flu.

We are told that the Warhol films are improvised, and certainly they begin and end abruptly, move jerkily from point to point, and pay no attention to the sort of details the continuity girl was supposed to look after. Still, there is a kind of storyline in *Trash*. Joe, the previously beautiful hero of *Flesh*, is now a drug-addict, spotty and unhealthy-looking, and continuously in a semi-stupor as he roams around looking for the next fix. Heroin has deprived him of his potency, and the main joke is that various women try in vain to excite him. He is constantly taking his clothes off to oblige or to earn a few dollars (and also, no doubt, to give the audience a view of that valuable property which presumably has been insured by now, as film stars' legs once were), but each attempt ends in a fiasco, usually with recriminations. He remains woodenly impervious to this and keeps drifting back to the filthy room he shares with his girl (or boy?) friend, Holly, a grotesque weirdie whose occupation is salvaging bits of garbage from the tip and treasuring or selling them. As a side-line, she pushes drugs to schoolboys in the hope that, having stupefied them, she can submit them to oral rape. In one nightmarish scene, she does just this, after assuring the bespectacled youngster that the stuff in the syringe is "just like penicillin". I think Miss Holly, with her fuzz of dirty hair, her bird-like movements and her mad chatter, must take the all-time prize for ghoulishness. If Bette Davis has seen this film, she is no doubt green with envy, because nothing she did in her heyday was anything like as intense. There is no suggestion that Holly is an actress, although in a way I suppose she must be; she just exists in her sheer and total awfulness.

It is clear that Joe and Holly form a kind of pair, like Vladimir and Estragon in *Waiting for Godot*, but Beckett's play is almost jolly compared with *Trash*. Why does Joe take drugs and why are we submitted to slow close-ups of him sticking the needle into his arm? Presumably because life has no meaning and one may as well commit suicide in that way as in any other. Drugs don't give access to any higher reality; they merely rot the body and anaesthetise the mind. Why is Holly a sort of dung-fly fluttering around the dust-bin? Because civilisation is essentially the production of waste; nature itself is a senseless process of consumption. And the couple is convincingly differentiated in that the man, though impotent, is male; he ultimately doesn't give a damn and remains as impassive as— to use the American expression—a cigar-store Indian. The woman, or female impersonator, goes on fussing, as a bird will try to build a nest in hopeless circumstances.

As I suggested before, the horror doesn't lie simply in the masturbation scene, the oral rape, and another sequence which shows attempted copulation with a naked woman in an advanced state of pregnancy; it also comes from contact with so-called normal people, in two long sequences.

In the first, Joe wanders into a middle-class apartment to try and steal something, but instead comes across a young housewife who takes a fancy to him. Her husband comes home and also shows a rather greasy interest in the drop-out. Joe has a bath, during which the young woman stays with him, fondling him and telling him in a shrill, wailing voice about obscene encounters in her past. She proposes various orgies to him but all he wants is more dope, which she goes to get from somewhere else in the block. Then Joe takes the drug and falls into a stupor, while the young couple insult each other in the most hysterical manner, as they lug his body around to prevent him becoming comatose. In this strange episode, his naked form is seen lolling in the various attitudes of the descent from the Cross, as the slanging match proceeds, revealing the falsity of their relationship. Finally, they push him out on to the landing and throw his clothes after him; so much for the Good Samaritan act.

The other scene is a visit from a Social Security official to Joe and Holly's slum. Inspired by her sister's real pregnancy, Holly has the idea of slipping a cushion under her skirt and asking for "Welfare". It is, incidentally, her ambition to "get on Welfare", which she feels is her right, since "I was born on Welfare and raised on Welfare". However, the dapper, talkative official is a shoe-fetichist, who is fascinated by a pair of elaborate silver slippers Holly has found in the garbage. He proposes a bargain: he will fill in the form favourably, if he can have the shoes. But Holly will not part with the shoes, which are her only ones, and in any case she considers them to be irrelevant to the central point, that is, her absolute right to Welfare. In the excitement of the debate, she stands up and the phoney bun drops out of the oven.

The ghastly thing is that real children are no doubt born quite frequently into this sort of situation, which is equal to the worst miseries of the 19th-century slums. It would be interesting to know whether the Warhol Factory has deliberately done a Zola on the drop-out myth or, perhaps tried to produce the *Uncle Tom's Cabin* of the drugs-and-sex scene. Or is *Trash* not really a work of art at all, but just another spontaneous boil on the face of contemporary American culture?

19. A French No-Play

Marguerite Duras' play, *The Lovers of Viorne (L'amante anglaise)* at the Royal Court Theatre, is a complete negation of traditional drama, an extreme example of the anti-play, which makes no concessions whatever to entertainment or to the average staying power of audiences. Both titles, the French as well as the English, are perversely misleading, because there are no lovers at Viorne and no Englishwoman in love. The action is even more inward than in classical tragedy. There are only two characters, but they do not appear on the stage at the same time; they merely occupy the same chair in turn and talk. If the playgoer can sit through this experience, and in a curious way enjoy it, he has clearly passed some kind of test.

I am glad to say that I stood the strain. I am now in a better position to admit that, a few weeks earlier, I had walked out of Arrabal's *The Emperor and the Architect* at the National Theatre. Nothing would have persuaded me to face the second half of that load of Hispano-French rhetoric. Even during the first half I could only check my impulse to flee by counting the pimples on Jim Dale's naked behind, for which exercise I was conveniently placed, being in the second row. But whereas Arrabal is just neurosis (or dottiness) rampant, Marguerite Duras has a weird something, even though she has been partly affected by the present rarefied Parisian atmosphere, where structuralists speak only to semiologists and semiologists commune darkly with the synchronic Idea.

The setting has the chic of utter bareness, like those expensive French restaurants where it is quite in order to anti-eat by toying with a hard-boiled egg and a stick of celery. There are only three canvas-and-metal chairs and a little table with a tape-recorder, against a dark background. Since the stage never contains more than two persons at a time (a character and a non-character), one chair seems austerely superfluous; but perhaps it is meant to represent the universal audience, the people in the body of the theatre and all other possible listeners, *i.e.* the anonymous *one* for whom the work of art exists. The work itself appears, at first sight, to consist of two successive dialogues. An undefined interrogator questions first a husband (in Act I) and then his wife (in Act II). But it soon transpires that this interrogator is neither a policeman nor a psychiatrist; he is the voice of the writer questioning the character in order to get the character to speak to himself or herself. The dialogues are disguised monologues.

Or, to put it the other way round, any monologue, any use of language, any attempt at understanding, involves a division of the self into Subject and Object. Language is that which, from the start, alienates the self from the self by introducing the presence of society into the inner sanctum. As soon as a baby lisps its first word, it is well on the way to schizophrenia. And so three chairs can represent the division within the speaking self, plus the listening ear of the third person. It is a pity, really, that Mme Duras weakened a little and introduced the tape-recorder as a piece of stage business. It is played back at one moment, so that the woman character can be surprised by the strangeness of her own speech, but she is surprised enough by it, as it is. The tape-recorder is surely a borrowing from *Krapp's Last Tape* or *Les Séquestrés d'Altona* and could have been dispensed with in the interests of greater purity.

Although there is no play in the traditional sense, the underlying subject inclines to the melodramatic. A murder has been committed. Claire Lanne, the wife, has slaughtered her deaf-and-dumb cousin, Marie-Thérèse, who kept house for her for years, and has dropped the various parts of the dismembered body on to trains passing under the local viaduct, which is in a provincial town outside Paris. The different sections have all been reassembled by the police from the far corners of France, except the head, with which she did something special that she refuses to divulge. The psychological action, such as it is, depends on the two questions: Why did she commit the murder when she had no particular animosity against her cousin? And what has she done with the head?

Act I, the interrogation of the husband which fills in the situation for us, is the longest *exposition* I have ever heard in the theatre. I wonder if Mme Duras borrowed the technique from Pinget's *L'Inquisitoire*, a whole New Novel written in the question-and-answer form. This first act might, I think, have eliminated a fair proportion of the audience at the interval— *"Un coup de massue pour les philistins!"*, I heard a gleeful French voice say—had they not had the promise of Peggy Ashcroft in Act II. To mention this is not to underestimate the brilliant performance of Maurice Denham, who had to give a non-boring display of boring minimality as the uninspired husband. He had married his wife because of her physical attractiveness, when she was on the rebound from a previous affair. She had quickly slumped into neurosis and he had consoled himself with a series of other women. Although he is not treated very harshly, he is obviously meant to come across as the humdrum foil to her interesting madness. He gives us a prosaic, common-sensical account of the circumstances in which the crime was committed, and expresses honest bewilderment at the realisation that he himself might well have been the murder victim.

Here, another literary parallel comes to mind. *Thérèse Desqueyroux*, probably the best of François Mauriac's novels, is about a husband with a murderous wife who cannot quite grasp the fact—nor indeed can she—that her crime is the outcome of higher spiritual sensitivity. But whereas Mauriac's heroine is meant to be a modern, inverted saint, Mme Duras's Claire Lanne is the Absurd heroine, whose maladjustment to life is "truer" than the apparent sanity of more balanced people. She has had many literary predecessors: Camus's Meursault and Caligula, for instance, or the heroes of some of Sartre's early short stories.

Actually, when Peggy Ashcroft gets into her stride in Act II, we realise that the action exists on two levels, the sentimental and the Absurd/phenomenological. Claire Lanne hails from Cahors where, as a pious young girl, she was seduced by a

policeman with whom she had an ecstatic affair. She transferred her feminine devotion from God to the policeman, and
when he was unfaithful to her she was crippled by traumatic
shock. This is, to some extent, a repetition of the theme of the
film, *Hiroshima mon amour*, where the heroine has been in love
with a German during the Occupation. In the play, the name
"Cahors" is repeated like a hypnotic invocation, just as
"Nevers" was in the film. Mme Duras, in this respect, seems to be
working off some personal obsession with a persistent memory.

But Claire Lanne could, perhaps, have become deranged
without this external shock, through the now well-known
process of the Existentialist revelation. Once the relationship
of the consciousness with the world has been called into
question, paralysis of the will can ensue, together with various
other symptoms. Claire neglects the house (this is why the
deaf-and-dumb cousin comes to stay) and sits most of the time
thinking in the garden. She cleans her own room with maniacal
thoroughness every day, presumably because this is the immediate area around her own body, but is indifferent to filth
elsewhere. She has to have time, she feels, to allow the thoughts
buzzing in her head to work themselves out as they will. She
sometimes senses them trying to rise up through her skull and
go off like gunshots. This is the gaseous nothingness of the
Pour-soi passing through the material density of the *En-soi*. She
sees other people as objects or animals. Marie-Thérèse is too
fat and looks like a heifer from behind; the husband, Pierre,
is too thin and tall, so that his head seems to scrape unbearably
against the ceilings. This is the break-down of categories, when
all the *En-soi* outside the consciousness begins to lose its recognisable, conventional contours. Claire has a horror of eating,
particularly certain dishes such as stew, although Marie-
Thérèse is an excellent cook; this is the mystery of the nourish-
ment of the *Pour-soi* by lumps of *En-soi*; the real horror of
transubstantiation is not that the bread and the wine should
turn into flesh and blood, but that the spirit should be dependent on stew.

However, in this phenomenological nightmare, there are
oases of reassurance. Claire is devoted to a bed of mint in the

garden, *de la menthe anglaise*, no doubt because of the pun, *l'amante anglaise*, which is meaningless in the context—but with that significant meaninglessness that some modern minds find intriguing. She is very fond of an illiterate Portuguese, Alfonso, a woodcutter, who is "perfect", perhaps through some coincidence between his simple personality and his function. Possibly, there is an echo-effect from his cutting-up of the trees to the de-limbing of the body. To cut, to segment, to subdivide, to quarter—these are profoundly satisfactory activities, because the *Pour-soi* can have the impression of neatly conquering the *En-soi*. To prune a rose bush or a hedge is to indulge in herbaceous sadism, as we would probably realise if we could read the thoughts of gentle ladies armed with secateurs. Snip! that relieves my castration lust! Snip! that establishes the reign of mind over matter and subordinates the world to my *Pour-soi* in the proper Object/Subject relationship. . . .

In fact, I wonder if the main concept behind the play is not murder as a form of phenomenological poetry.* Claire—to whom Peggy Ashcroft gives a wonderfully musical, detached, upper-middle-class English pathos—presumably kills Marie-Thérèse in an explosion of Absurd disgust, as she might have killed anyone, or even her own body. Then she drops the parts of the corpse on to trains which distribute them to the different corners of the French "hexagon", whence they are reassembled by the police. Dismemberment is followed by reconstitution.

---

* My suspicion that the dismemberment is the deep, central image is increased by the ambiguity of the source. In an early version of the play, *Les Viaducs de Seine-et-Oise* (1960), Mme Duras refers to a real-life murder which is supposed to have occurred in 1954. The programme notes to *The Lovers of Viorne* quote another, different, real-life murder, which is said to have happened in 1966. The common element in both is the dropping of the body segments from a bridge on to trains and their distribution and reassembly. I don't remember what the papers said at the time, but it occurs to me that Mme Duras may have invented the "real-life" incident and drawn two plays and a novel from it, because of its disturbing poetic power.

In the second play, the character of the deaf-mute is certainly her invention, and one can see a justification for the choice of character. A deaf-mute, being deprived of language, cannot be a true *Pour-soi*, and therefore, although she has a head, cannot be fully aware of the perpetually anguished emptying out of the Godless consciousness. She is said to have been "happy."

The beautiful simplicity of this operation sets off by contrast the terrible problem which will beset us all on Judgment Day, when we shall have to retrieve our limbs from the multiplicity of conflicting forms they will have assumed in the evolving universe.

But the head is missing. Why did she not distribute it along with the rest? Only when she looked at the head, she says, did she realise that she had killed a human being. The head is that part of the *En-soi* which is the seat of the *Pour-soi*, and is therefore a particularly ambiguous piece of matter. This raises the question: what is the appropriate phenomenological thing to do with a head when you have cut it off? Claire travels up to Paris with the head in a bag and disposes of it in some way that clearly satisfies her. But she refuses to let on, and so, as in so many modern literary works, we are left with an unresolved suspense.

It is at this point that we, the playgoers or readers, must renounce the facilities of old-fashioned completed literature and stir our imaginations into healthy, creative activity. What would you do with a severed head . . . and you . . . and you? I confess that I have racked my brains in vain in the waking state. But I am going to be really modern and wait for the answer to come to me in a dream.

20. Centre 69?

After attending a performance of Andy Warhol's *Pork* at the Round House, ex-Centre 42, and after experiencing showers of obscenity in some other theatres, I have been trying to reflect on the implications of the theatre as public brothel. I must confess—and this may seem a damaging admission on the part of a French specialist—that I have never been inside a real brothel, although I once lived for three months in a hotel in Montmartre which was partly a *maison de passe* and where, as I sat translating rather austere *avant-garde* texts for *transition*, things were going bump all around me. But since I was what is called happily married even before the beginning of time some twenty-five years ago, my knowledge of such institutions is largely derived from literature and art. They would suggest that the brothel, with the theatre and the church, has always been a basic social organism, more so indeed than the school or academy, although the latter—as literature amply testifies—has often combined a modicum of book-learning with vigorous erotic, dramatic and pseudo-religious functions. At a pinch, a society might do without schools, if instruction were passed on from individual to individual, but can it, I wonder, do without churches, theatres, and brothels?

Modern English society may appear to have got almost to the point of dispensing with churches, but one has to inquire whether the religious function has not been taken over, in a slightly disguised form, by other activities. For example, does pop-singing not to some extent replace the hymn-singing of the Victorian era? The intellectual content is often just as deliberately abysmal and the hypnotic effect quite similar; they are parallel instances of making a reassuring collective noise in face of the mystery of the Unknowable. I often feel that there is a live, though very raw, metaphysical excitement in *Top of the Pops* which is missing from *Songs of Praise*, as if one corresponded to a religion in the making whereas the other echoed a dead belief. The fact that the former is a kind of commercialised voodoo, with dervishes and buttock-wobbling, and the latter polite and distinguished, merely emphasises the difference in vitality.

Then again, it has been repeated *ad nauseam* since the popularisation of the ideas of Antonin Artaud that the theatre, "holy theatre", should be total social ceremony. Originally it came out of the church; now it should move back to being a church in its own right, with ritual, catharsis and audience participation. Hence the intensity of the Living Theatre and all that experimental theatre of sado-masochistic rites associated with Genet, Grotowski, and Peter Brook. There is, of course, little or no attempt to organise the theology of this new ecclesiastical theatre; its god is not the traditional transcendent deity who was thought of as a person, a coherent being, and whose rules and regulations could therefore be given some rational dress. The new god is the individual or collective unconscious, which lies beneath the puny, superficial structures of reason—a magnificent, steamy, inarticulate smoking like the witches' cauldron or the sybil's censer. One could no more put it into a theological strait-jacket than one could tame a volcano; one worships it with tremulous awe, and the non-believers are those dull, conventional people who do not realise that they are divinely inhabited or, to adapt a traditional phrase, that they are sitting on something which may or may not be a gold-mine, but is certainly a *numen*.

I now get back to my main point: just as the church has re-converged on the theatre, might we not explain the universal outburst of theatrical obscenity by saying that the brothel too has moved into the theatre? No doubt, the theatre has always had a brothel aspect; up to 1914 at least, it was, all over Europe, a reservoir of ladies of easy virtue and young men of accommodating charms. The theatre-owner in Zola's *Nana* corrects someone who refers to *"votre théâtre"* by replying *"mon bordel"*. Also, French bourgeois who watched bedroom-farce or

English middle-class people who attended Christmas panto-
mimes laughed at jokes that they would not usually have
tolerated in their own drawing-rooms. The collective naughtiness of the theatre was to some extent a liberation. But what
has happened now, I think, is that the concept of naughtiness
has been carried almost to its final expression. Not quite,
however, because the physical sex is still simulated instead of
being really enacted, as it would be in certain kinds of true
ritual, such as a black mass. Still, the exposure of nakedness
(particularly in *Pork*, where the girls and boys display their
pudenda in a blaze of light, as if they were in the venereal
ward of a hospital) and the indecency of word and gesture are
complete.

All obscenity is, I suppose, lyrical and para-religious, since
profanity means a negation of the sacred. Sex appears to be the
most easily accessible form of sacred lyricism for most people,
or at least for most men; the universal obscenity of folk-culture
is a confirmation of this, and takes that form because it is less
embarrassing to blaspheme than to worship. But blasphemy is
only the other side of worship, and so the theatre-as-brothel is
not so far removed as one might at first think from the theatre-
as-church. It is perhaps the theatricality—the playing of the
part, the attempt of the consciousness to project itself so as to
become an object of knowledge to itself—which is the central
human characteristic, and the sacred or profane are only
modalities.

Now the evidence of French literature would seem to suggest
that the brothel had at least three clearly distinguishable
functions; to sell immediate sexual intercourse untrammelled
by the conventions of courtship or class; to facilitate the working-
out of sado-masochistic fancies connected with orgasm by the
arrangement of *mises-en-scène* (this is well documented in Proust,
Genet and elsewhere); and to allow the client to be completely
frank in word and deed about purely bestial impulses that he
might not be able to admit to his wife, or even to his conventional mistress. If one can overlook the fact that the brothel
used human beings as instruments, all three functions had a
therapeutic value, and the last might even be said, in addition,

P

to be graced by a philosophical point. There is something in human nature which wants to explore all possibilities, to be true to the fundamental animal, irrespective of cultural inhibitions, and to name everything with names so that nothing, however extreme, is left unsaid.

How far *Pork* corresponds to the first function, I cannot say. I did not check at the box-office whether the telephone numbers of the performers were available to the public, but the programme notes, I see, obligingly remind us which of the young men are circumcised and which are not. But I think *Pork* corresponds very definitely to the second function, and still more so to the third. It is an exercise in outrage, and if it has a genuine purpose behind it, other than easy money-making, this can only be to correspond to the audience's own obscure desire to be outraged. It is deliberately and thoroughly nasty, as if to show that the truth is nasty and that some profound satisfaction is to be gained by admitting this and by rubbing our own noses in it.

Not much effort has gone into the dramatic structure. The stage is furnished with a number of characters—a telephone-operator, a bald lady, a fat, epicene gentleman, etc.—who are mainly there to look quaint and make up a background: *ces messieurs-dames sont au salon.* The actors are constantly to-ing and fro-ing through swing-doors and there is a lot of moving about of objects—telephones, drug-syringes and electrified dildoes—again to give an appearance of busy-ness. The scene-shifters are two naked young men with startlingly dyed pubic hair and blank faces. The centre of attention is a caricature of Warhol himself in a wheel-chair, a twisted, effete *voyeur* with a drawling voice, who is listening to, or provoking, monologues from three women and one transvestite. The main woman is called Pork (I am told that this is an old Negro slang term for female flesh) and the transvestite Vulva, presumably because that is precisely what a transvestite wants to be but is not. The two women other than Pork are not really necessary, although one of them has points, and their monologues could equally well be delivered by her. The basic pattern is that a *voyeur*, non-operative and probably homosexual, is listening to the frenzied blatherings of a woman and a pseudo-woman. The prurient intellect is lending a curious ear to the peculiarities of physiology.

The monologues are as definite as "To be or not to be", but on a different literary level. One is about the pains of abortion, another about the coprophagous perversion, another about a three-way masturbatory session in a cinema, and the most striking about the varieties of excrement. This last is delivered by the transvestite with the voice and gestures of a pantomime dame, and gives one a sudden vision of the marvellous continuity of a theatrical tradition which probably goes back in a primitive form to the farces of Ancient Greece. It is strange to reflect that the most sophisticated thing one can do at the moment in the theatre, on TV or at a party is to say "shit" with a certain knowing, philosophical, God-defying air, when the term has been used for centuries as a swear-word by people who did not understand its implications. It has now almost superseded that other short, sharp term which was the first to break the decency barrier. Not being scatologically inclined myself, I suspect that the shift from the sexual to the scatological is perhaps a bad sign, because the sexual is a positive, forward-looking aspect of the life-cycle, whereas the scatological, except on the level of gardening, is a negative one.

I haven't said yet whether I enjoyed these two hours in the theatrical brothel. Actually, no. I was almost sick at one point, and if we are getting to a stage where one has to be provided with a paper bag in the theatre as in an aeroplane, I shall stay at home. I am too old to adapt to the idea that being sick might be part of the sound cathartic process. If we are to have brothel-theatres, could they not be jollier, more centrally sexual, more directly adapted to the happy perversions of *l'homme moyen sensuel*? There was no glimmer of sentiment or human kindness or balance in *Pork*. The Marquis de Sade would have been quite pleased with it, and it was this, I think, that depressed me most.

21. Modalities of Sex

My best friend, who is candid almost to a fault, accuses me of wasting my time on trifles, such as the modern theatre and cinema, and says that I always write the same article. "I see you've done your sex piece again", he remarks gloomily, before settling down to put me right about the current political situation and the nobler cultural phenomena of the past two thousand years.

"George", I invariably reply, "that is unfair. As you very well know, I have not one article but two—my sex piece and my moral values piece. If the first comes round rather more often, it is obviously because, at a crucial stage, I was deprived of sex and given a surfeit of moral values. Even at this late hour, when the problem has become academic, I am still trying to strike a balance. Being the Prussian you are, you ought to admire my persistence. Anyway, how can you just dismiss the theatre and the cinema, decadent though they may seem to the truly adult mind like your own? Everything is significant; there are no privileged subjects. So why shouldn't I try to squeeze an idea or two out of show business? . . . etc. . . . etc."

Actually, within show business itself, it would be correct to say that there is still a major, privileged subject, which is precisely sex, with or without violence. After giving the cinema a miss for about three months, I recently made an attempt to catch up by going to see six films in a row. In watching four of them (*Straw Dogs; W.R. or The Mysteries of the Organism; Carnal Knowledge;* and *Klute*), I was surprised to notice how much further contemporary taste has moved towards disregarding love and replacing it by sex. One would have thought that, by now, the sexual high-water mark would have been reached, but there may still be some way to go before the tide turns, if it ever does. Four-letter words, displays of pudenda, galumphing animality—all these prove that Puritanism has now been almost completely reversed. Whereas, in the old days of the cinema, the characters first fell in love, and then if necessary discovered sex in very discreet forms—*i.e.* began by the emotional superstructure before moving down to the physiological infrastructure—they now begin by physiology and then, perhaps, look round for some idea or emotion with which it can be linked. They start with the animal and make a gesture in the direction of the spirit. There is no point in being scandalised by this; it is just an alternative approach, to which the whole of culture has been tending for generations. When so much of culture is anti-cultural, this means that man is trying to animalise himself in the hope of discovering his true nature. He is caught, of course, in a vicious circle. Even Diogenes the cynic, one of those forgotten fellows who lived "in B.C.", did not succeed in being totally dog-like. He performed his organic functions (including masturbation, if I remember rightly) in public, in a very modern manner; but he went on using language and even said that he was looking for "a man." In other words, the soul may be a fiction, but man is the animal who knows he is an animal, and the knowledge makes all the difference. The rough, ugly, hairy, contemporary hero may be trying to look pubic all over, but he is not simply a set of walking genitalia, as someone has claimed. To exaggerate the animal within oneself is to do something beyond the scope of any animal.

These thoughts occurred to me as I was reading some shocked reactions to the new Sam Peckinpah film, *Straw Dogs*, and wondering why it had left me quite unmoved. I have only one slight intellectual worry; I haven't been able to discover what the title means. Can it be a learned pun on the Diogenes complex? The characters think they are dogs, but are only dogs of straw? However, the film itself I take to be an entertainment in the Gothic mode, incredible in many of its details, but good fun while it lasts. The theme is sub-Lawrentian. An American professor of mathematics (Dustin Hoffman) is on leave in a remote Cornwall village, where he is writing a book on mathematical problems in astronomy and, possibly, taking refuge from the political confusions of the United States. His English wife, a former native of the village, mopes around the house because, instead of making love to her during the day as well as during the night, he tries to get on with his work. Half-a-dozen male villagers, one of them an ex-lover of the wife, are sniffing around the couple like a pack of hounds. The air is heavy with menace. The American is conscious of primeval British lusts whenever he goes into the local pub to buy a packet of cigarettes. The yokels hang the wife's cat in her wardrobe; they try to involve the husband in a road-accident; they decoy him away from the house with the oldest trick in the book, so that two of them can rape the wife at leisure.

None of this part can be taken very seriously, because it is based on unlikely assumptions. Most British villages, in my experience, have the normal quota of peculiarities, but they do not reek overtly with sex, like Sodom and Gomorrah. Professors are not necessarily less sexy than farm-labourers or game-keepers. On the whole, intellectuals seem to do more than their fair share of copulation, and by now it appears rather comic that D. H. Lawrence should have thought of Keynes and Russell as sexless brains. Women do not depend simply on brute force for their sexual stimulus. Any manifestation of power can arouse them: money, eloquence, or intelligence. I am willing to bet that many a wife would be highly excited to have a husband who could cover a blackboard with abstruse formulae and would never dream in that situation of showing frustrated breasts to the builders mending the garage. In human beings, sex is hardly ever straightforwardly animal; if it were, a great many happy relationships between the ugly and the beautiful or the old and the young would be incomprehensible.

As for the rape scene, it is not really shocking, since the young woman wants to be raped, at least by one man, and the second can be looked upon as a bonus. In any case, the elaborate simulation signifies nothing but the bestial adjustment of bodies, which is scientific or medical. Years ago, when my grandfather took a cow to the bull, we small boys would accompany him and look on while, with a similar alternation of thwacks and expletives, exhibit *A* would be brought into line with orifice *B*. This free rustic entertainment (now replaced, I suppose, by men in white coats operating quietly with syringes) provided a definite satisfaction, because it was a real event in nature and a powerful statement of generation. But why pay 75 new pence to see a phoney performance in Piccadilly? I found myself wondering *in petto* what my grandfather would have said—he who never set foot inside a theatre or cinema—and I thought I could sense rumblings of deep, dialectal mirth.

The last third of the film moves on from sex to more purely physical violence. Because the American has acted as Good Samaritan to the village idiot, whom the yokels propose to beat up, they lay siege to his house on the outskirts of the village. He does not know that his wife has been raped; she has not told him, no doubt because of the ambiguous pleasure of the experience. What irks him is that the sanctity of his house is being violated. The American's sabbatical home in Britain is his castle; or, to put it another way, his virility is only fully aroused by Ardrey's "territorial imperative". He therefore resists with all the stubbornness of which the meek are capable and, in a splendidly organised sequence, kills in turn all five or six of his assailants, Again, the whole thing is totally unrealistic, because no group of contemporary British yokels would behave like this, and in any case the noise would have attracted a crowd from miles around. But the episode is enjoyable as a mythic battle between a goodie, a human being, and a group of baddies, bestial brutes with no higher feelings at all. The American may be unable to satisfy his insatiable wife, but he has slaughtered half-a-dozen rival phalluses. Before the last fade, he smiles quietly to himself at the thought of having wiped the slate clean. The appeal of this film is really escapism through violence. Life would be so simple and satisfactory if, like animals in the jungle, we could kill each other with a clear conscience, or with no conscience at all.

There is no love in *Straw Dogs*; the American does not really love his wife, nor she him. Lust is rampant, and the only disinterested emotion is the American's feeling that he ought, in common decency, to protect the village idiot, and this is only a liberal reflex. No love either in two other films: *W.R. or The Mysteries of the Organism* by Makavejev and *Carnal Knowledge* (Mike Nichols, scenario by Jules Feiffer).

W.R. has been referred to as a "great" film. It seems to me to be far too scrappy and uncertain in its intentions to be that, but it is undoubtedly a curio. The overt thesis appears to be that sexual liberation can be used to loosen up totalitarian oppressiveness. The starting-point is Wilhelm Reich, the post-Freudian crank, who had the idea that happy orgasms put one in tune with the cosmic process. A good part of the film consists of documentary snippets, in the Godard manner, about Reich's disciples in America, his institute which still belongs to his widow, and the Encounter groups which try to apply his principles. However, none of this adds up to a comprehensible statement of Reich's views, and it is impossible to say whether Makavejev takes him seriously or not. Probably the Yugoslav director is just using him as a stick with which to beat East European Victorianism; on the other hand, the vistas of crankiness opened up by these glimpses of the Neo-Reichians would give any average liberationist the creeps.

As a matter of fact, Reich is not necessary to the argument that sexual emancipation would further the cause of political freedom. Nor is the argument itself developed very convincingly. I suspect that Makavejev has not bothered to think out the problem; he has probably not read Huxley's *Brave New World*, in which total sexual promiscuity coexists with perfect social regimentation, sex being merely the opium of the people. For sexual freedom to have a pervasive moral influence, it would have to be more than casual; it would have to be accompanied by genuine human relationships, that is by love. There is little sign of this in *W.R.*, and the most notable sequence, the one for which the film will remain famous, is fascinatingly inhuman.

It was presumably shot in America, since the man and woman concerned are American and the interior has the elaborate messiness one associates with a certain kind of hippie mentality. The lady appears to specialise in making plaster casts of penises, which she then reproduces in glossy plastic. The young man takes off his trousers and lies down on a couch; she caresses him with absent-minded professionalism until he reaches the required state of firmness, and then she covers his member with a transparent sheet—none too clean, by the look of it—and builds a little plaster mound over it. Cut to the point where she is putting the finished red object on a shelf alongside other trophies. Cut again immediately from the red phallus to Stalin, standing among his group of sycophants. Stalin was, presumably, a big phallus, in a field (politics) where phalluses should be irrelevant. The implication may be that all power tends mistakenly to be sexual; Stalin was everybody's Big Daddy through the confusion between crypto-sexual authoritarianism and genuine political health.

This is quite a good joke, but I cannot claim to have understood the sequence as a whole. Why has the American lady taken to making these plastic replicas? Has sex without the accompanying personality become so important that we have got to a stage when the individual lingam is to be perpetuated as the significant part of the whole? Instead of saying: "Here is a bust of my late husband", the widow will point to the mantelpiece, murmuring "That was Percy in his prime. . . ." Divorcées, loose women, and homosexuals will make collections. One foresees moments of great suspense at Christie's and Sotheby's and Parke-Bernet when some prestigious piece comes on to the market and, through a Freudian reversion, there will no longer be any demand for souvenir models of the Eiffel Tower.

Carnal Knowledge could be sub-titled "Or Spiritual Ignorance". As a film, I found it rather slow-moving and tedious, like so many big-screen pictures in which the vastness of the screen is inappropriate to the intimate nature of the theme; but it fits perfectly into my argument, since it deals with the American male's inability to move on from sex to a heterosexual relationship.

Jack Nicholson and Arthur Garfunkel are two college friends, one handsome and brash, the other ugly and fairly sensitive, who are obsessed with the need to get rid of their virginity. The former is the dominant partner, and in fact, although there is no suggestion of homosexuality, their friendship has a slightly male/female pattern. Perhaps, in a culture where the "buddy" is a dominant concept, it is difficult for men to graduate to a full relationship with women. When I was young, it seemed to me that this was to some extent the case even in France. All young men tended to have a best friend, with whom they lived on terms of close intellectual and emotional intimacy, which made women seem rather unnecessary, except on the physical level. Hence the curious mixture of ceremoniousness and insensitivity which often characterised inter-sexual relations. Why this pattern should be repeated in America, where the bourgeois mentality and arranged marriages are much less prevalent, I don't know. Perhaps it is a survival from the pioneer days, when male friendship was more important than the sexual bond.

At any rate, we are asked to believe that these two buddies are eminently successful in their professional lives (one is a lawyer, the other a doctor), but that their sexual relationships all fizzle out in disappointment. Garfunkel gets married and has children, and claims for a while to have a "mature" understanding with his wife, but then quickly reverts to bachelor adventurism with Nicholson. The latter can think of women only in terms of their vital statistics; an inch too many or too few on the erogenous protuberances and his operational capacities are jeopardised. Sexual attractiveness is not a subtle perfume compounded of psychology and physiology; it is a question of physical "points", as if one were dealing with prize dogs or horses. Here, again, I am reminded of a traditional French approach. I remember a middle-aged Frenchman at a male dinner-party explaining his current dilemma in solemn tones, as if it were a really serious matter. His new secretary had indicated her willingness to go to bed, but he was not sure that he could do himself justice, because she was a shade too thin: *"Moi, il me faut de la viande!"*

The development of the two friends is parallel but different: Garfunkel has a series of mistresses with whom he becomes bored; he ends up, long-haired and mustachio'd, as a middle-aged, weekend hippie with a shaggy teen-age girl who, he claims, is initiating him into the secrets of the younger generation; in other words, he has become a self-deceiving verbaliser. Nicholson at least is honest about the onset of impotence; the film closes tragically on a vision of him lying back on a divan and being ministered to, at a hundred dollars a time, by a plain, flat-chested prostitute who, with a mixture of words and osculations, can conjure up a phantom tumescence. In manner, she is uncannily like the plaster-cast lady in *W.R.* An efficient prostitute, it would seem, like any other woman, is not a person with whom a man has a reciprocal relationship. She is a mirror in which he reflects his own virility, and that virility is a recurrent and pointless finality, a perpetually exploding short-term *project*, that is, the most poignant symbol of contingency. On reflection, I think *Carnal Knowledge* is one of the saddest films I have seen. It presents heterosexuality as being as barren as the most sterile forms of homosexuality.

For a ray of hope, we have to look at the last of the four films, *Klute*, which on the surface is just a well-made thriller. The title is the name of the private detective who is investigating the disappearance of a friend, an impeccable business and family man who has gone missing in Chicago. There is a slight lead to a New York call-girl (Jane Fonda), and the basic subject of the film is really a study of her mentality, so that the title is a misnomer. It is not surprising that Jane Fonda should have got the Best Actress award; she gives a quite remarkable performance as the New Woman who has only got rid of her bra the better to flaunt her advantages under the noses of gullible males.

She forms a more intelligent counterpart to the Jack Nicholson character in *Carnal Knowledge*. Whereas he, the Don Juan type, is in the grip of an insatiable hunger which takes him from woman to woman, because he can see no woman as a person (they are all the same anomymous pudenda surrounded by different but necessary frills), she sees all men as lustful adolescents who can be milked of their substance by a bright woman who treats sex as a form of mental and physical massage that men need and that women can do without. Being up to date, she actually encourages her clients to indulge in their extreme whims and, as usual, the greater the perversion the higher the price. In her professional patter, which we hear several times, she puts forward the view that everything is natural and cannot therefore be wrong. However, it is precisely by this argument that she has revealed to the villain of the piece that he has repressed homicidal tendencies associated with sex. He is responsible for a series of murders, including that of the missing business man, his colleague, and he would murder her too, did Klute not come to her rescue in the final sequence.

Klute, of course, is the "good" individual who, by his patience, firmness and kindness, brings her to the realisation that happiness is to be found in loving one man, not in treating them all as enemies whom she can exploit one by one. We know from her long conversations with her psychiatrist (all prostitutes have, traditionally, gone to fortune-tellers, but this is the first time I have come across a prostitute-character who discusses herself with her analyst, as if she were the subject of an Existentialist or Freudian seminar) that she has non-sexual ambitions. She wants to be an actress or a stage-designer. Meanwhile, prostitution gives her a comfortable living, and she also enjoys it, because she derives pleasure from treating men as objects whom she can manipulate. When Klute is first kind to her, she seduces him to put herself in a position of dominance but then, when he persists in being decent, she suddenly discovers that her body is responding to his, and that she has made the acquaintance of love. Instead of the old stereotype of the warm-hearted whore comforting the distressed male, we have the stony-hearted prostitute being thawed into humanity by a virtuous dick. Although the film makes no pretence to be other than commercial, the development is managed without sentimentality and the obvious happy ending is avoided; the two people will go their separate ways, now that her sentimental education has been achieved.

There remains the question of the "naturalistic" view of sex. The villain, after making a speech in which he proclaims his feeling of innocence, is allowed to commit suicide by defenestration. It is thus more or less recognised that he is not really a villain; he is just an unfortunate person for whom orgasm happens to be linked with killing and destruction, just as for some middle-aged men it is associated with stealing female underwear from washing-lines. This makes one wonder what happens in Encounter groups if a liberated individual begins strangling another in the interests of the perfect orgasm.

Pace Wilhelm Reich, it is difficult to imagine an orgasm which is not in line with the cosmic process. But what one has doubts about is the cosmic process itself.

22. The Light and the Dark

The two major show-business successes of the moment—the rock "oratorio" Godspell and the Stanley Kubrick film A Clockwork Orange—have been commented on a great deal already, so that I risk boring the pants, rather than charming the knickers, off the gentle reader by re-opening the discussion at this late stage. My excuse is that no one seems to have thought of comparing them. I attended the two performances within the same fortnight, and they struck me as being in some mysterious way alike. Now, after a stroll among the tombstones of the Hampstead Cemetery, that useful thinking-ground, it has come to me that they have the similarity of opposites: Godspell is an exercise in angelism, A Clockwork Orange a venture in diabolism. It is difficult to say what the proportions of genuineness and commercialism may be in either, but on the whole, in respect of interest, the devil wins, as he usually does.

I take it as axiomatic that Christ is a super angel and the Devil a fallen one, with the result that they balance each other as brothers in God, operating on the right hand and the left hand of the Creator. Alex, the diabolical hero of A Clockwork Orange, is presented as an attractive young thug with a band of recalcitrant disciples, and he is given the charm of innate and independent wickedness. The hero of Godspell is Jesus himself, another personable young man, but of positively honeyed sweetness and with something of the soulful clown surrounded by a harlequin band of fey worshippers. Whereas the group of the wicked are dressed in black bowler hats and white track-suits with bulging jock-straps and are armed with sticks and bicycle chains, the band of the blessèd are in various kinds of motley and play with feathers and yo-yos. Both groups are completely balletic and their movements are set to music. To complete the parallel, the Devil, no less than Jesus, undergoes a Passion. Actually, in *Godspell*, the *chemin de la croix* is prettified almost out of existence, but in *A Clockwork Orange* it is rich and variegated: Alex is betrayed by his disciples, stripped of his raiment, scourged, spat upon, given a crown of torturing electrodes and ends up as a plaster cross on a hospital bed. Then, in the last scene of the film, he resuscitates with the same diabolical impishness as he had at the beginning. By comparison, Jesus' implied resurrection in *Godspell* is very insipid, because God has been on his side all along. One show is so angelic that it doesn't even begin to give the Devil a run for his money; the other is so diabolical that it gives the Devil the inverted prestige of a black Christ.

It would be interesting to know if the two performances appeal to the same schizophrenic public in different moods. The vast queue in Leicester Square waiting to see *A Clockwork Orange* seemed to be made up of the same mixture as the enthusiastic audience at *Godspell*, except that there was a sprinkling of dog-collars among the latter; perhaps a clergyman who goes to see *A Clockwork Orange* feels obliged to remove his vestimentary sign so as not to dishonour the cloth. But I thought I noticed some rather red ecclesiastical faces during the interval at *Godspell*. "I suppose it's like a medieval mystery play", said one parson to another without much conviction as they stood behind me in the back of the stalls, watching the audience rush up on to the stage to partake jovially of the blood of Christ in the form of free plonk.

A moment's reflection is enough to persuade one that *Godspell*, music and lyrics by Stephen Schwartz, conceived and directed by John-Michael Tebelak (both twenty-three years old, according to the programme, which however refrains from specifying whether or not they are Christians), is very far from being a mystery play. It is not a naïve and spontaneous presentation of Christian myth within an illiterate Christian society; it is show business in a literate, predominantly non-Christian society, a jazzed-up version of the Gospel according to Saint Matthew, which does not require any Christian belief at all on the part of the makers. They could have done the same with the Old Testament or the Koran, and may indeed be already at work on these other holy libretti for different publics. The emotional conviction is all in the beat of the music, not in the imaginative treatment of the material. If it is objected that the same might have been said of the Salvation Army in the good old days when it blew into cornets and rattled tambourines, I would reply that the Army was, or is, an activist organisation applying Christianity literally. Its music was functional and served the purpose of bolstering faith in cold winds on street corners. The score of *Godspell*, like the dancing, the music-hall tricks, the miming and conjuring, stands in a contingent relationship to the Christian message; being neither functional nor illustrative, it is at best entertaining. Of course, one had only to overlook the intellectual contingency for the throb of the music and the vitality and mobility of the young performers to create a sense of collective excitement, which the audience, judging by their unwillingness to go home at the end, took to be a confirmation of faith. In fact, it is religion turned into *divertissement*, a development that would have surprised Pascal.

Let me give one or two examples. The show begins with "The Tower of Babble", a chorus in which the company jig up and down bearing placards identifying them individually as noted miscreants: Gibbon, Nietzsche, Sartre, etc. I couldn't make out the words they were singing, but I suppose that was the point. They weren't meant to be intelligible; they were only there to be swept aside when the horn blew and John the Baptist began his refrain: *"Prepare ye the way of the Lord."* This tune, the best in the show, consists of one strong, splendid phrase indefinitely repeated without development. However it emerges from nothing, because disbelief and evil have not been given their effective music—no Monostatos or Queen of the Night here—and it leads into nothing, because Jesus, when he appears, is just a winsome, bare-chested young man in soccer shorts (there must be a degree of nakedness in any contemporary show), who does a curiously effeminate little dance, the import of which escapes me. This Jesus didn't attempt to be the Lord; he was sugar and spice and all things nice. When he delivered the Gospel words straight, he said them with carefully rounded vowels, like a child reciting a lesson written by a grown-up. None of the harsh statements of the New Testament would have fitted into his mouth, and in fact he wasn't provided with any. Obviously, all disturbing implications have to be filleted out of show-business Christianity.

As a matter of fact, very little of the Gospel text was delivered straight. The parable of the mote and the beam was given as an "I say, I say" dialogue; that of the sower was mimed by different groups, and the seeds which fell on stony ground or grew among weeds got very good laughs; that of the Good Samaritan was done as a kind of charade, and again was great fun. But in each case, the theatrics, as they now seem to be called, were independently amusing and were not geared to the significance of the parable. In other words, the show mainly exemplified the aesthetics of publicity, not of art or conviction.

After all, Mr Tebelak's young life may have been nurtured on the television commercial, the technique of which is to fuse an obsessive musical jingle or verbal phrase with some memorable little action so as to drive home the name of the product. Sometimes these commercials can be very enjoyable; I loved the recent one about Tetley Tea Bags, with acrobats inside white sacks somersaulting out of a large box; it had a kind of lunatic poetry. But there was no inherent relevance to tea; I was not moved to buy a tea bag, and the white packets could have contained bicarbonate of soda for all I cared. Similarly, Messrs Tebelak and Schwartz might have been doing a commercial for Christianity, reminding us of its existence, helping us to sit through the sermonising part by disguising its nature with rhythms and stage business and implying, without argument or organised aesthetic force, that religion, like Tetley Tea or Shredded Wheat or Omo, is a *totally good thing*. That part of advertising which is not based on fear or envy depends on the myth of angelism, that is, on the belief that evil can be eliminated. Even Christ's lament on the Cross was deliciously pretty and unreal; who would not like to die so charmingly? Mr Schwartz, more perhaps than Mr Tebelak, is a man of talent, but *Godspell* is not a notably Christian work. At most, it is a parasitical product depending on the fact that a lot of us thirst vaguely for religion, as we thirst for gracious living or the perfect car.

I have forgotten whether Anthony Burgess's novel, *A Clockwork Orange*, contains an explanation of its title, but I suppose the expression refers to man, who can be thought of in both mechanical and organic terms. Alex, the diabolical hero, takes a lyrical delight in thuggery and rape, "the ultra-violent and the old in-and-out". This is his organic aspect; his "soul" is at home in evil. After being caught and imprisoned, he is subjected to reconditioning according to Pavlovian behaviourism. He is forced to watch films of sex and violence after being injected with a powerful emetic. From then on, whenever he is caught in a violent or sexual situation, he will be paralysed by sickness. The government hopes to neutralise all common criminals in this way, not for humanitarian reasons but in order to be freer to deal with political offenders. The plan backfires, because the "liberal" opponents of the government get hold of the freed Alex and subject him to such painful stimuli that he attempts suicide and creates a scandal. Confusion and eating of words on the political level, but Alex is happy again, because he realises on recovery that the shock has nullified the conditioning and reinstated his wicked soul.

In the April 6 1972 number of the *New York Review of Books* Christopher Ricks excellently demonstrates how the Kubrick film, although Anthony Burgess has expressed approval of it, softens and distorts the book in several respects in order to make Alex's evil more attractive and to turn him into a sacrificial victim. For instance, the violence he commits is purified by the aesthetics of the dance (influence of *West Side Story*?), whereas the violence done to him is sordidly realistic. I agree, and this confirms my point that the Devil becomes a Christ-figure. But I think the essential affirmation is already present in the book. Alex *is* a hero; the book contains no representative of the good at all; the victims are despicable and get their own back when they can. The book, like the film, forces us to identify with Alex, because we are shown things only from his point of view and he is the only character credited with a soul, although that soul is evil. The message is neo-Sadism: in a world of zombies, dare to be a devil; the lyricism of destruction is the only dignified response to the scandal of the Hidden God or the Absent God. It is significant that the film alters the book by giving Alex/Satan a pet in the form of a snake with the regal-*cum*-ecclesiastical name of Basil; it is almost as if some Freudian structuralist has been at work on the script to round off the implications.

A central point is that Alex, in addition to doubly distancing himself from prosaic reality by wearing special gear and using his own jargon, made up of transliterations of Russian words and Germanic syntax, has one great passion, Ludwig Van, and more especially the Ninth Symphony, that hymn to brother-hood which some critics have tended to have reservations about, precisely because they think it is tinged with facile angelism. Does Mr Burgess wish us to understand that the angelism of the Ninth is an illusion and that all music, whether "great" or not, is at bottom an amoral patterning of vitality? Could one, for instance, perform a delicate and measured operation of torture to the accompaniment of Gluck's *Dance of the Blessèd Spirits*? Mr Kubrick seems to think so, because the most brilliantly executed scene in the film is a rape and beating carried out by the gang of thugs as they gaily chant "Singing in the Rain." On this reading, the statement that *"Music hath charms to soothe the savage breast"* is quite wrong, and all those people (like myself) who think that their feelings become nobler as they listen to Beethoven are confusing a musically induced sense of mental and physical well-being with the perception of moral good. The experience of well-being may be equally attuned to sadistic glee. If there is no moral law in the universe, music merely enhances individual functioning; it is an un-differentiated psychological booster, on the same level as alcohol and other drugs.

Well, I cannot altogether accept this. I sense a difference between the Emperor Concerto and a double whisky, and so I would accuse *A Clockwork Orange* of being as one-sided in its diabolism as *Godspell* is in its angelism. A character who can kick an old man in the face to the rhythm of "Singing in the

Rain" must be suffering from some kind of mental hiatus. The weakness of Burgess's book, as of the film, is that it does not succeed in its attempt to convey a qualitative lesson by moral negation, because the hero who is consciously negating morality goes over the edge into the pathological, that is, he himself is more clockwork than orange, in spite of the constant effort to suggest the contrary. The implication is that he represents the only spark of poetic vitality in the spiritual desert of the new England. His parents are footling, the police are professional brutes, the probation officer has an ambiguous interest in his charges, the prison is a monument of bureaucratic stupidity and the politicians on both sides are shallow tacticians. One sees the grain of truth in each of these criticisms. But it is nothing like enough to bestow metaphysical dignity on Alex by contrast. If it is poetically right for four thugs to beat up an old man, it is also poetically right for two policemen to beat up one of the thugs; the book and the film imply a qualitative difference which isn't there.

Alex's evil is not caused by the surrounding spiritual vacuum, or at least no proof is offered that it is. It is inherent and gratuitous, and its only superiority over the evil of adult society is that it is fresher and more vigorous, since Alex has the appeal of youth. To give the Devil a young face and body and to weight the emotional scales in his favour is to mix up metaphysics with sentiment and sensuality. It is true that a lot of traditional paintings do exactly this in the case of Christ, but one form of artistic excess does not justify, although it may encourage, the opposite excess. Whole art, let us say, is always genuinely Manichean in that it strikes a convincing balance between good and evil.

Having said this, I add that my criticism of the metaphysical core of the film does not make me insensitive to its occasional beauties. Particularly impressive, I thought, was the first rape sequence. The camera dwells to begin with on the ornate proscenium arch of a deserted theatre, then it moves down to reveal the stage, where a gang of leather-boys are ripping the clothes off a nicely plump young girl, who is running wildly to and fro in an attempt to escape. As she is gradually exposed in her tender nakedness, her flesh glows warmly against the black rippling movements of the boys. Eventually, an interruption allows her to dart off into the wings with bobbing breasts. The scene, set in the gilded theatrical frame, is like a moving mythological picture of pearly innocence beset by the forces of darkness. Here the balance is right because the sadistic charm of the episode contains an implied recognition of its own dubious nature.

III

LITERATURE

23. King Phallus

This, it would seem, must count as a historic volume,* since it is the first serious, non-clandestine edition of the Marquis de Sade's writings ever to appear in English. The translation reads well, in spite of a number of perhaps misleading archaisms or gallicisms, such as "luxury" for "lust" (*luxure*) and "inconsequent" for "inconsistent" (*inconséquent*). The choice of texts is quite representative; in addition to seven letters by Sade and a dialogue on atheism, there are two "black" items, *Justine*, in one of the later, fuller versions, and *La philosophie dans le boudoir*, and one "white" item, *Eugénie de Franval*, a tale of incest and murder with a conventional moral ending. *Eugénie* is rather a bore, but at least it shows that Sade could bow to the moralising conventions of the 18th century when he chose to do so, just as he could deny authorship of the "black" works with a fine display of moral indignation worthy of Diderot or Rousseau. *Justine* and *La philosophie* are not quite so overpoweringly ghastly as *Les 120 journées de Sodome*, which has been omitted; still, they are obscene and sadistic enough to give a fair idea of the Marquis in his most typical mood and to put any *homme moyen sensuel* completely off sex for a day or two.

The volume also contains two essays by Jean Paulhan and Maurice Blanchot, which were landmarks in the 20th-century rehabilitation of Sade in his native France as one of the neglected glories of that already richly endowed nation.

It is easy to see why Sade, after a hundred and fifty years of clandestinity, has been finally brought out into the open again. With the recent development of sexual frankness from André

* The Marquis de Sade, *Justine, Philosophy in the Bedroom and Other Writings*, compiled and translated by Richard Searer and Austyn Wainhouse, with Introductions by Jean Paulhan and Maurice Blanchot (1965).

Gide to Proust and Jean Genet, or from D. H. Lawrence to Henry Miller and Norman Mailer, it was to be expected that the Marquis would eventually come into his own as the most concentrated and forceful exponent of the sexual obsession. As far as my reading goes, in his own particular line there is no one to touch him; he ranks as King Phallus. Shut a man up for some thirty years in jails and asylums and, if he does not rot, he is likely to work out such thoughts as he has to their ultimate conclusion. Sade had an obsession and he had ideas about it, and for the better part of his adult life he lived in the sort of confinement that could be imposed on an 18th-century French gentleman. He did not go into a decline, his spirit was not broken, and he wrote at such length and with such gusto that one even suspects he enjoyed the transcribing of his erotic dreams as much, or perhaps even more, than he would have enjoyed erotic practice.

It has been suggested that all his stories are masturbation fantasies. I doubt whether they would be so vigorous and exultant if they were. My impression is, rather, that they represent a quite exceptional case of verbal and imaginative sublimation; or, if sublimation is too noble a word, of verbal relieving of instinct. As Blanchot claims, he is the embodiment of an absolute; his books are the apotheosis of obscene graffiti.

This is not to say that we need adopt the current attitude of some of the Marquis's French or foreign admirers and look upon him as the *poète maudit* of sex who was locked up by a hypocritical society because he dared to tell the truth about human nature.

This attitude is reflected in the Foreword and the Preface to this volume and it lies behind the whole of Paulhan's essay. It is strange that people should be so sentimental about the Marquis when he himself, in his genuine works as opposed to his conventional declamations, is so ferociously unsentimental. True, his actual misdemeanors—flogging prostitutes, upsetting their stomachs with Spanish fly, bisexual copulation in his Provençal *château*, running off with his sister-in-law—can be looked upon as the minor indiscretions of an 18th-century

French aristocrat. But it was natural enough in the circumstances of the time that his mother-in-law should use the device of the *lettre de cachet* to restrain so embarrassing a character, and it is rather comforting to note that the 18th-century police considered even prostitutes to have some rights as citizens. In any case, Sade's admirers cannot have it both ways; if his vision of human nature is true, his mother-in-law was perfectly entitled to persecute him as much as she liked, and there can be no appeal to humanitarian principles on which he himself poured scorn.

However, it seems obvious to me that he was crazy. I think his contemporaries knew that he was and that he himself sometimes suspected he was. To refer to him as "a clear-minded and eminently sane rebel", as Paulhan does, is to indulge in a silly paradox. Leaving aside the works themselves, the seven long letters reproduced in this volume show many signs of mental derangement. M. Gilbert Lély, the most eminent living Sadist and the author of the apparently definitive two-volume biography, is said to have a hundred and fifty manuscript letters by the Marquis in his possession; since fifty-nine of these still remain unpublished, one wonders if they do not contain still more emphatic evidence of Sade's madness. Nor do we know how mad were the manuscript volumes that were burned, with the agreement of Sade's son and heir, after the Marquis's death. Perhaps the 18th century did not find the best way of dealing with this madness, although, after all, shutting him up and allowing him pen and paper may not have been such a bad solution.

At any rate, those people who romanticise about him now and turn him into a martyr who suffered in the cause of sexual or spiritual emancipation either have not read him very carefully or themselves have rather aberrant ideas about freedom. It may be a fact that each of us, in the depths of his unconscious, has a Gothic castle in which he works his will on an endless supply of appetising victims of both sexes and eventually finds his supreme pleasure in self-immolation. If so, it is to Sade's credit that he exteriorised this fantasy in the completest manner possible and so allows his readers to grasp it objectively. It is hardly to his credit that he seems firmly to have believed in the fantasy as a valid way of life, or death.

Paulhan and Blanchot set Sade in his 18th-century context to some extent and make a number of interesting points about the way in which he anticipates Nietzsche, Freud, and Kafka. Paulhan, especially, compares and contrasts him with Voltaire, Diderot, and Rousseau, implying that he is more interesting, because more radical, than any of these three. In a sense, this is true, although Voltaire, Diderot, and Rousseau in their best works are great writers in a way that is quite beyond Sade's scope. Yet at the same time Sade can be considered as being much more typically 18th-century than either Paulhan or Blanchot admit. It is difficult to imagine him occurring with the same peculiar concentration of characteristics at any other point in history. Only in the mid-20th century have we returned to something approaching the intellectual extremism and emotional ambiguities of late 18th-century France.

To begin with, Sade's headstrong character and the ruthless egotism he preaches may not be unconnected with his aristocratic birth. He belonged to one of the last generations of the *ancien régime*, that is, to a privileged class that had been ripening in idle eccentricity for about a century-and-a-half, and it contained a great many weird individuals. Then, for reasons which have never been fully elucidated, the diabolical libertine who gloried in wickedness, especially of a sexual kind, had been developing as a European literary figure for quite a long time. There had been the various types of Don Juan, Richardson's Lovelace, Prévost's bold, bad barons, Diderot's Rameau and Mme de la Pommeraye, Crébillon's seducers and then, in Sade's own day, the devilish hero and heroine of Laclos's *Les liaisons dangereuses* as well as Restif de la Bretonne's villain, Gaudet d'Arras. All these characters are obviously first cousins to the male and female monsters in *Justine, La philosophie dans le boudoir,* and *Les 120 journées.* Sade removes all the psychological subtleties present in the other writers, endows his heroes and heroines with supreme power and superhuman genitals, and describes their complex orgies with an appalling zest for detail. To read him after reading the others is to feel that a historical tendency has been taken to a dreadful, logical conclusion.

The copulations and flagellations of Sade's characters are buttressed by a philosophy of Nature which is a sort of parody of Enlightenment speculation. The literary form used is the 18th-century *conte philosophique*; *Justine ou les infortunes de la vertu* follows the pattern of, and makes exactly the same basic point as, Voltaire's *Candide*, which could have been subtitled *les infortunes de l'innocence*.

Like Candide, Justine always tries to do the right thing and invariably comes to grief, until in the end, just when she thinks her troubles are over, she is killed by lightning, that is by an act of "God". But Sade, echoing Diderot, says that if God is all-powerful, he is incomprehensibly erratic, and that if he is not all-powerful, he is not God. It is more logical to suppose a Godless Nature, working aimlessly according to its own accidental laws. Sade's *Dialogue d'un prêtre et d'un mourant*, which puts forward this view, is almost exactly the same as Diderot's dialogue between the parson and the blind English mathematician in the *Lettre sur les aveugles*. In reading *La philosophie dans le boudoir*, one is reminded of Rousseau's *Emile*. Eugénie, the heroine, is carefully instructed in sadistic, sexual horror as Emile is instructed in virtue and chastity, and bang in the middle of all the sodomisings and tortures is a theoretical statement—"Yet another effort, Frenchmen, if you would become Republicans"—not unlike the profession of faith of the *vicaire savoyard* which occurs in the middle of *Emile*. Sade's "black" didacticism is the exact counterpart of Rousseau's doctrine of nature. Whereas Rousseau preaches that Nature is good and positive, Sade sees it as a collection of destructive, warring impulses. He therefore advocates complete anarchism; nothing the individual wants to do can be wrong, except in a conventional sense, so let him rob, rape, torture, and murder to his heart's content. If he espouses all the abominable promptings of Nature, he will achieve peace of mind. As Dolmance, the arch-villain of *La philosophie dans le boudoir*, remarks after indulging in innumerable horrors:

> "I never dine so heartily, I never sleep so soundly as when I have, during the day, sufficiently befouled myself with what our fools call crimes."

In defence of this "black" doctrine, we can say that it is just as tenable as Rousseau's wholesale whitewashing of Nature in his simpler writings. The point is that any didacticism based on the hopelessly ambiguous concept of Nature is self-refuting. For instance, one of Sade's favorite themes is that sodomy is "good", because it is an impulse found in Nature. Rousseau, as far as I remember, does not discuss this question; but he says enough on kindred subjects for us to know that, in his view, sodomy would be "bad", because it goes against the primary arrangements of Nature. The truth surely is that sodomy, like so many other things, is either "good" or "bad", or at least harmless or harmful, according to one's assessment of the complexities of the particular human and psychological situation in which it occurs; and the word Nature is rarely of much use in making such an assessment, since Nature has given human beings uncertain guidance on this score.

Rousseau is sentimental, because he assumes that the primary arrangements of Nature are always clear and can always be followed. Sade is crazy, because he reduces the individual to a phallus, or to a system of sexual nerves, and decrees that any sexual act is good, especially if it is destructive. He is also crazy in that he wants anarchism and destructiveness to be organised on sound, civic lines. Like practically all other French writers of the 18th century, he describes his Utopia, a feature of which would be free, bisexual, municipal brothels, where the clients would be entitled to do as they liked with the inmates, and the inmates would be promptly punished if they tried to resist. However, with the dottiness of the maniac or the assurance of a seigneur, he overlooks the vital issue of deciding who are going to be the clients and who the inmates, or indeed of how to run any institution on a basis of universal destruction. His dream of power is, in fact, just as romantic and unrealistic as the enormous genitalia with which he credits his heroes and their ability to function for hours on end like erotic machine-guns. For this reason he often produces the curious impression of being a cruel little boy in the first flush of adolescence, with a fantastic, intuitive knowledge of the possible varieties of sex.

As a writer, Sade can hardly be counted as belonging to literature at all, since his characters are so wooden, their exploits so specialised and monotonous and the supporting framework of reflection and observation so perfunctory. If Sade is a "great" man, it is because he left behind him an overwhelming pathological document, shot through with intimations of the Absurd and constituting a kind of mad hymn to the mystery of sex, and more particularly to the strange link in the human psyche between creation and destruction. Of course, all obscenity is really mystical; even the graffiti in public lavatories are like pathetic votive offerings to the great god Pan. Sade's transcendent obscenity is an atheist's maniacal tribute to sexual energy conceived as an immanent divine, or diabolical, force. This is no doubt why he has excited so many eminent writers whom one would have expected to be put off by the all-pervading stench of blood, excrement, and sperm.

24. Sartre versus Flaubert

Jean-Paul Sartre's awe-inspiring book about Flaubert* is without a doubt the most extraordinary work ever composed by one writer about another; it is even more remarkable than his previous enormous tome on Genet, *Saint Genet, comédien et martyr*. I have been reading it for a month in varying moods of exasperation, humility, exultation, and despair, and I have still not got to the end of the 2,000 odd pages. But to speak about an end is probably inappropriate. Sartre promises us more volumes, and indeed if his intention is eventually to analyse Flaubert's major novels with the same exuberance as he has brought to bear on the *oeuvres de jeunesse*, there is no reason why the book should ever be completed. So far he has only got to the foothills of the subject; to deal with it completely he will have to digest the universe, because, strictly speaking, no one detail in creation is ever adequately defined until its relationships with all the rest have been minutely worked out.

As I have whirled along in this spiralling tornado of words, there have been times when I have thought that Sartre cannot be addressing any living person, not even Mme de Beauvoir. Perhaps the only reader really competent to understand him fully is the late G. W. F. Hegel, provided the professor has not been idle in the Elysian fields but has kept up with all the major intellectual events since his demise, and is conversant with every kind of French from technical vocabularies to *la langue verte*. *L'Idiot de la famille* is an attempt at *totalisation*, and those of us who put together our little crumbs of thought and knowledge in different corners of the field must hang our heads in shame; we are not in the same league.

* Jean-Paul Sartre, *L'Idiot de la famille—Gustave Flaubert de 1821 à 1857* (Paris: Gallimard, 1971).

Of course, if this were a Ph.D. thesis presented by a research student, the report would not be too difficult to write:

"The candidate has not made up his mind what subject he is dealing with. The fundamental argument indicated by his title is that Flaubert, through being permanently crippled by his alienation within the bourgeois family, evolved an *actively passive* attitude which led him to realise himself in his particular kind of literature. There may be some truth in this interpretation, but it is developed with a total disregard for the ordinary niceties of scholarship.

"M. Sartre has read widely—indeed, he is almost incapable of writing a sentence that does not contain a concealed quotation—but his critical apparatus is so defective that one often cannot tell whether the facts he is analysing have any objective reality or whether he has invented them on the spur of the moment for the purposes of his demonstration. He is obviously one of those modern young men, very active at present in literature and the arts, who believe that because no final truth is available, the search for relative truth is a waste of time and may conveniently be replaced by interesting suppositions and lurid distortions. It need hardly be emphasised how contrary this is to sound academic method.

"But above all, instead of keeping to the point, he allows himself lengthy digressions on any subject that takes his fancy: the meaning of statues, the psychological explanation of laughter, the phenomenology of excrement, etc. I suggest that he be asked to resubmit, after working out an intelligible plan and cutting the text by two-thirds. It should be impressed upon him how unfortunate it is that, among other mistakes, he should misspell Dr Starkie's name as 'Sterkie'. In view of his undoubted fluency, I fear that a *viva* at this stage might only serve to confuse the issue still further."

The common sense arguments against what Sartre is doing are, in fact, very strong and can be reinforced from his own earlier writing. It will be remembered that Roquentin, the hero of *La Nausée*, gives up writing the life of the 18th-century figure, M. de Rollebon, because he comes to realise that an aspect of the existential dilemma is the non-recoverability of the past. The truth about M. de Rollebon is lost forever, because the documents concerning him are fragmentary and in any case can only be given a meaning by being interpreted in the present by the historian. In other words, history is bunk, in the sense that it is an imaginative reconstruction which can never be verified; as Voltaire put it, history is a series of tricks we play on the dead. This is not an amusing paradox, as some people seem to think; it is strictly true, and therefore all our thinking about the past is an anguish, because it is a perpetual manipulation of uncertainties. And if we are constantly aware, as we should be, that the past began a moment ago, all thought will be experienced as an anguish.

Why, then, should Sartre now set out so confidently to write the life of Flaubert? First, for reasons that one can speculate about, he has always been obsessed with the novelist; as he says, he has long had the feeling that there was an old score to be settled. In spite of his assertions that Flaubert and he are very different, my suspicion is that he is haunted by the need to exorcise a certain idea he has of the Flaubert within himself. Secondly, just as he jumped, without any explanation, from Existentialist despair about the impossibility of meaningful action to the policy of commitment, so he jumps from the belief that the life of M. de Rollebon is unwritable to the opposite conviction that he can intuit the truth about Flaubert.

In both instances, he begins by showing that the game makes no sense, and then his intellectual vitality forces him to play it, because his tremendous brain cannot accept the insignificance of its own operations. But he plays the game with a sort of mad impatience, which is his particular form of *mauvaise foi*. It is not simply that he is intellectually arrogant; he is, but he has a lot to be arrogant about. It is rather as if he could not slow down and weigh the pros and cons in any average fashion, because he would blow apart with despair. Ingenious dogmatism is his only form of self-therapy or self-preservation. He can be seen pulling the wool over his eyes when he declares in his Preface:

> . . . *chaque information mise en sa place devient la portion d'un tout qui ne cesse de se faire et, du même coup, révèle son homogénéité avec toutes les autres.*

(. . . each item of information put in its place becomes part of a whole which is constantly in the making, and at the same time reveals its homogeneity with all the other items.)

This desire to replace the universe by its total verbal counterpart is later illuminated in a brilliantly poetic passage (pp. 960 *et seq.*) where Sartre, in speaking of Flaubert, is clearly describing his own linguistic frenzy as the atheist's response to the nonexistent God. Literature, he says, is *la Contrecréation*, which is meant to make up for the inadequacies of the existing creation. The writer writes "[*pour donner*] *l'être au non-être dans l'intention de manifester le non-être de l'être* ([to give] being to non-being so as to manifest the non-being of being)". Literature is demiurgic, and *"Ecrire est le plus beau délire* (Writing is the finest form of delirium)".

As I have already indicated, the composition of the book is rhapsodic rather than ordered, but Sartre can eventually be seen to be dealing with Flaubert on three main levels:

1. The child within the family. He was the second son of a dominant father and a recessive mother. His elder brother was a "replica" of his father; his sister, Caroline, a "replica" of his mother. Gustave himself was lost in between; at first apparently a backward child, *l'idiot de la famille*, a victim of estrangement, conscious of being unable to play any adequate role, etc. He eventually had a breakdown, and thereafter lived a secluded life as a *rentier* devoted to literature. From an early stage, he saw life from the point of view of death.

2. The adolescent at school and the young man with his friends and mistresses. At this level, the bourgeois was inserted into mid-19th-century society, with its peculiar political nature, during the aftermath of Romanticism. Gustave played various fantasy roles, and would have liked to be an actor; since the theatre was impossible for family reasons, he had to fall back on literary composition, which is another form of role-playing. In his sexual relations, he also opted for "active passivity"; he was not homosexual, but he liked to play a feminine role in conjunction with masculine women, although at the same time he could act a comedy of virility.

3. The individual in his metaphysical relationship to the

universe. The great "Naturalist" hated nature. He saw life as *"une brève folie de l'inorganique"*. Like Camus, he felt that the fundamental question was whether one should commit suicide or not. In his case, art was a substitute for suicide.

To my mind, level one is the least satisfactory part of the thesis. Sartre repeats once more, and at still greater length, his analysis of the bourgeois stereotypes, and asserts that, in the case of Gustave, *"la Malédiction paternelle . . . a réglé sa vie jusqu'à la mort"*. Now one may know from direct observation and from abundant literary evidence (Balzac, Zola, Mauriac, Hériat, etc.) that the French bourgeois family is, or was, one of the toughest sociological inventions of all time; but it is difficult to believe that it is quite as Gothic in its all-pervading awfulness as Sartre makes it out to be. Although he rejects the Freudian unconscious, he seems to be ultra-Freudian in his acceptance of the fatality of family relationships. Curiously enough, he constantly describes the bourgeois family in feudal terms: Flaubert senior is *"le Seigneur"*, the children are *"des vassaux"*, etc. His gleeful insistence on the restrictiveness of the family even leads him to imply that Mme Flaubert killed her unwanted (?) children by suggestion:

> . . . *au suivant, elle se serait écriée: "Encore un!" Le nouveau-né devant cet accueil, se serait hâté de rentrer sous terre.* [p. 723]
>
> (. . . when the next came along, she must have exclaimed; "What! another one!" Faced with such a welcome, the new-born babe must have lost no time in giving up the ghost.)

A great deal of this part is based on wildly tendentious interpretation of anecdotes, when it is not pure invention. Gustave may have been a slow developer in his earliest years, but the stigma, if there was one, cannot have continued indefinitely, because his literary ability was already apparent in his early teens; he was, in fact, precocious.

There are, moreover, two major difficulties in Sartre's Existentialist psychology, with its Freudian and Marxist overtones: the first relates to his elimination of "human nature", and the second to the exercise of "freedom".

He declares categorically in his Preface: *"un homme n'est jamais un individu; il vaudrait mieux l'appeler un* universel singulier (a man is never an individual; it would be better to call him a *singular universal*)." This means, if I have followed his thought, that Flaubert was only Flaubert because he was born and brought up in that situation. Anybody else would have done as well in that position. Therefore, if we explain the family setting, the historical moment, etc., we define the reality of Flaubert. Sartre omits the physiological uniqueness, the given genetic identity of the individual Gustave, because the concept of predetermined "human nature" is as hateful to him as the concept of the bourgeois. He loathes it as a limitation of freedom.

But anyone who has brought up children knows that each child *is* an individual from the day of its birth; it may grow up in many different ways according to circumstances, but each way will be a compromise between the possibilities of its temperament and its conditioning. There is a sense in which Gustave is Gustave and no one else, just as Sartre, heaven knows, is Sartre. The identity may be ultimately incomprehensible, being hidden in the recesses of physiology, but it is there. In the course of his narrative, Sartre often spontaneously assumes this, but he will not incorporate it into his thought.

Then his tone implies that the people he is writing about, and chiefly Gustave, were guilty of *mauvaise foi* in their various positions and did not fully exercise their freedom. It has always appeared to me that Sartre wants freedom to be exercised internally *in vacuo*, although externally *en situation*. If there is no density of the given individual nature. if there is no weighting to be derived from the various different possibilities within the temperament, how can anyone get the inner leverage necessary for the exercise of freedom? Freedom cannot be rootless; it must be the margin of uncertainty in the possibilities of the given. After all, Flaubert chose to write his books, which Sartre refers to as *"ses grands romans"*; was this not a proper exercise of his freedom? I may have misunderstood, but Sartre gives the impression that Flaubert ought to have been different. I would agree if this means that the novels could have been still better, if he had been a still greater genius. I don't agree if it means that he ought to have gone in for *praxis;*

he might simply have got bogged down in the *"pratico-inerte"*. In this case, he wouldn't have become Flaubert, and Sartre wouldn't have had occasion to write a book about him.

Levels two and three are much more convincing, and even in those places where the text is hardly credible, it is often animated by great intellectual excitement. Sartre hammers away at Flaubert, as if he were under some irresistible compulsion to prove that the novelist was full of multiple forms of *mauvaise foi*: class prejudice, false forms of friendship and love, fluctuating aggressive or recessive personae, ingratitude, self-centredness, and psychosomatic symptoms. However, through a curious reversal, this complex onslaught only serves to make Flaubert more interesting, especially as it is accompanied by dazzling improvisations on all sorts of themes, from the meaning of the Romantic movement and the psychology of the aristocrat to the function of language.

Someone has reported Sartre as saying: *"Je n'ai pas l'admiration facile* (Admiration does not come easily to me)."* It is true that his favourite mode is to think *against*, just as his favourite intellectual device is to argue from *le néant*, as if it were a solid entity. Fundamentally, I suppose, he is worried about God as a solid absence. At any rate, the more he attacks Flaubert, the more substantial Flaubert becomes. This celebration by negativity may not conjure up everyone's idea of Flaubert, but it turns him into a fascinating and monstrous character, the central figure in a kind of delirious philosophical novel.

What still remains to be shown is how this crippled monster came to write masterpieces, if they are masterpieces, and this presumably will be one of the functions of the future volumes. It might be thought that Sartre, because of his violent hatred of the gratuitous and the apparent lack of tenderness and warmth in his make-up, would be incapable of appreciating literary beauty, but, paradoxically, this is not so. In several pages of quite breathtaking felicity and ingenuity (pp. 1,277 *et seq.*), he gives an anticipatory *explication de texte* of the *fiacre* episode in *Madame Bovary*. If he cares to turn his hand to expository criticism of this kind, we shall soon be overwhelmed by a new aspect of his remarkable ability.

25. Céline's Paranoid Poetics

There can be no doubt about the historical importance of
Louis-Ferdinand Céline in the literature of anarchistic revolt.
He was the first great foul-mouthed rhapsodist of the 20th
century to proclaim a satanic vision of a godless world, rolling
helplessly through space and infested with crawling millions of
suffering, diseased, sex-obsessed, maniacal human beings.
Voyage au bout de la nuit, which appeared in 1932, was not simply
a continuation of the pessimistic literature of the 19th-century
"realists". It was Zola-esque in its blackness, but it had a
frenzy, a speed, and a virulence which made the average Zola
novel suddenly seem almost as old-fashioned as a horse-drawn
bus. Zola had toyed with the idea of using the working-class
vernacular as a medium for the expression of social reality, as
had Jean Richepin and a number of minor satirical poets, but
no one before Céline had exploited the figurative obscenities
and racy syntax of the spoken language in such a thorough-
going and masterly fashion. It was as if the underdog had
suddenly found a voice.

Céline's anti-hero, the penniless, disreputable slum-doctor,
Bardamu, was a sort of eloquent Caliban, expressing the nether
side of civilisation. The effect was as startling in the 1930s as
that of the comparable cry of revolt in the '40s and '50s by Jean
Genet, who also emerged suddenly from the anonymous mass,
this time to proclaim a complete subversion of "normal" values
in the name of the criminal, homosexual outcast.

Since nothing is ever absolutely new, Céline would probably
not have been what he was without the French tradition of
revolt, which one can trace back almost as far as one likes—
through the Surrealists (with whom he was contemporaneous,
although he appears to have had no dealings with them) to

Jarry's *Ubu Roi* and to Rimbaud, to the Romantic movement, to the Marquis de Sade and the other *révoltés* of the 18th century, such as the hero of Diderot's *Neveu de Rameau*, to the scurrilous and picturesque writers of the 17th century, to Rabelais in the 16th and Villon in the 15th. God-defiance or God-rejection, wild satirical exaggeration, scatological and pornographic hyperbole are not novel elements in French literature, but they have appeared with increasing density as each fresh wave of revolt has broken on the historical scene. Céline may not have absorbed much of this tradition consciously, but it was in the air he breathed. Also he had suffered the terrible shock of the First World War at the tender age of eighteen and had emerged from it with serious head-wounds, which caused chronic insomnia and may have permanently affected his personality. He admits to only one important immediate literary influence— the writings of Henri Barbusse, the author of *Clarté* and *Le Feu*, who had a similar impatient, erotic temperament but rather less force and staying power.

It would be interesting to know whether or not Henry Miller had actually begun writing his "Tropics" before he read *Voyage au bout de la nuit*. The very short letter he contributed to the special number of the periodical *L'Herne* devoted to Céline (1962) leaves the matter in some doubt. Yet the similarities between his books and Céline's two major novels, the *Voyage* and *Mort à crédit* (1936) seem too striking to be explained merely as a coincidence, or as two separate manifestations of the *Zeitgeist*. One gets the impression that Céline pulled out some kind of stopper and released a flood of vituperative literature, which since his time has flowed as strongly in the English language as in French. The vengeful, apocalyptic note, which sounds first in Miller, then in Mailer, Kerouac, Baldwin, Ginsberg, *et al.*, has also been characteristic of a great many of the younger British writers, although in England it has perhaps been heard more frequently in the theatre than in the novel or poetry. I have lost count of the garrulous heroes who have stood on the British stage during the last twenty years or so and shouted their disgust with society and life in different varieties of the demotic. Whether they know it or not, Céline had a lot to do with the development of the poetics of paranoia, which they have illustrated so exhaustively.

The dust-jacket of *Castle to Castle** says that it is "a novel by Louis-Ferdinand Céline". Actually, Céline is a novelist only in the limited sense that he produces imaginative variations on his autobiography. This book is the middle volume of a trilogy, including *Nord* and the recently published *Rigodon*, which gives an account of his experiences in Germany during the last phase of the Second World War, just as the *Voyage* dealt mainly with the First World War, while *Mort à crédit* went back to his childhood and adolescence. The expression "gives an account" is perhaps misleading. The writing is demential in that Céline does not tell a story nor explain anything, but instead produces a vast, swirling monologue in which glimpses of real-life episodes, worked up to Céline's usual feverish pitch, alternate with repetitive diatribes against all those people against whom he has a grudge—the mob who ransacked his flat in Paris at the time of the Liberation, the Danes who put him in jail as a suspected collaborator, his publisher, Gallimard, his various literary colleagues who have come through the war unscathed, and anybody else who, for one reason or another, has provoked his bile.

He found himself in Germany with the retreating puppet French government because he had been a collaborator; but why he should have become one is a major problem that has never been properly clarified. After producing *Voyage au bout de la nuit* and *Mort à crédit*, which were widely and justifiably assumed to be expressing a predominantly left-wing sensibility, he suddenly turned into the most scurrilous kind of anti-Semitic pamphleteer and, when the Germans occupied France, allowed himself to be associated with one of their most revolting enterprises, the anti-Semitic exhibition in Paris.

Some of his defenders have put forward the view that he had looked upon the Jews as war-mongers and had been so horrified by the First World War that he couldn't stand the thought of another. It is surely a feeble excuse to say that anti-Semitism

* Louis-Ferdinand Céline, *Castle to Castle*, translated by Ralph Mannheim (1969).

is a metaphor for pacifism; the indiscriminate expression of hatred can never be expected to ensure peace, and even if there were Jews who were thirsting, and not without reason, for a crusade against Hitler, it was as plain as a pikestaff between 1935 and 1939 that Hitler himself was itching for war. Then, after the German invasion of France, it was still possible, for someone who had no faith in an ultimate Allied victory, to adopt an attitude of minimal cooperation with the Germans, at least during the initial phase, in order to save something of France. But Céline seems to have gone far beyond the attitude of sorrowful acceptance that was legitimate in the circumstances and therefore he had little grounds for complaint when his property was confiscated after the German defeat. He was, in fact, condemned to death *in absentia* and, had he not been held in Denmark until the proclamation of the amnesty, he would not have remained alive to make such a fuss about the disgraceful treatment he received at the hands of the Danes.

Another argument advanced in his favour is that his attack on the Jews was really a criticism of capitalism and of what is now called "the consumer society". We are asked to look upon him as a prophet of the contemporary disgust with money and commercial values, and this no doubt is why he is quoted in Jean-Luc Godard's film, *Pierrot le fou*. It seems to be true that he was in some ways a generous man; during his last years, he apparently gave his medical services free of charge to such poor people as came to consult him in his retreat at Meudon. But he had no social or economic philosophy that I can discern. His reason for going to Denmark by way of Germany was that he had salted away his literary earnings there in the belief that Denmark would be able to keep out of the war. This shows a certain individualistic self-interest rather than a detestation of commercial values. In any case, all his railing against people with money is nullified by the fact that his publisher, Gallimard, is one of the rich men he attacks most violently. Since Gallimard is serenely drawing revenue from this attack upon himself, Céline is reduced to the role of licensed, anti-bourgeois jester. It is impossible to take him seriously as a thinker, although it is also impossible to forgive him his more disgusting outbursts.

I think one has to assume either that Céline was not quite right in the head, or that his metaphysical despair was so great that he thought it didn't much matter whom he attacked or what he said, provided the theme he was dealing with could be translated into his particular, brand of rhapsodic prose. The most one can say on his behalf is that he didn't play safe. His literary reputation stood high in the late '30s and, since anti-Semitism was not a popular theme in France, he had no personal axe to grind in suddenly switching to it, apart, perhaps, from the technical need to find a new source of invective, after using up the material of his early life in the two major works. Nor are the later volumes in any sense an apologia. He doesn't try to explain or justify his behaviour; he just carries on in his usual tone, hitting out in all directions, although he has one or two kind words incidentally for Pétain and Laval, who appear to have maintained their personal dignity during the shambles of the German collapse.

Castle to Castle oscillates between Céline living in the present at Meudon after the war, with his second wife, Lili, his cat, Bébert, and his horde of dogs, Céline at various stages in his childhood and youth, as in the *Voyage* and *Mort à crédit*, and Céline during the German collapse and after. The style is characteristic of his later manner, *i.e.* it bears as little resemblance to traditional narrative writing as Turner's last pictures do to representational painting. The reader has to surrender himself to an impressionistic, paranoiac monologue, in which more often than not the sentences are left unfinished, the transitions from one idea to the next are not explained and many of Céline's contemporaries are referred to elliptically and derisively under transparent nicknames (Larengon=Aragon and Tartre=Sartre), as if their misdeeds were too obvious to need recounting. Occasionally, there is a more sustained passage where Céline is describing some tragi-comic scene in Germany—crowds arriving at a railway station, French collaborators scattering as the English bombs fall, or the extraordinary Hohenzollern castle of Siegmaringen, where the French refugees were temporarily lodged.

The technique is always the same: detail is piled upon detail in a mad rush, as if the intolerable nature of creation were being suggested by a proliferation of instances. The phenomenon is very close to the hysteria of the Absurd in Ionesco, which expresses itself through the multiplication of chairs on the stage, or a sprouting corpse, or the transformation of humanity into a herd of rhinoceroses. Céline has swarms of refugees milling around one overworked hotel lavatory (the excremental side of human nature was almost as hateful to him as to Swift; *cf.* the description of the New York public lavatory in *Voyage au bout de la nuit*), or he conveys the horror of the castle by dwelling on the endless labyrinth of its rooms or the all-invading clutter of objects and Hohenzollern portraits, *e.g.:*

> From one side to the next, I got lost . . . I'm telling you, I admit it . . . Lili or Bébert found me . . . women have an instinct for labyrinths, for ins and outs . . . they find their way . . . animal instinct . . . it's order that stymies them . . . the absurd is their dish . . . to them the whacky is normal . . . the fashion for cats . . . attics, mazes, old barns . . . they're drawn irresistibly by Gothic manses . . . that we'd better stay out of . . . they're funny that way . . . that's embryogeny, the pirouettes and somersaults of the gametes . . . the perversity of the atoms . . . animals are the same way . . . take Bébert! . . . he'd peekaboo me through the transoms . . . *brrt!* . . . *brrt!* . . . big joke! . . . I couldn't see him . . . teasing me . . . cats, children, ladies have a world of their own . . . Lili went where she pleased all over the castle of the Hohenzollerns . . . from one maze of corridors to the next . . . from the bell-tower up in the air to the armory on a level with the river . . . by sheer instinct! . . . reason'll only mix you up . . . wood, or stone spirals, ladders . . . bends . . . up or down? . . . hangings, tapestries, false exits . . . all traps . . . troubadours, bats, vagrant sprites . . . there's nothing you won't run into, I'm telling you, from one false exit, one false drapery to the next . . .
>
> . . . . the *Schloss* and its library! labyrinths . . . woodwork! porcelain and dungeons! . . . into the drink with its memories! . . . and all its thousands of princes and kings! down into the delta . . . ah, crashing, impetuous Danube! the river will carry it all away! . . . ah *Donau blau!* . . . my ass! . . . crashing fury, carrying off the Castle and its bells . . . and all its demons! . . .
>
> . . . porphyry Apollos! . . . ebony Venuses! all carried away by the torrent! and the Huntress Dianas! whole floors of Huntress Dianas! . . . Apollos! . . . Neptunes! . . . the loot of demons in breastplates, ten centuries of pillage! the work of seven dynasties! you'll see when you get there, the warehouse of superloot . . .
>
> . . . I thought of this and that . . . I'm boring you again . . . Yes, I thought of the way she was at home in that castle . . . never lost . . . the way

she'd find me in some corridor . . . fascinated, looking at one more
Hohenzollern . . . Hjalmar . . . Kurt . . . Hans . . . another . . . a hunch-
back . . . yes . . . yes . . . I didn't tell you . . . they were all hunchbacked!
Burchard . . . Wenceslas . . . Conrad . . . they're driving me nuts . . .
twelfth . . . thirteenth . . . fifteenth of the name! Centuries . . . centuries!
. . . centuries! . . . hunchbacked and no legs! . . . cloven goat's hoofs . . .
all of them . . . Landru Devils! . . . ah, I see them! I see them all! their
warts too! . . . that family wart! . . . on the ends of their noses . . .

The basic feeling in paranoia may be that the individual
consciousness is being stifled by the infinite number of other
existences and by the pressure of the unassimilable weight of
material things. Here the *objets d'art* are treated with a certain
respect because they are precious and the skills that produced
them have largely disappeared (this is a subsidiary obsession
with Céline, because his mother was a lace-maker, *i.e.* a
devoted, old-fashioned artisan), but at the same time they are
hated, because there are so many of them, just as the generations of Hohenzollerns who amassed them are hated and seen
as an endless series of warts on predatory noses.

Céline is both fascinated by the castle and looks forward to
the day when it will collapse into the Danube with all its
contents. This again is typical; the twin poles of his sensibility
seem to be endless proliferation or total destruction. This would
fit in with his anti-Semitism, which is a tendency to see Jews
everywhere and make them responsible for everything, while
calling for their complete obliteration.

Independently of its moral obtuseness, this all-or-nothing
rhythm is, in the long run, very monotonous, and *Castle to
Castle*, apart from one or two good, nightmarish passages, is
quite a tedious book. He himself seems to have realised this,
because he says in an interview included in this volume that
he had written himself out with *Voyage au bout de la nuit* and
Mort à crédit. I would suggest, rather, that after 1936 he went
so peculiar that he involved himself in experiences which did
not correspond to the whole of his personality as it had existed
in the earlier phase. The increasing stridency of his later works
shows that there is something wrong with the experiences
themselves and that he is not digesting them properly into
literature.

26. O'Brien's Sexy Cross

When this study* of Mauriac, Claudel, Waugh, Greene, etc., was first published some years ago, its author, "Donat O'Donnell", was unknown except to a few intimates. He is now world famous as Conor Cruise O'Brien, and his recent history has been as exciting as any of the plots devised by the lurid imaginations of the writers he chose to study in his days of comparative obscurity. Everybody's man in Katanga has been involved in a great deal of black mischief, and he became (1963) Vice-Chancellor of an African University, which is exactly the sort of post that Greene or Waugh could make great play with. (He has, more recently, been a militant man of the left as a Professor at New York University and, on his return to Dublin, a moderate M.P. between the barricades.)

The name, Conor Cruise O'Brien, has a sinewy improbability and punning potentialities that would make it absolutely appropriate for a character in a Claudel play: "Conor"—I try, in Latin, but in French two words of golden suggestiveness; "Cruise"—at once world-ranging and a small vessel that might contain holy oils. At the height of the controversy surrounding his name, Dr O'Brien was divorced and remarried, thus linking the personal and the cosmic in a way again very typical of the more Providentialist writers in his selection. These intimations are not misleading. *Maria Cross* is not an ordinary critical work; it is one of those rare books which, under the guise of criticism, express a contemporary personal and philosophical dilemma.

The professed aim of the book, which is perhaps rather different from the deepest impulse behind it, is to react against

* Conor Cruise O'Brien, *Maria Cross: Imaginative Patterns in a Group of Catholic Writers* (1963).

the vagueness and inconclusiveness of most "Catholic" criticism, and to speak sharply and frankly about the authors under discussion. In an excellent footnote, Dr O'Brien rebukes Jacques Madaule for saying in tones of hushed reverence only too typical of Catholic critics, *"On n'analyse pas Claudel"*. "A critic," remarks Dr O'Brien, "has no business to be so modest. Jacob might as well have said, 'One doesn't wrestle with angels'." Dr O'Brien wrestles manfully with all these angels, and if they turn out to be in some respects Luciferian, he does not hesitate to say so. Indeed, a quick glance through his book might lead one to think that he has investigated the major Catholic writers of the day in order to explode them one by one. Mauriac ceased to write good books in his forties, when he compromised with his class background. Waugh's effectiveness as a writer, even in his better, earlier works, is based on a snobbish contempt for the modern world and an incurably childish and romantic approach. Geene's basic emotion is "pity", but it is a soft sentiment, very different from the astringency of genuine Christian love, and it may surround his heroes with a fuzz of modest self-indulgence. Léon Bloy thought at times that he was God, and it is debatable whether or not he was certifiably insane. Péguy and Claudel are a mass of shifting symbolism, which seems to show that they are trying to creep back into the womb at the same time as they betray a suspicious complicity with certain aspects of Fascism.

More serious still—and this is why Dr O'Brien has taken the significant name of a Mauriac heroine, Maria Cross, as his general title—sexual ambiguity, sexual guilt, and cruelty are at the root of their attitudes. They all believe in suffering connected with sex; they confuse the mother with the mistress, passion with the Passion, copulation with the Crucifixion. None of them has the sane, broad-minded approach to the subject which is sometimes said to be characteristic of Catholics as opposed to Protestants. They are, in fact, Puritans, whose repressed instincts flower in all sorts of peculiar ways. Mauriac's obsession is indicated by the inability of his heroes to transfer their passion from the mother-figure to some real woman with whom they can have an adult relationship. The separated lovers in Claudel think of themselves as spending what should have been their wedding-night nailed to separate crosses. Greene brings in joyless sex as a way of increasing the atmosphere of doom already indicated by flapping vultures and hostile nature. Behind Waugh's view of sex lies a streak of cruelty, which explains his interest in necrophilia and cannibalism. Bloy, who in real life sometimes tried to equate sex with Christian mysticism, goes furthest by declaring, in so many words, that there is a parallel between the emission of semen by the copulating male and the expulsion of the Holy Ghost from Christ's body on the cross. Such a comparison does little to make sex "healthy" or "normal", but certainly serves to increase its intensity.

Well, you might say, all these poor fellows, whatever their stylistic gifts, are in pretty sad case and ought to be despatched to the nearest clinic for guidance. They feel themselves to be exiles from some impossible heaven; they want to return to their childhood dreams of romance, which were cushioned in bourgeois security; they long for the Middle Ages when God's finger could be clearly discerned directing the course of pre-industrial, pre-scientific events; they have a horror of post-Renaissance rationalism and pine for the values of the blood, for tradition, race, ancient landed families or noble representatives of some reassuring mystic order, such as policemen and priests. What a good thing that Dr O'Brien, a pillar of the Enlightenment, a former international civil servant, a carrier of academic light into dark places, should have cleared up and disinfected this mess by the acuteness of his analysis and the corrosiveness of his wit!

Actually, the situation is not as simple as that. Not for nothing has Dr O'Brien come out of Ireland. If he has written a book about eight Catholics, it is because, despite his reservations, he believes in their greatness; they are, for him, the best modern writers, the ones he has thought it worthwhile to write about. It is true that a whole side of his nature revolts against them and this is why, in his chapter on Claudel, he invents a character, "the logical, post-Freudian materialist," who steps forward and declaims against the "eloquent French somnambulist" under discussion. But I am not sure that Dr O'Brien is really fair to his own doubts, because he turns the post-Freudian materialist into a caricature of dogmatic certainty. One may question the ultimate quality of these Catholic writers without going to the extreme of declaring:

> Everything which we now call by this archaic name of *spiritual*—art, religion, and various glorifications of sexual inhibition, "chivalry," for instance—is about to crumble away. . . . To a new generation, completely carnal and completely rational, the idea of poetry will be as incomprehensible as the idea of typhus.

Having led his objector out on to this limb, Dr O'Brien proceeds to demolish him, by arguing that he is missing the point:

> Where the materialist goes wrong is not in discernment of a set of facts, or even in his interpretation of the facts, but in his unscientific assumption that only one set of facts is relevant and only one interpretation on one level is possible.

I wonder how many modern "materialists" (supposing they feel they can define "matter" clearly enough to lay claim to the appellation) believe that only one set of facts is relevant and one interpretation possible. Nor am I convinced by the further arguments put forward by Dr O'Brien to offset his criticisms of these writers. He says, for instance, that although Claudel and Péguy had similar obsessions, they cannot be lumped together negatively, because their works are very different. This strikes me as a non-sequitur; one may readily admit that Claudel and Péguy make very different uses of their obsessions and are, in their outward manifestations, two very different types of Catholic, without agreeing that either has a satisfactory philosophy. Dr O'Brien also claims that their value can be perceived by a simple contrast with the work of a highly intellectual, non-believing poet, to wit Valéry, perhaps the outstanding French sceptic of the 20th century. This particular passage is worth quoting, because it seems to me to contain both a misinterpretation and an intellectual abdication:

> There is probably no poem, in any language, of greater verbal brilliance than Valéry's *Le Cimetière marin* and no poem in which the religious sense is so conspicuously and glitteringly absent:
>
> *Tout va sous terre et rentre dans le jeu.*

T

In the result, this perfect jewel of cultivated materialism is curiously null, an eternally abandoned pyramid of virtuosity. Its conclusion, with

Le vent se lève! Il faut tenter de vivre!

gives, in a literal sense, the game away; all that elaborate and impeccable felicity was no more than a game, of which the ivory pieces are put away when the serious business of "living" is resumed. The beauties of *Le Cimetière marin* have more in common with the goldsmith's art than they have with such a work as Baudelaire's *Crépuscule du soir—*

Recueille-toi, mon âme, en ce grave moment—

for in Baudelaire we know that poetry is not being used as a game or decoration but with profound seriousness, as incantation for admission to another dimension. That is to say that for the religious poet poetry is a kind of magic. This is "bad" from the materialist—and suspect from the orthodox—standpoint but it is undeniably true to the origins of poetry, in ritual, in magic, and in hymns, and true also to what all of us, whether consciously or unconsciously, expect from the highest kind of poetry. If we resent in *Le Cimetière marin* a kind of profanation or vacuity, it is because of this expectation, this magical conception on our part of the nature of poetry. We do not like to be told at the end of the story that "it was only a dream", for we know obscurely that this represents an arrogant and philistine intrusion of the rational mind.

The misconception, in this excellently written paragraph, is that for Valéry, poetry is a game or a decoration. On the contrary, it is precisely an incantation (hence the title: *Charmes*, carmina), but one which relies on no gratuitous belief and attempts to carry the rational faculty along with it—which it succeeds in doing to an astonishing degree. *Il faut tenter de vivre* does not wipe out what went before; it marks a regretful transition from the contemplative to the active state.

The abdication is in the statement that Valéry, by using his intelligence, is allowing "an arrogant and philistine intrusion of the rational mind". Why should Dr O'Brien be so keen to denigrate rationality? Here we can turn his own phrase against him and say that a critic has no business to be so modest about his stock in trade, and in particular should not be condescending about those artists who manage both to create and to remain intelligent.

The basis of Dr O'Brien's admiration for his chosen authors is that they strike down deep into things common to humanity and touch "some essential all-underlying tufa". He appears, indeed, to consider them as great, intuitive Unconsciousnesses, who offer a placenta-like broth of dark, nutritious saps. In praising them, he attacks not only sceptical rationality but also Protestantism:

> Modern Protestantism, which is dead from the waist downwards, which conceals the Cross, refuses devotion to the Mother of God, ignores the Communion of Saints, lays its emphasis on the reasonable rather than the mysterious, has nothing to offer imaginations like these.

And imaginations like these are so tuned to suffering that they see both their personal lives and universal history (or the history of their country) in terms of the Crucifixion. This is their great distinguishing feature:

> The power of conviction which the best in these writers has over others, who are not conscious of sharing either their religious outlook or their pattern of feeling, comes, I think, from this intuitive harmony of mystery and suffering, the reverberation, even at the oblique touch of a fingernail, of the great Catholic bell. However much we may disclaim the tie, we are all related, like Raymond and his father—through Maria Cross.

My reaction to this is the vulgar one: speak for yourself. If religion is a projection of the mother/mistress mix-up on to a cosmic backdrop, then I think it ought to be condemned very heartily. I am not denying that there is a mother/mistress mix-up and that it is often acutely expressed by these authors. What I find shocking is the attempt to write a sexual dilemma across the sky, as if it were of universal spiritual significance, or to annex God to one's particular neurosis. In so far as the cross is a sexual symbol, it is deplorable, and could with advantage be replaced by the phallus, which is at least clear and unpretentious.

My uneasiness about Claudel, Péguy, Bloy, Mauriac, and Bernanos arises from the feeling that they are dramatising frustrations that result from local social or personal prejudice, that is, from non-essential forms of evil, and which would be seen as non-essential by keener intelligences. This is not the whole story, of course. At the same time, they have great literary gifts and make many incidental points with consummate skill; but they all confuse issues instead of clarifying them. Claudel and Bloy are the greatest transgressors in that they are constantly assuming, with an arrogance far greater than that of any rationalist, that they have some definite inkling of God's great purpose in putting them in the situation in which they find themselves. Bloy's *Journal* is consistently entertaining precisely because of its mad extravagance, and some of Claudel's dramatic works, such as *Tête d'Or*, *Le Soulier de Satin*, and *Christophe Colomb* are interesting pieces of self-absorption masquerading as statements about the universe.

It is not enough to say that these writers strike down to "some all-underlying tufa". As much could be said of all authors of bad best-sellers. Literature, and therefore criticism, is concerned not only with the tufa but also with all the layers of being above it, and if these are not properly organised, then the works are defective. Dr O'Brien proves that, in many instances, the symbolism is drifting and interchangeable, and that what the writer is really expressing, unknown to himself, is a web of emotions about sex and God that are not necessarily connected with each other. Then, without producing any valid theological or literary reasons for his change of attitude, Dr O'Brien suddenly backpedals vigorously and asks us to accept the web as having some mystic rightness.

Consequently, to me at least, his book seems to be cracked down the middle. But I wish there were more vital critical works of this kind, cracked or uncracked.

27. O is for Orifice

There is an old joke which runs: "Have you stopped beating your wife yet?"—"No, she won't let me." This book* corresponds to the idea behind the joke. It is the conscientious flagellant's vade-mecum, the apotheosis of whipping as a fine art or practical religion. It is also the most famous pornographic work to have appeared in France since the War, and it comes to us now in a rather shaky anonymous translation, but with several impressive recommendations on the dust-cover —from Graham Greene and Harold Pinter, amongst others.

Yet I can't say I like it any better now than I did several years ago when it was first lent to me in Paris. I think I see the point, and I grant that the book has a certain hallucinatory quality, in the well-established style of Sade's *120 journées de Sodome;* but to tell the truth mystic pornography embarrasses me. Whereas funny indecency, in the manner of *Myra Breckenridge* or *Portnoy's Complaint*, adds to the gaiety of nations, solemn, highbrow eroticism, of which there is quite a large supply in contemporary French, runs counter to that fizzy energy which is the real charm of sex, and bogs everything down in psychological viscosities.

No one seems to be sure whether *L'histoire d'O* was written by a man who likes beating women or by a woman who likes to be beaten. Since it was published with a precious and ambiguous preface by the late Jean Paulhan, rumour had it for a time that he himself was the author, but later the attribution was shifted to one of his female associates. I find it hard to make a guess at the authorship on internal evidence. Normally, women are far less interested in erotic elaboration than men, but some strongly Lesbian women seem to have a taste for

* Pauline Réage, *Story of O* (Olympia Press, 1970).

pornography, and indeed the heroine O herself, in the intervals of suffering incredible tortures, enjoys a kind of phantom masculinity in her relationships with certain women. So perhaps the author is a woman, wallowing in imagined violations and beatings which satisfy her femininity, yet deriving subjective pleasure from the spectacle of herself as victimised object, *i.e.* also satisfying a strong, narcissistic, masculine streak.

No doubt, the psychological necessity for this kind of writing rests on the fact that all sexual relationships have to have a fundamental sado-masochistic pattern. The Marquis de Sade himself was not simply a sadist, but a sado-masochist, nearly a hundred years before Sacher-Masoch came along to provide the second half of the compound adjective; and I suppose everyone is to some extent a sado-masochist, with sadism more on the masculine side and masochism more on the feminine.

The kind of pornography exemplified by *L'histoire d'O* can presumably only occur in an advanced society, where there is relative equality between the sexes and the sado-masochistic demands of human nature are no longer fully catered for in the everyday forms of culture. Where women are actually treated as inferiors and beaten as a matter of course, few people, either men or women, would require a rapist/flagellatory fantasy. And where primitive religious beliefs are strong—*e.g.* in the backward Catholic countries—the sado-masochistic symbols of the cross, the crown of thorns and the flagellation are still operative.

The problem that arises in an advanced civilisation, where equality between the sexes (and/or social equality, since class relationships can operate to some extent like sex relationships) has been largely achieved, is that the patterning becomes blurred. There is a gain in decency and refinement, but a loss of essential primitivism. I imagine that quite a few marriages go wrong nowadays not because the husband is cruel and oppressive, but because he does not know how to be cruel and oppressive at the right time and in the right way. This, I take it, is what D. H. Lawrence was often trying to suggest, although I am not sure that he ever sorted the matter out completely.

L'histoire d'O redresses the balance with pathological intensity. The heroine, O, is a modern Parisian professional woman with a lover, René. Although they are deeply attached to each other, their relationship apparently leaves something to be desired, because he takes her to a sort of private brothel, where for a fortnight she is beaten and prostituted in all imaginable ways, while he looks on with sympathetic interest. This Dothegirls Hall is a modern equivalent of Sade's Gothic castle in the *120 journeés*, and the closed world of the Gothic castle is, of course, an inverted Utopia, where the principle of evil is used as a source of lyricism instead of the principle of good. By the end of the treatment, O is mystically happy (*cf.* the heroine of Buñuel's film, *Belle de jour*), because she has been turned into a pure, will-less void, a trinity of acquiescent orifices open to infinity.

However, this is only the first stage of her mystic ascent or descent. René himself lives in the shadow of the will of an older man, an Englishman, Sir Stephen, one of those saturnine gentlemen who have stalked through European literature ever since Richardson (a sado-masochist *avant la lettre*) invented Lovelace. Perhaps we should be flattered at the fact that the French, in particular, credit us, and more especially our aristocracy, with such proficiency in highbrow vice. We are the whipping experts of the West, so much so, in fact, that a common French term for flagellation is *l'éducation anglaise*.

I once expressed surprise at this to a French colleague of mine and he assured me that when he lived in a Soho flat during the '30s people carrying bundles of canes were constantly ringing his doorbell and asking: "Do you require correction?" One wonders if this interesting class of itinerant artisans was composed of Old Etonians and Harrovians; at any rate, it is significant that when O requires still more correction it is arranged for by Sir Stephen, who flogs her manfully at home, in the intervals of sipping his whisky and soda, and then puts her into another specialised institution, where he finally brands his mark (his noble crest?) on her buttocks with a red-hot iron, and rings her vaginally as bulls are ringed nasally, so that—having reached erotic sainthood—she can be led everywhere on a chain.

Of such is the kingdom of heaven, you may say, if you take this kind of allegory seriously. I would not wish to spoil anybody's fun, and I hope every sadist finds his masochist to read this book aloud to, for their mutual satisfaction; it may even save them the trouble of actual physical activity. But I am pretty certain there is something wrong with it as literature. I would call it a black novelette for people who have got their eroticism mixed up with, rather than organised by, their religion. Let us secularise eroticism! would be my motto.

28. Myth of the Butch Bitch

To say that Gore Vidal's novel* is queer would be an under-statement; it is a queer, queer book, a virtuoso exercise in kinkiness, a draught of fizzy hemlock, a strikingly intelligent attempt to go as far as possible in outrageousness. Literature about sex is so often soggy and embarrassing, or clinical and sick-making: Mr Vidal pitches his narrative in a key of slightly demented funniness, and sustains this note right to the end.

Wit and intelligence can disinfect almost anything. It is such a relief, after reading, say, Miller, Kerouac and Burroughs, or watching American underground films in a spirit of social inquiry, to come across a book which deals with the same kind of decadent material in a sparkling, ironical way. If it is true that an important part of American culture has gone straight from provincial primitivism to metropolitan decadence, then this book stands in more or less the same relation to the deca-dence as Laclos's *Les Liaisons Dangereuses* to the gameyness of late 18th-century French society. It is both part of the pheno-menon it describes and a marvellously spirited comment on it.

The novel takes the form of a diary that the heroine, Myra, a girl entranced by her own loveliness, is keeping as a matter of mental hygiene to send to her psychiatrist, Dr Montag. But Montag may have been preceded by Sontag, because Myra helps along her chatter with lots of knowing references to the French New Novel and the mass media and Lévi-Strauss. She has come to California to claim her share, as her husband's widow, in a profitable drama academy run by her husband's uncle, an ex-cowboy star. While she is battling with the uncle, she is taken on as a teacher of Empathy and Posture, and this allows her to comment at length on modern American youth

* Gore Vidal, *Myra Breckenridge* (1968).

in general, and on California and its denizens in particular.

Myra is a girl with ideas, perhaps not very coherent ones, but mostly relating to the central Existentialist principle that there is no given human nature, only an infinitely variable pattern of behaviour-types. The average man is a pale reflection of the hero or heroes he has taken as his models, and these heroes themselves may not be real people, but only actors impersonating certain parts. A fundamental fact about American culture is that a range of personality-types was more or less fixed by the cinema during the heyday of MGM. The students at the academy have no individualities; they are all imitations of imitations. The bewilderment of the modern American young arises from their awareness of being superfluous and interchangeable in an over-populated world, where living can mean no more than working out one's fantasies, harmfully or harmlessly. As far as sex is concerned, the collective orgy is a harmless form of group therapy, in which the indefiniteness of the average human being is allowed full expression, with a resultant feeling of catharsis. The brighter people, who realise this, are the "swingers":

> It is true that the swingers, as they are called, make up only a small minority of our society; yet they hold a great attraction for the young and bored who are the majority and who keep their sanity (those that do) by having a double sense of themselves. . . .
>
> It is the wisdom of the male swinger to know what he is: a man who is socially and economically weak, as much put upon by women as by society. Accepting this situation, he is able to assert himself through a polymorphic sexual abandon, in which the lines between the sexes dissolve, to the delight of all. I suspect that this may be the only workable pattern for the future, and it is a most healthy one. . . .

Further, the cinema is now in decline, and the truly living art form is the television commercial, in which art pretends to imitate life so that life may imitate art.

But while professing this philosophy and commenting amusingly on everything around her in the light of it, Myra herself belies it by a kind of strange, puritanical drive to maintain the integrity of her personality. She wants to be herself, whatever that may mean, and force her will on other people. She doesn't care for orgies, for instance, although she is a dab hand at describing them, and, when invited, replies with reserve that she "Perhaps might just . . . *watch*, you know, and perhaps help out, in little ways. . . ."

Her consuming passion is for dominance. She is a manipulator, like Laclos's Mme de Merteuil, and it gradually emerges that her aim is to destroy the male principle, to unman the virile and so negate creation. In this sense she is quite metaphysical and truly diabolic. If all life is ultimately shadow and nothing has any final meaning, the only acceptable intellectual course is to turn the vital energies against life itself, that is against the Creator.

It follows that the central episode in the book is the account of Myra's attack on the outstanding he-man among the students, the symbolic Genitor, whose attributes, primary, secondary and tertiary, are catalogued with the exquisite precision of love-hatred. In the English edition this long passage has been trimmed somewhat in deference to "the high moral climate that currently envelops the British Isles", but enough remains to give a good idea of the beautifully graduated, suavely wicked original, which is one of the most delicate pieces of sadistic writing I have come across, and as a student of French literature I have had to read quite a few. Myra breaks down the young man's assurance step by step and finally subjects him to utter humiliation, which he both wildly resents and, in a curious way, accepts. He goes on to become a world-famous star under the programmatic name of Ace Mann, but is now no more than a virile shell with a homosexual inside. Physical virility is just a mirage; true virility is a matter of character, and Myra has it—at least in a sterile, destructive form—although she is a woman.

But, of course, in the end she turns out not to be a woman at all; she is her own so-called husband, Myron, a homosexual who has had the operation. Her passionate assault on men is due to a mad desire to exalt the female principle within herself at the expense of the male. Or possibly all her talk about the female principle is just a mistake and she is the kind of homosexual in whom there is a heterosexual clamouring to be out, and the only way he can get out is by turning femininity itself into a masculine drive.

All this suggests hormones within hormones, until the mind begins to boggle and one wonders what exactly the author is up to. Most pornographic or erotic works are depressingly simple; but one of the charms of this book is the difficulty of deciding whether it is a pure spoof, written for the fun and the money, or a spoof with a core of genuineness. Since the author has taken the unusual step of putting a double bronze image of his handsome face on the dust-cover, it is just possible that he is partly serious.

29. *Omelette à la Ponge*

What would we think of a cook who served up an omelette with the broken egg-shells and the egg-whisk on the plate? Or of a builder who built us a house and left the scaffolding against one wall and his cement-mixer in the garden?

Yet something similar happens in many branches of modern art. The work—whether it be a painting, a drawing, a film, a piece of sculpture or a poem—often includes the remnants of the process of its making; the work, one might almost say, is the record of the artist's attempts to reach some ideal that has remained beyond his grasp. This selfconsciousness of the creative process may emphasise the difference between the crafts, which remain fundamentally utilitarian, and the arts, which can never be sure that they have a point at all. The cook does not need to display the egg-whisk nor the builder the cement-mixer, because the omelette or the house, whether good or bad, are there to be eaten or lived in. The artist, on the other hand, may suspect that his initial stabs at the canvas are "truer" or "better" than the more elaborated stages of his composition and so he leaves them in. Likewise, a television producer, in his desire to overcome the limiting illusion of his medium, may use a second or third camera to show the first and second in operation. When this kind of device is resorted to the work of art is being made to exist, as it were, in depth or perspective as a fluctuating system of values about which the artist is not finally prepared to make up his mind.

The method seems now to have been applied, perhaps for the first time, to a work of criticism. M. Francis Ponge, the whimsical French prose-poet with a passion for objects, has brought out a large book on Malherbe,* which consists of the notes he

* Francis Ponge, *Pour un Malherbe* (Gallimard, 1965).

made at intervals between 1951 and 1957 in preparation for a book on Malherbe which, as it happens, he has never written. We can make various guesses about why the volume has come out in this form. Perhaps M. Ponge, in despair, just bundled all his notes together and handed them to M. Gallimard, who said: "Oh, very well. You're sufficiently famous now for us to publish your incidental droppings." Or M. Ponge, on re-reading his notes, realised that to recast them as a continuous text would be to deprive them of the freshness of incipience. Or again—and this is the most interesting possibility—he may never have intended to produce an ordinary work of criticism; it may have been his aim all along to compose a prose-poem on Malherbe, in the typically Pongian, fragmentary, tentative style. Certainly, he takes Malherbe as an object, like a pebble or a glass of water or any other of the given phenomena he has dealt with in his previous works, and reacts to this object with his whole personality. The notes can be read as a diary; their substance is as much Ponge in the light of Malherbe as it is Malherbe in the light of Ponge.

It is clear that M. Ponge, in producing an unbook or an antibook of this kind, is deliberately reacting against the fluency of academics—*"les incapables professionnels de la critique"*—whom he considers as being coherent and authoritative in the wrong way about subjects they do not understand. Their form of reason is not the genuine sort which M. Ponge, with a characteristic verbal play, calls *raison* and *réson, i.e.* intellectual rightness embodied in the appropriately expressive physical structure of words. Malherbe is presented as the first great exponent of this type of *raison* in French poetry; M. Ponge, in composing his own poems, is trying to be faithful to the same principle—*"c'est notre façon de servir la République"*. As he himself puts it, he is one of the highest and newest leaves on the tree of French poetry of which Malherbe is the trunk. Therefore in glorifying Malherbe, he is not indulging in that sterile rooting in the compost of history which is the mistaken occupation of professors; he is bracing himself for the immediate task, which is to save the French language in the current welter of bad taste. M. Ponge sees himself as standing almost alone, as needing,

indeed, to found a school of *raison-réson,* in opposition to the
various forms of committed literature or *littérature d'évasion* that
occupy the field.

All this is very attractively expressed, even though the
obsessive repetitiveness occasionally makes the reader feel that
he is going round and round inside some labyrinthine *nouveau
roman.* But if we apply the hated, and alas inevitable, method
of academic analysis to M. Ponge's notes, we may wonder
whether he is not lumping together in a lyrical blur statements
of very unequal value. For instance, he makes great play with
the fact that Malherbe grew up in Caen and then spent a
number of years in the Midi, while he, M. Ponge, spent his
childhood in the Midi and his adolescence at Caen. This
geographical parallelism savours of the most discredited
academic conventions about local conditioning. Nor does the
circumstance that M. Ponge attended the Lycée Malherbe and
passed Malherbe's house twice a day on his way to and from
school seem any more relevant to literature; it is the kind of
point that would be made much of in a despicable *conférence
mondaine.* M. Ponge gives a good, traditional account of Malherbe's historical period as lying happily half-way between the
disorderliness of the Renaissance and the excessive regimentation of Louis XIV's court, but he implies a similarity between
Malherbe and himself which is hardly convincing. Whatever
the asperities of Malherbe's temperament, he was primarily a
court poet, *i.e.* he was *engagé,* he was a sort of royalist Aragon,
with more refined literary scruples than Aragon, no doubt, but
an equal readiness to put his poetic instrument at the service
of the official cause. How can M. Ponge, who is an incorrigible
individualist and despises Aragon, dismiss Villon and Théophile
as *"geigneurs"* and *"roucouleurs"* and profess total admiration for
a court poet with an eye to the main chance? Would M. Ponge
actually like to be invited to compare a celebratory ode on one
of General de Gaulle's tours of the provinces? It seems improbable, yet we begin to wonder. Does he really think that
Malherbe is to be put on the same level as Shakespeare?
Would Malherbe have made anything of the statement: *Notre
patrie est le monde muet* which M. Ponge, ever faithful to his

objects, keeps repeating as his slogan? And how is it that M. Ponge, an exponent of the modern, open, broken form, is so keen on a poet who wrote in regular verse? If he believes that the Malherbe of today would write in free verse or poetic prose, he does not say so, nor explain why he should do so. What he conveys most forcibly is the conviction that there ought to be a modern Malherbe, and he seems to be hoping that some future Boileau will be able to write: *"Enfin Ponge vint . . .".*

However, since his antibook is not an academic treatise but, presumably, a contemporary work of art, it contains its own negation. In the second half of the volume M. Ponge goes into a recessive mood and tells himself that his view of Malherbe is probably an illusion, that Malherbe may have prepared the way for 17th-century totalitarianism and that he himself is no poet at all. It is as if the cook, after thrusting the egg-shells and the egg-whisk under our noses, said: "Don't touch the omelette, it's too *baveuse*". But we have eaten it by now, and must admit to enjoying its peculiar, endearing flavour.

30. Genet's Black Chivalry

The French have a reputation for carrying intellectual attitudes to extremes and especially for being doggedly persistent in negativity. They are not motivated in this by any misty kind of *Schadenfreude*, but rather by intellectual glee at forcing their own logicality on that Janus-faced nonentity known as God or the Devil. "If this is Your creation," one can hear the French genius saying, "we are damned well going to define it as we see it." This is the common Frenchness linking the most dissimilar individuals—Jean-Paul Sartre, General de Gaulle, Paul Valéry, François Mauriac, the Marquis de Sade, Baudelaire, etc.

As for Jean Genet, although he is a real person, he is such a perfect example of thoroughgoing negativity that he might almost have been invented as a synthetic demonstration of this tendency of the French mind. What is absolutely certain is that, if he had not existed, Sartre would have had to invent him; fortunately "God" invented him to provide Sartre with a perfect Existentialist subject for his *Saint Genet*. His system of values is as symmetrical as a French formal garden, and his sense of hierarchy and ceremonial detail is almost as acute as if he had been brought up under the *Ancien Régime* at Versailles. But what he presents us with is an inverted mirror-image of the "average" world. His is literally an underworld or counterworld, a realm of night or hell which stands in black opposition to the moderately tragic operations of daylight existence.

It is a remarkably consistent development of his personal situation. As a parentless bastard, a reform-school boy from the age of ten, a habitual thief and jailbird for whom social rehabilitation could have no meaning, a familiar of drug-peddlers, a homosexual prostitute with a despairing view of homosexuality, he was an almost ideal dropout character, or

U

Existentialist outsider, or *poète maudit,* or rogue genius, or Bohemian versus the Bourgeois. To complete the pattern, he should also perhaps have been a Jewish Negro. One or two other people have come along to remedy this deficiency. He has done his best, as his plays testify, to become an honorary or spiritual Negro, although, for the sake of the peace of the world, it is to be hoped that most Negroes reject his view of them with loathing. I don't remember any pronouncement by him on Jewishness, but I suppose he considers Jews, in spite of their persecuted wing, to be too firmly ensconced in the citadels of power and riches and average morality to rank among the irredeemable have-nots. At any rate, there are no Jews as such in his novels, whose heroes are criminal riff-raff, often with exotic names indicating international origins. But they all speak French argot, and over them all Genet spreads the rich decoration of his own sumptuous literary French.

Not the least surprising thing about him is that a child brought up in what one imagines to be a desert of illiteracy should have acquired this unerring distinction of language. His underworld speaks its own peculiar tongue, which is also, of course, his own native idiom, but he himself constantly describes it in the most refined style of the upper world. If, as Valéry says, syntax is a faculty of the soul, Genet was born with the soul of a medieval aristocrat, and it was only an accident of his situation which made his knightly sword a burglar's jemmy and his coat of arms a lavatory graffito— buttocks, testicles, and a penis rampant. Aristocrats, after all, are only people who are confident that they are the best. Genet decides to have this confidence, at least linguistically, and so he turns prison yards into courts of love, condemned murderers into holy martyrs, and tattooed thugs into Lancelots and Guineveres. This extraordinary imaginative effort succeeds to a surprising extent, and it is none the worse for also containing its own ironic negation. Genet's books are typically modern works of art in that they build up a deliberate illusion as if it were the truth, while at the same time suggesting that, in matters of this kind, there is no truth other than varieties of willed illusion.

Although there are no bibliographical details in the French edition, *Miracle de la Rose** seems to come after *Notre Dame des Fleurs* (already translated as *Our Lady of the Flowers*) and before *Pompes Funèbres* and *Querelle de Brest* (both untranslated) and *Journal d'un voleur* (already translated as *The Thief's Journal*). All five books belong to the same kind of writing and might in fact be considered as different volumes of the same work. They take the form of rambling, fantastic memoirs, which dodge about between the first person and the third, and show no respect for clarity of narrative. They are not ordinary books written with an eye to the reader, but rather private ruminations or celebrations in which Genet goes over the past and works it up to the poetic pitch at which he can, in a sense, become reconciled to it. A special feature of *Miracle of the Rose* is that it deals with childhood and early adolescence in the reformatory, as well as with adult life in prison or on the streets. This almost puts it into the category of "confessions of an old boy". It reminds one a little of accounts of English boarding schools in their worst phases, when the masters were as remote as warders and the detailed government of the community was carried on by the "bloods", behaving like pashas among their feminised underlings. No doubt, all closed monosexual societies, when they go wrong, deteriorate in the same way, and old-fashioned reform schools and prisons, being permanently wrong, develop elaborate rituals of power and perversion. Parts of *Miracle of the Rose* read very much like the account of the English boarding school in Céline's *Mort à crédit* or Julien Blanc's nightmarish description of the practices of the Foreign Legion.

The difference is, perhaps, that Genet's writing expresses strong emotion only in the direction of sublimity. He is so steeped in pornography and dirt that he deals with it quite unselfconsciously. It is there and, whenever the need arises, he refers to it directly by means of the obscene terms (which the translator, the late Bernard Frechtman, struggles with—shall we say?—manfully). But his real interest is in psychological detail and the poetic superstructure. He both wants to see the situation as it is and to transmute it into noble terms.

* Jean Genet, *Miracle of the Rose*, translated by Bernard Frechtman (1967).

v

Hence a very curious oscillation; Cinderella turns into the Princess but, before we know where we are, she is Cinderella again, or even one of the Ugly Sisters. Moreover, she is a boy playing the part of a girl, just as the Prince, who flexes his muscles-so charmingly, may suddenly become somebody else's Princess. To read Genet is to be whirled through a succession of appearances: male changes into female and vice versa, darkness into light, horror into ecstasy. And the doomed sump of humanity appears more moving and obscene through being lit by this fitful glow than if it were described with straight and conscientious sordidness.

Unlike most of the under-the-counter authors, Genet actually claims to be a stimulating, masturbatory writer; but I doubt whether he is, even for the homosexual reader. His most memorable scenes have a sad, detached poetry about them, and sex and excretions are present only because these are what his imagination has found to work on. I am thinking for instance, of the touching episode in *Miracle of the Rose* in which Villeroy tries to introduce the narrator to the manly delights of active fornication, and valiantly covers up the fiasco of the occasion. Genet has a marvellous way of suggesting the strange and ludicrous aspects of sex as well as its lyricism and mystery. This comes out most clearly not in *Miracle of the Rose* but in the astonishing copulation scene in *Querelle de Brest*, which is like an amplification, in poetic prose, of Rimbaud's powerful homosexual sonnet.

Since I have a high opinion of Genet's writing and, indeed, think he is quite unique within his given range, I would like to indicate his limitations. Being a rapturous monologuist like Céline or Henry Miller, he has little sense of over-all literary structure. You just have to accept each "novel" as a flux in which he moves from incident to incident without warning or explanation. Sometimes an episode is completely elaborated, but often the scenes are merely hinted at or not developed enough to become fully intelligible. Some readers may feel that this adds to the literary effect of sinister chiaroscuro; but I often find it disappointing and think it arises from the fact that Genet is writing primarily for himself and not completely objectifying his experience. Also like Céline or Miller, he is an egoist with little or no gift of characterisation. In *Miracle of the Rose*, he keeps referring to different boys by name—Villeroy, Divers, Bulkaien, and Botchako—but it is impossible to get an individualised picture of any of them. They are all in a sense the same boy, and no doubt versions of the author, wavering between masculinity and femininity, fidelity and betrayal, courage and cowardice, defiance and abjection. They have hardly more substance to them than figures in a courtly romance, such as *L'Astrée* or *The Faerie Queene*.

This may be because petty criminals, even when they commit murder, are not evolved enough to be really interesting as individuals. More probably the reason is that Genet is only concerned with their sexuality and the emotions of power and humility connected with sex. They have no personal quirks, no ideas, hobbies, or ambitions. Even burglary is, in the first place, a form of sexual excitement. The burglar is a representative of the nether world raping the upper world and leaving the stains of his virility on bourgeois silks and satins. The murderer, even though he may have strangled only some defenceless little girl or decrepit old man, has committed supreme rape against the bourgeois social order and, by paying for it with his life, is raised to the level of a saint and martyr. Those of us who live within the bourgeois social order may wonder at this simplicity of approach, which sees the social order as such a coherent entity that it becomes a sort of person with sexual attributes. But for Genet, respectable society is a compact, foreign bloc, like capitalist America for a naïve Russian Communist or Soviet Russia for a naïve American right-winger. In *Miracle of the Rose*, he can thus build up Harcamone, the condemned criminal, into an august sacrificial figure, around whom the prison community moves, like the faithful around the figure of Christ during the Passion. This is the ultimate point of inverted Romanticism, and I don't believe in it for one moment. But I think I see why he needs it to complete his topsy-turvy psychological structure and maintain his imaginative stance.

To my mind, the real quality of his writing lies not in his description of the opposition between the nether and the upper worlds but in the instinctive way in which he shows how, in the masculine nether world itself, there is a hopeless straining after happiness and fulfilment through the creation of an artificial polarity between the "sexes" and a pattern of dignity and tenderness, which is a sort of heart-rending parody of the pattern in the "normal" world. Although Genet will not admit the fact in so many words, the whole enterprise is a failure from the start, since a convicted criminal, however potent, has been classified as an object, and therefore feminised, by society. The dandyism of the "big shots" in their carefully modified prison uniforms is pathetic, since they are to some extent false males, virile within captivity, and their persecution of the "females" is a form of overcompensation. The "females," on the other hand, can never become women. Their receptivity, being psychological and not part of a physiological cycle, has no end to it, and so, if they do not revert to masculinity, they can only sink further and further into defilement, as they fumble towards an absolute in submission, betrayal, and abjection. Genet himself clearly followed this downward path, and he suggests the stages of the descent in beautiful and appalling scenes.

Perhaps most jailbirds are mercifully spared the ability to see their plight as Genet describes it. It may even be that what Genet says about them is only true for those who, like himself, have got their predicament inextricably involved with their sexuality; this may not be the case with the majority. But statistics are not very important in this connection; if his account is valid only for a small minority or for himself, it gives one of the most convincing and moving visions of psychological distress to be found in contemporary literature.

31. Nathalie Sarraute

On those rare occasions when one meets well-known people, more often than not one is disappointed by their failure to display any of those characteristics for which they are famous. The celebrated poet discusses the Reports and White Papers he has bought from H.M. Stationery Office and is anxiously poring over in an attempt to understand the modern world. A Minister of the Crown will give the impression that he is far less interested in foreign affairs than in Proust. But sometimes one strikes lucky. I have heard of an admirer of Ionesco who was invited to lunch at the dramatist's flat and was delighted when, in the middle of the meal, the postman delivered an enormous parcel, the unwrapping of which occupied the company, filled the room, and created the proliferating absurdity of an improvised Ionesco play. I myself have a comparably significant memory of one of my meetings with Nathalie Sarraute.

We were sitting in a rather crowded café and, wanting to attract the attention of a waiter, I asked her advice on a point of etiquette about which I had been wondering. Would I be justified in raising a finger and calling out *"Garçon!"*? Certainly not, she said. To call *"Garçon!"* would be to act like those bourgeois who deny their subordinates individual reality by addressing them as if they were stereotypes. No sensitive, right-minded person could behave like that. Obviously, to snap my fingers without giving tongue would be still more insulting. On the other hand, if I cried *"Monsieur!"*, several unsatisfactory consequences would ensue: I might appear ridiculous, or too heavily ironical, or no one would be sure whom I was addressing. What, then, was to be done? Nothing, she said. We must just sit and wait.

A little later, a member of her family hurried in to discuss with her the buying of a baby's coat that was to be given as a rather formal present. They settled the question of the size and colour and, as the other person was dashing out again to make the purchase, Mme Sarraute called after her: *"N'oublie pas qu'il faut le nom du faiseur!"* In other words, the coat, to be a valid bourgeois present, had to bear the name of one of the recognised makers.

Mme Sarraute's books, which have made her famous among the *literati* of two continents as an exponent of the French New Novel, are about such tiny points as these. If I utter a word in a café, what surging complexity of inarticulate attitudes, both in myself and others, lies behind it? Every day, of course, hundreds or thousands of French bourgeois stereotypes raise their fingers and cry *"Garçon!"*, and every day hundreds or thousands of waiter-stereotypes hurry to do their bidding and, on both sides, bourgeois and waiters probably assume that this is quite in order; this is what life is like; this is "reality". But they are mistaken. Each individual is a teeming mass of original movements (tropisms) from which convention, habit, or inertia have selected a simplified pattern; this pattern is taken to be the "truth" when, in fact, it is a sediment or ossification. Most people live their lives in terms of this ossification, and everyone is forced to submit to it in certain cases; for instance, when one French bourgeois family, even an enlightened one, makes a present to another, the ultimately significant detail is not that the present should be appropriate or aesthetic in itself (although the French tend to be exceptionally particular on both these scores) but that the label should at once eliminate doubts about whether or not the object belongs to the accepted, closed, bourgeois system of exchanges. To be a bourgeois or a waiter, or any other type of "character", is to submit to the range of signs defining that limited identity; it is to speak a language that is living in the sense that it is still used, but dead in the sense that it is not being reinvented.

Now a function of art as a whole, and of literature in particular, is to see behind existing convention into the wealth of possibilities that the convention does not cater for. Each genuine artist introduces a new vision, a fresh selection from amongst the infinite possibilities of reality. With the passage of time, this vision itself will become conventional and appear inadequate to some new and genuine artist. But such ageing is not a cause for dismay; on the contrary, what could be more bracing than to become aware of the inexhaustible newness of reality?

Mme Sarraute's basic tenets, which I have thus roughly summarised from her book of essays on the novel, *L'Ere du soupçon* (1956), are obviously not far removed from those of Jean-Paul Sartre, and it is not surprising that Sartre should have contributed an enthusiastic preface to her first novel, *Portrait d'un inconnu.* His conception of *la mauvaise foi,* that half-conscious dishonesty that leads people to accept borrowed attitudes instead of exercising their freedom, is close to her view that most "characters" are a simplification in comparison with the raw material of psychological reality from which they are drawn. But it cannot be said that Mme Sarraute owes anything to Sartre or that she started from a philosophical attitude and wrote her novels to exemplify it.

In the first place, she began writing along her chosen line before Sartre published any of his important books and she has never followed him on the specific issue of "committed" literature. Although her political sympathies seem to be with the Left, she denies that it is the artist's business to do anything but express his vision as he sees it, in connection with that limited, and perhaps very humble, section of life with which he has first-hand acquaintance. Most probably she looks upon Sartre's committed writings as a mistake, as a crude manipulation of ready-made counters, the concept of Existentialist freedom operating only in the manipulation, when it should be used instead to break down the counters into a truer representation of life. Also, she has explained that she began writing her first book, *Tropismes* (1939), before she had worked out intellectually what it was she was trying to do. Her subsequent novels—*Portrait d'un inconnu* (1948), *Martereau* (1953), *Le Planétarium* (1959), *Les Fruits d'Or* (1963) and *Entre la vie et la mort* (1968)—are all elaborations of aspects of the early book. In holding so doggedly to the same course, Mme Sarraute resembles other exponents of the New Novel; whatever doubts one may have about the ultimate importance of their work, one cannot but admire their singlemindedness.

A tropism, according to the dictionary, is the response of an organism to a stimulus. Since childhood, Mme Sarraute says, she has always been aware of the fact that our mental life is made up of masses of infinitesimal movements, many of which, perhaps even most of which, have spent themselves or become blurred with others, before we have had time to be fully aware of them or to put a name to them. It is here, in this fundamental vibration of our being, that truth and sincerity are to be found, and the problem of realism is how to translate it into words. On the subject of realism, Mme Sarraute makes some impeccably thoughtful remarks:

> But, people will ask, what do you mean by a realistic writer? Well, quite simply—and it could not be otherwise—a writer who, above all, however great his desire to amuse his contemporaries, to reform them, to instruct them, or to fight for their emancipation, applies himself, while making an effort to cheat as little as possible, and to neither trim nor smooth anything for the purpose of overcoming contradictions and complexities, to seizing with all the sincerity of which he is capable, to scrutinising as far as his sharpness of vision will permit him to see, what appears to him to be reality.
>
> His passion for this reality is so great and so sincere that he shrinks from no sacrifice it may entail. Indeed, he accepts the greatest of all those a writer may be led to make: loneliness and the moments of doubt and distress that this involves. . . .
>
> Style (whose harmony and visible beauty are such a constant, dangerous temptation for writers) is for this writer merely an instrument, the only value of which is that of serving to extract and embrace as closely as possible the fragment of reality he is trying to lay bare. All desire to write "beautifully" for the pleasure of doing so, to give aesthetic enjoyment to himself or to his readers, is quite inconceivable to him; style, from his standpoint, being capable of beauty, only in the sense that an athlete's gesture is beautiful; the better it is adapted to its purpose, the greater the beauty. And this beauty, which is composed of vigour, precision, vivacity, suppleness, boldness and economy of means, is merely the expression of its effectiveness.
>
> *(The Age of Suspicion)*

However, there still remains an important linguistic problem. Words begin, as it were, at a much more superficial level than this basic reality Mme Sarraute is interested in. She has published no full-scale critique of language, but from the incidental remarks in her novels it is easy to see that she is bothered by the generalising tendency inherent in linguistic expression. Every word, except a unique proper name (if there is such a thing), is a generalisation, *i.e.* brings under the same label a very large group of ill-defined phenomena: "house", "chair", "garden", "good", "bad", "black", "white", etc. are rough approximations which we repeat indefinitely without stopping to reflect that, for instance, when we say "a white house" in connection with a particular house, we are not grasping its true individuality (it may be more or less of a "house", more or less "white"), but putting it into a class of constructions so large that we are saying nothing at all about its uniqueness. The situation is even worse in the case of words referring to feelings. It is difficult to imagine any character in a Sarraute novel saying to another: "I love you" because the term "love" is an impossibly clumsy piece of shorthand. How can a sensitive person ever sum up all the fluctuating variety of an intense relationship by means of one, much used word? Actually, "love" occurs, almost inadvertently, in *Portrait d'un inconnu*, but it is followed at once by the comment: ". . . again one of those crude words that stun like a blow with a club." Mme Sarraute, faced with language, is like someone who has been presented with a childish jig-saw puzzle in which the pieces are far too big and coarsely coloured to make a picture with anything like the grain of reality. She wants to cut up the pieces into ever smaller particles until she arrives at a mosaic of minute points of light exactly corresponding to our faculty of perception at its most acute. In this sense, she can be called a psychological pointillist.

This ambition is, I think, the key to all her work, both creative and critical. If she is almost as scornful of the "traditional" novel as Robbe-Grillet, this is because she looks upon it as a rudimentary jig-saw puzzle. The title of her critical study, *L'Ere du soupçon*, refers to the suspicion now surrounding "characters" in novels. A character, traditionally, was an entity with a name, a profession, and certain recurrent features. The author saw him from the outside as an object and explained him from the inside with divine omniscience. Both procedures are now inadequate; to harden the character into a finished, definable unit is just as impossible as to claim to know what goes on inside him. No character can be finished, since the process of living is perpetual psychological newness, whether it is accepted as such or not. Two people together in a room are not two "characters" but a flickering interchange of impressions, a double series of tropisms. At the same time, the writer is not God, nor is he a super-psychologist; he does not explain, he describes. Why should he bother to break up what he knows of his own nature into separate fragments and pretend that each fragment is a separate character? His function is, rather, to describe a field of perception of which his own subjectivity and other people's objectivity are interconnected incidents, perpetually reacting to each other like those plant-animals on the floor of the sea that live in a state of tremulous intimacy with their habitat. (Mme Sarraute is constantly using imagery involving tentacles and antennae.)

It will be obvious why Virginia Woolf is mentioned with approval. She too saw the stuff of life as a kind of unbroken and animate web, full of shifting lights. Mme Sarraute also praises Ivy Compton-Burnett for having evolved a form of dialogue which, while it is not "realistic" in the more superficial sense (few people speak, or ever spoke, quite in that way), produces a sensation of reality because it is the voice of subjective/objective truth floating between the characters. Mme Sarraute even argues that the most permanent part of Dostoevsky and Proust is not their character-drawing, since the characters, she says, already have a rather dated look, but their rendering of the basic psychological fabric from which the characters emerge. Paradoxically enough for one who is obsessed with the idea that it is the duty of literature to be "original", Mme Sarraute seems to believe that the most original literature, which strikes down to this fundamental reality, reveals a kind of undifferentiated material common to all individuals, "a new unanimism",

as she calls it.* To use another image from painting, it is almost
as if an artist were to delve so conscientiously into the truth of
material creation that he ended up by painting nothing but
hydrogen atoms, or fundamental particles, or whatever the
scientists now say the world is made up of—supposing these
ultimate units were paintable. Why Mme Sarraute wants to go
as far down as this and why she thinks truth is universal at that
level, she does not explain. I shall have to touch on the problem
again later, because there may be a metaphorical confusion
here, as in some theories connected with the New Novel. The
idea that truth is truer deeper down may itself be an old-
fashioned convention; the implications of modern science seem
to be that there are various strata of truth and that we have no
means of deciding whether the lower ones are any more valid
than the upper ones. This has a bearing on the problem of the
"character" in literature.

Since Mme Sarraute is primarily interested in the subjective/
objective fabric of life, she might be said to be more of a poet
than a novelist. *Tropismes* is a collection of twenty-four very
short prose-poems, each of which attempts to grasp the complexities of an apparently simple situation: parents trailing
through the streets with their children and looking dispiritedly
into shop-windows; rather drab domestic situations in which a
husband is exasperated by his wife's pettiness and can do
nothing about it, or bourgeois women chatter emptily like
birds. I confess I cannot work up much more enthusiasm for
this volume than for a comparable short collection of prose
pieces by Robbe-Grillet called *Instantanés*, and I am not surprised that, as Mme Sarraute says, it aroused no comment
when it first appeared in 1939. The writing is neat and scrupulous, but each item seems puzzlingly slight. The collection has
no general theme, except perhaps the dim unsatisfactoriness of
French bourgeois behaviour. I would say that just as telling
fragments of the same kind, written without any references to

* The word *unanimisme* was popularised in the earlier years of the century
by Jules Romains, who wanted literature to stress his conviction that in the
complex, modern world, individuals are more completely "members of one
another" than in previous ages.

"tropisms," could be culled from a number of traditional, sensitive novels: from those of Colette, for instance. It is true that Colette, like Virginia Woolf, often overwrites, whereas Mme Sarraute is too honest ever to do so, but when Colette and Virginia Woolf are good, they seem to be saying more in the same space. For instance, the following "poem" which is meant to be complete in itself, presents the kind of subject that Colette, Virginia Woolf, Katherine Mansfield or even Francis Ponge might have dealt with, adding to it their own particular psychological penetration or verbal conceits. Mme Sarraute treats it so puritanically that the question arises: Is she saying anything at all? The sentences read like notes for a short story or a poem that has not yet been written:

> On the outskirts of London, in a little cottage with percale curtains, its little back lawn sunny and all wet with rain.
> The big, wistaria-framed window in the studio, opens on to this lawn.
> A cat with its eyes closed, is seated quite erect on the warm stone.
> A spinster-lady with white hair, and pink cheeks that tend towards purple, is reading an English magazine in front of the door.
> She sits there, very stiff, very dignified, quite sure of herself and of others, firmly settled in her little universe. She knows that in a few moments the bell will ring for tea.
> Down below, the cook, Ada, is cleaning vegetables at a table covered with white oil-cloth. Her face is motionless, she appears to be thinking of nothing. She knows that it will soon be time to toast the buns, and ring the bell for tea.
>
> *(Tropisms)*

With *Portrait d'un inconnu*, which Sartre called "an anti-novel which reads like a detective story," Mme Sarraute's intentions are clearer. We are in the mind of an unnamed person—a man, presumably, since the grammatical endings are masculine—who, for reasons unstated, is keeping a sort of watch on two— dare I say?—"characters," an elderly man and his daughter, between whom no love is lost. Either of the two could have figured in *Tropismes*. They appear to fluctuate uncertainly in the narrator's field of perception. The elderly man has some of the characteristics of a miser; he fusses about the things his daughter takes away from his flat, and about her inability to live on her allowance. She, for her part, seems to be trying to avoid the narrator. One or two passages clarify into recognisable episodes: for instance, the father has a quarrel with his daughter and locks her out of his flat, and at the end the book emerges into the light of common day when the daughter becomes engaged to a commanding positivistic man, who is presumably meant to be a caricature of bourgeois definiteness and efficiency. He steamrollers through the flurried uncertainties of the narrator, the father and the girl, and the vulgar reader is thankful to see him do so. Has Mme Sarraute put him in to show that she can draw a character if she wants to? She certainly has a remarkable gift for catching the rhythms of spoken French. But I cannot say that I find the book easy to read or satisfactory in its final impression. I fail to see the point of the narrator, who is, I suppose, the unknown man whose portrait we are promised in the title. Why does the story of the uncomfortable, even cruel, relationship between father and daughter need to be told through the medium of his anonymous consciousness? As a matter of fact, he seems to disappear occasionally to be replaced by the omniscient voice of the "traditional" novelist; but whether this is deliberate or inadvertent is not deducible from the context. I agree that Mme Sarraute is saying something about the changing, unfinished nature of the relationship between a father and his daughter; I doubt whether it is of great interest or absolutely needs to be said in this particular way.

The "plot" of *Martereau* marks a step in the direction of clarity. The narrator, this time, is a delicate young man living in his uncle's household, again in the Paris bourgeois setting. The uncle and aunt maintain a state of more or less permanent conjugal warfare; she is shallow and cruel, he is bumbling and crass. The story, such as it is, concerns the purchase of a house on the outskirts of Paris. The uncle has a large amount of spare money which he wishes to spend quickly to avoid paying income tax. He asks a much less prosperous friend, Martereau, to buy a house for him with this money, but through an accident does not get a receipt. Martereau seems to want to hang on to the house and then, in the end, appears to relinquish it. It is not certain whether he is honest or dishonest.

The story is, once more, just a pretext to allow the author to describe the changing relationships within a small group of people. The ultra-sensitive narrator is a repetition of the anonymous observer of *Portrait d'un inconnu,* and I do not find him any more essential. He too fades out from time to time and the novelist quietly takes over to describe things that the narrator could not possibly know. But in this book there are some outstandingly good passages, in particular one of the best descriptions I have read of the painful, and almost spurious, pleasure of visiting a house one may, or may not, buy. Mme Sarraute admirably catches the interplay of attitudes between the three people who go off on this expedition; she shows how they are honest, or dishonest, with themselves and each other. The clash of character is also more interesting than in the previous book. Martereau, seen at first from the outside, appears definite and rounded in comparison with the other psychological quagmires, but he too eventually turns out to be no more certain in his characteristics than the uncle. Incidentally, I cannot see why the book should be called *Martereau*; it is true that he is the only character with a name, but he is not the central one.

The bourgeois obsession with property—already touched on in *Portrait d'un inconnu,* where the elderly father works himself into an enjoyable frenzy through imagining that his daughter is stealing his soap, and continued in *Martereau* in connection with the house—reaches a climax in *Le Planétarium,* which is largely about emotions centred on material objects. This time there is no narrator; we are inside each consciousness in turn and we gradually realise that there are three main characters: an elderly aunt living alone in a large flat and very upset because some workmen have put the wrong sort of handle on a new door she has had specially made; her nephew, Alain, who is living with his wife in a small flat and would like to exchange it for the aunt's large one; he is also a social climber and wants to impress the third character, Germaine, a society lady who is at the same time a writer. Alain and the aunt are both weak characters, whose moods oscillate wildly. In the end, Alain and his wife get the flat and Germaine comes to visit them there.

Another storm in a teacup, then; but as the narrator in *Martereau* says, speaking obviously for Mme Sarraute herself, "Storms in teacups are my great speciality." Never has a wooden door been discussed at such length in literature; Flaubert's elaborate paragraph on Charles Bovary's cap, or Balzac's minute account of the Pension Vauquer in *Le Père Goriot* or even Proust's variations on the hawthorn bushes, are outstripped by Mme Sarraute's treatment of the door, which assumes the importance of a character in the novel. But Mme Sarraute's obsession with "the object" is not quite the same as that of her fellow New Novelist, Robbe-Grillet. He defines objects with pseudo-frigidity in order to emphasise the mind's alienation from the material universe, or he uses certain objects as "objective correlatives" (T. S. Eliot's expression which he has accepted), *i.e.* as supports, or reference points, for emotions that they do not, properly speaking, symbolise. Mme Sarraute's objects are obviously meant to be futile receptacles for all the anguish of living. The elderly aunt, and then Alain, worry about the door because their minds are incapable of posing any metaphysical problem. The door is copied from one the aunt first saw in a church, where everything bored her until her eye lighted on the carved wooden surface set in a wall. There may be a satirical intention here; unbelieving French bourgeois are often fond of refectory tables from monasteries or fragments of carving from churches, without seeing that they fuss over them with an intensity that amounts to the worst form of idol worship—that is, the form which is neither religious nor truly aesthetic, but merely proprietary.* This, like the miser's passion, is a misplaced interest, and Mme Sarraute does it proud in terms of "tropisms". Here for instance, is the nephew producing an effect in society by giving an account of

* This particular form of "obsession with the object" crops up more frequently in France than in England, and is an important theme in Georges Pérec's *Les Choses* and in Robert Pinget's *L'Inquisitoire;* it is interestingly used by Alain Resnais in his film, *Muriel.* (See Ch. 2, "The Obsessive Object".)

how his aunt rang him up at eleven o'clock at night to go and see how the workmen had bungled the fixing of the door:

> "I saw right away, as soon as I got there, that she was in a bad way. She looked fairly haggard. And the entire place was in what, for her, was terrible disorder; a can of furniture polish on the floor. . . . She let me in, a rag in her hand. Come and see, it's incredible what they've gone and done, your friend Renouvier is no good. . . . Look at the door. . . . I saw an awful new door such as you see everywhere, a pretentious, interior decorator's sort of door, which was there nobody knew why. . . . A mad idea she had had all of a sudden. . . . But I didn't say anything, it was too late, there was no longer any question of that . . . the fingerprint plaque had been removed and it had left holes in the wood, tiny marks that had been stopped up with putty and which she was rubbing, painting with all her might. . . . Almost weeping, she begged me. . . . Look . . . tell me the truth, I can't judge any more, I can't see anything but that. . . . The nail marks were undoubtedly visible. . . . If she had said nothing, I shouldn't have noticed anything, but now that she had told me. . . . It was, indeed, too bad, but there was no doubt about it, I did see them. Some devil must have prompted me, I couldn't help saying to her: Oh, if you don't think about it, you can hardly see anything, but now that you've told me, I do see the filled-in spots. . . . But so tiny . . . you have to know they're there. . . . But that was just it, that little defect, that minute flaw, the little wart on the face of perfection. . . . It must be dominated, annihilated, she must rub. . . . She stepped back. . . . And at moments, in certain lights, if you stood in certain places, you couldn't see anything, but then it would reappear, she couldn't see anything else . . . the door, the room itself, were gone, but the little round spots were there, her eyes guessed them, made them appear at regular intervals, counted them . . . it was torture . . . he hears their laughter, gentle chuckling, dove-cooing, a caress, an encouragement, a vote of thanks. . . . They allow themselves to be led, they let themselves go in brotherly fashion, and he feels that he is gaining in confidence, he would like to splash about and shake his feathers. . . . But do you know that, two years ago, she got like that for even less. . . . She noticed that a bit of wood had been scraped off her bed-post, the one against the wall . . . well, it had to be matched, filled in . . . and you could see it . . . or you couldn't. . . . She was constantly pulling the bed out. Finally she decided to replace the entire bed-post."
>
> *(The Planetarium)*

With *Les Fruits d'Or*, she breaks rather new ground, although still remaining within the same Parisian milieu. The hero—the blank hero, one might say—is not a wooden door but a new literary work that has just appeared. In a mosaic made up of fragments of interior monologue or dialogue, Mme Sarraute traces the various and changing reactions to this book, *Les Fruits d'Or*, which at first startles by its newness and then is finally discarded as old hat. The impression conveyed is that no one has really understood it; the book has been thrown into the Parisian literary pond and has produced a series of croakings, all of which are more or less irrelevant and indicative of the tropisms of the public in its relations with itself rather than of any critical appreciation. The theme may be meant to have some connection with the reception of the New Novel and, as such, should perhaps be taken as a dreadful warning to anyone so bold as to write about Mme Sarraute. However, I can only record my opinion that it is an interesting exercise which, in the last resort, fails to carry conviction. The flaw may be that the nature of *Les Fruits d'Or* is never suggested, even by implication, and so we can hardly judge how appropriate or inappropriate the reactions are; the book is ingenious but has a hollow in the middle.

It will be clear that, although I have the highest respect for Mme Sarraute as a person and an intelligence, she has not converted me to a belief in the New Novel. As after reading Robbe-Grillet or Michel Butor, I am left with a feeling that a genuine impulse, valid within a limited field, has been generalised into a system which warps the writing, or at least makes it rather boring.

More than one critic has said, of course, that the boringness of the New Novel is a feature of its authenticity. Whereas the old-fashioned novelist strove to entertain, to cut out the dull parts where nothing happens and to present even boring people as being amusing when seen from a particular angle, the best present-day writers (like some contemporary filmmakers) do not cheat in this way; the boringness of their writing is meant to correspond exactly to the boringness of existence, so that if the aunt in *Le Planétarium* fusses about her door for pages on end, she is actually intended to be as excruciating as some old dear who corners you in real life. But it is difficult to accept the view that the New Novelist actively intends to bore. Ministers of religion and university teachers may be resigned to being professionally boring, artists cannot be, and Mme Sarraute speaks of the expression of artistic truth as being exciting. In any case, if the aim of art were simply to reproduce the boringness of life, there would be no need for it; life itself would suffice. It is much more likely that all art is intended to be a victory over boringness, through the substitution of a stylisation for the undifferentiated, unthinkable muddle of living. All art *is*, of course, a stylisation, absolute realism being logically impossible, since life could be totally rendered only by life itself. Mme Sarraute, like every other novelist, is offering us a stylisation, and if I find the New Novel stylisations unsatisfactory and rather wearisome, this must either be because I am too stupid to understand them (a lamentable circumstance beyond my control) or because the stylisations are leaving out something I feel to be essential. Why is it, for instance, that I am rather bored by the aunt in *Le Planétarium* but not by fussy old Miss Bates or Mr Woodhouse in *Emma*? It must be because Miss Bates and Mr Woodhouse are part of a philosophy I can accept, which is the ultimate pattern behind Jane Austen's books. This is not really connected with their being picturesque "characters", now out of date. They are mediocre enough to satisfy the most earnest 20th-century writer, and have hardly dated at all. Nor is it concerned with their having a part to play in the plot; Jane Austen's plots, although well-managed, are, like all plots, tedious once you have got to know them. The devices of the "traditional" novel are, after all, just the apparatus the writer is using to organise his or her field of perception. Jane Austen's organisation is not absolutely impeccable; she is exactly right about Miss Bates, I think, but too kind to Mr Woodhouse. She is tainted with 18th-century sensibility, pre-Romantic flabbiness, misplaced piety, and ingrained snobbishness; but these defects are as nothing compared to the strong, even miraculous, clarity of vision which keeps them at bay.

In the last resort, her books break down into "the good bits" and the traditional or inferior passages which only serve as bridges from one good bit to the next. Fortunately, the good bits are numerous enough to make one feel happy and excited, during the process of reading, at being able to borrow her strength of mind. With the New Novel, I feel that the good bits, such as the visit to the house in *Martereau*, are too few and far between; most of the time, I am being told the obvious, plainly and minutely, and what I would really like to know about the author's mind is being, almost perversely, withheld.

Something missing in all the books, except *Les Fruits d'Or*, is a shape (but even in *Les Fruits d'Or* the shape is not organic; it is engineered from without). I am not asking for an abhorred and old-fashioned "plot", because I agree that the story element is often the least interesting part of a novel. But aesthetic shape means that the artist knows which parts of the work are most important for his sensibility and intelligence. Mme Sarraute's attempt to catch the tiniest movements of the sensibility all the time seems to involve a destruction of perspective. She often appears to be needling away at the fabric of perception to no purpose, just as Robbe-Grillet or Butor will describe some object at inordinate length and leave the reader wondering: "Why this object and not any other of an indefinite number of objects?" In a good, "traditional" novel, "characters" do not occur just because the author is adopting facile stereotypes, but because character is a function of perspective. We see people as "characters" in proportion as they are remote from us. The subjective consciousness cannot see itself as a character because it is aware of itself as a welter of conflicting tropisms, but it is always living in an improvised, real-life novel, peopled by characters of greater or lesser complexity and definiteness. The fact that I see a given person as a stereotype is no less "true" than the fact that he himself inevitably looks upon himself as anything but a stereotype. Miss Bates is a stereotype when looked at from Emma's point of view, but ceases to be a stereotype in the moment of self-awareness when she apologises for being the fussy old chatterer she has suddenly realised she is. Emma herself, being the heroine, is never entirely a stereotype, etc. This whole problem is magnificently studied and demonstrated by Proust and, frankly, I cannot see what the New Novelists add to his great achievement. There are lots of dead bits in his work and he is not always completely in control of his magnifying apparatus, but I can think of no one who has managed to

w

describe "tropisms" on such a scale while incorporating them into a general statement about life. I disagree about his characters being now worthy of relegation to a sort of literary Mme Tussaud's. For the most part, the characters, whether complex or flat, are still very much alive, though of course they could not be re-invented today with the same historical and social details, because the world they belonged to has disappeared. Only certain of Proust's ideas or manias have become defunct, or were still-born even at the time of writing.

By using the phrase "a general statement about life", I have come out into the open as the sort of pedant who wants a writer to say something, whereas, according to Robbe-Grillet, "a writer is someone who has nothing to say". My suspicion is that Mme Sarraute has something to say but that she is not saying it fully.

After all, most of her novels can be read as a critique, monotonous in its ruthlessness, of Parisian, middle-class *mauvaise foi*—a critique, moreover, conducted mainly by means of interior monologue and, inevitably, the interior monologue, even chopped up into very short phrases, is as dated and as artificial a convention as any. There would be nothing wrong with Mme Sarraute's use of it, if she included in her books some indication of the nature of the "authenticity", in the light of which she is presumably stigmatising *la mauvaise foi*. As in the café, I have to sit and wait without being told what an active form of living might be. Here again, it is not a question of asking for an old-fashioned "message", but of knowing what balance the artist is striking between the various tensions of life. If "tropisms" are pure responses to stimuli, the universe Mme Sarraute is describing is deterministic, and indeed the impression of claustrophobia her novels produce in me comes, I think, from the fact that her characters, however subtle their twitchings, are entirely passive. They never initiate anything; their emotions, which are consistently repulsive or contemptible, wash this way or that without the intervention of any act of conscience, as opposed to mere consciousness.

Now the New Novelists, generally speaking, have eliminated morality as being an antiquated encumbrance. The word is crude, I admit, and the phenomenon infinitely mysterious, and if any writer wants to be an out-and-out determinist, good luck to him or her. But it is impossible to be both a determinist and to convey moral disapproval of behaviour, as though one were standing outside the world one is describing—unless, of course, the writer argues that his moral disapproval is itself predetermined, and this lands him in an infinite regress. Mme Sarraute has moral feelings; one has only to talk to her to see that this is so, and her books imply the most traditional French form of social, intellectual, and aesthetic contempt for the bourgeois class to which she belongs. The element lacking in the "reality" described in her books is a most important one: the positive manifestation of the conscience which is passing the unfavourable judgment.

32. The Ludic Novel

Since 1955, when I spent a happy week at the Château d'Eu in Normandy listening to some of the practitioners of the French New Novel, then in the springtime of their fame, expressing their anti-Balzacian views among the imperial, and utterly Balzacian, bric-à-brac of the Orléans-Braganza family, I have puzzled intermittently over this relatively recent artistic phenomenon. The New Novel has been one of the major events during my career—or accidental involvement—as a teacher of French, and I have quite failed to respond to it in any positive way. Ought I to resign, or do they also serve who expound their own obtuseness? I hope so, because I have proved almost as insensitive as a French classicist reacting to the Romantic movement between 1820 and 1830.

This is not, however, because I cling deliberately to any conservative notions about what the novel ought to be. I find the theoretical statements of the New Novelists extremely interesting and, for the most part, intelligible and even acceptable as philosophical principles. Over the years I have had many opportunities of hearing them talk further about their creative beliefs; indeed, I have listened to M. Robbe-Grillet giving the same lecture at least three times in different places, although I have occasionally suspected that, in his case, it is artfully calculated to keep the debate alive through ambiguity rather than to settle it by clarification.

But, generally speaking, I have grasped the argument: it is now old-fashioned to assume, as everyone once did, that the function of the novelist is to show a character or a group of characters living through a phase of life in a recognisable social context. People, whether seen from the outside or the inside, are not "characters"; they are indefinitely complex series of appearances to which it is risible, and almost vulgar, to attach proper names. Time is a mystery—an always immediate mystery, since the past and the future are mere illusions of the shifting present. Any realism of the social context is out of the question, because reality is infinite and multifarious and can only be rendered linguistically by partial, and often mutually exclusive, grids. There are no plots in nature, so that to tell a story in terms of cause and effect is to accept a naïve, linear fiction.

So out go the characters, the story as a chronological sequence, the identifiable narrator or narrators, and any commonsensical description of social settings. All these things are said to smack of the false bourgeois certainties of the 19th century, and should be left to those retarded writers who repeat the automatisms of the past without realising that new forms have to be invented to convey new perceptions. On the whole, what the New Novel gives us in the place of the traditional story is very carefully arranged linguistic structures palpitating in a sort of void, as if they were autonomous patterns or puzzles.

My difficulty is that these patterns or puzzles provide me with little enlightenment and give me practically no pleasure, apart from the incidental enjoyment to be derived from savoring the French language, when meticulously written. But I can get that kind of enjoyment from a good textbook or technical treatise, in which case I also understand the necessity of what is being said. For me, the New Novel in some fundamental way lacks necessity, and the odd passages I appreciate and remember are unfortunately those which are closest to the traditional novel: the description of the dreary English landscape in Michel Butor's *L'Emploi du temps*, the aunt's obsession with the door in *Le Planétarium* by Nathalie Sarraute, an evocative paragraph or two in Robbe-Grillet, a few vivid, erotic sentences in Claude Simon, or a humorous fragment in Robert Pinget.

Taken as would-be aesthetic wholes, the novels strike me as very disappointing after the excitement of the critical theories, as if the writers had not adequately solved the problems raised by their own philosophical attitudes. Strangely enough, I think the disappointment is directly, or indirectly, admitted even by some people who have welcomed the New Novel and claim to support it. It is perhaps significant, for instance, that the most fashionable contemporary French critic, Roland Barthes, who was largely responsible for arousing interest in Robbe-Grillet's early novels, has not committed himself to any definite and extended judgment on the later ones. However, in 1963, in prefacing Bruce Morrissette's book, *Les Romans de Robbe-Grillet* (a descriptive work which gives no aesthetic evaluation), he made the following curious statement in connection with the apparent gratuitousness of Robbe-Grillet's books:

> What do things signify? What does the world signify? All literature is this question, but it must immediately be added, since this is what gives literature its special nature: *it is this question minus the answer*. No literature in the world has ever replied to the question it put. . . .
> What god, Valéry said, would dare to take as his motto: I disappoint [*Je déçois*]? Literature might be considered as this god; perhaps it will eventually be possible to describe all literature as the art of disappointment [*l'art de la déception*].

This is a very debatable assertion. Granted that the ultimate meaning of things is beyond our grasp, it has usually been assumed that literature, and art in general, is a means of producing a satisfactory, not a disappointing, response to the ultimately unknowable. The entire critical argument, we might say, has been about which responses are disappointing and which satisfactory and, as I shall try to show later, there may be a connection between this problem and the ambiguous concept of necessity.

In a recent study, *The New Novel from Queneau to Pinget*, an American academic, Vivian Mercier, who declares himself convinced of the permanent value of some at least of the characteristic New Novels, hedges his bet a little:

> It is of course possible to argue, as many critics still do, that the reach of Robbe-Grillet and the rest far exceeded their grasp: that their actual as opposed to their ideal novels are either so brief and lacking in content as to be negligible—Robbe-Grillet and Madame Sarraute—or concerned with working out an obsessive pattern at such enormous length as to be boring—Michel Butor, Raymond Queneau, Claude Mauriac. As for

Simon and Pinget, they may be seen as innocents ruined by evil company
—potentially great, warm-hearted writers who have made their books
unreadable by forcing good meat through the sausage-machine of dogmatic theory.

Since Mr Mercier himself dismisses Robbe-Grillet's previous
novel, *La Maison de rendez-vous* (1965), as being of no interest,
without however showing in what ways it differs from the
earlier ones, we may wonder if he did not grow progressively
wearier of the New Novel as his study proceeded. At any rate,
we are forced back on to our own judgment in dealing with
the latest product, *Projet pour une révolution à New York* (1970).*

To my mind, this "novel" has exactly the same characteristics as Robbe-Grillet's five preceding works, but the publicity
handout accompanying the French edition, which was written
by the author himself, is rather more explicit than some of his
earlier statements and is therefore worth bearing in mind as
one reads the book.

He begins by repeating, for the *n*th time, that the traditional
novel is "a fossilised use of language", surviving from the early
19th century, which tells, in chronological sequence, a story
which is "as definite as a judgment". Sociologists have shown
that this traditional novel reflects bourgeois values connected
with the destiny of the individual and the history of societies.
These bourgeois values having collapsed, the traditional novel
must be replaced by something else, "a new organising force".
To supply this force, the New Novel has evolved the theory of
generative themes *(le théorie des thèmes générateurs)* :

> From now on, it is the themes of the novel (objects, events, words, formal
> movements, etc.) which become the basic elements engendering the
> whole architecture of the story, and even the adventures which occur
> in it, according to a mode of development comparable to those employed
> by serial music or the modern plastic arts.

But what are these generative themes? Robbe-Grillet says
he finds them among the "mythological material" of everyday
life—in newspapers, posters, etc.—which reflects the collective

* Alain Robbe-Grillet, *Project for a Revolution in New York* (Grove Press,
1972).

unconscious of society. Then comes a very important paragraph, asserting that all moral judgments are a form of backward-looking escapism:

> In dealing with these modern myths, two attitudes are possible: one can either condemn them in the name of accepted values (erotic imagery may be condemned in the name of "true love," or even in the name of "true" eroticism, which is connected with psychological depth, pathos, and guilt); but this moral condemnation is no more than an escapist attitude, a flight into the past. Or they can be accepted, and without altering their flatness as modish images, I can recognise that they are all around me, that is, within me, and that instead of closing my eyes and veiling my face, there remains the possibility of playing with them.

As his imagination manipulates the mythological material, the novelist establishes his freedom, which exists only in language, the sole domain of human liberty. And this literary game, unlike bridge or chess, has no pre-ordained rules; they are made up and cancelled by the writer, according to his whim, and this is as it should be:

> After the bankruptcy of the divine order (of bourgeois society) and, following that, of the rationalistic order (of bureaucratic socialism) it must be understood that henceforth only ludic* organisations are possible.
>
> Love is a game, poetry is a game, life must become a game (this is the only hope for our political struggles) and "revolution itself is a game", as was said by the most conscious of the revolutionaries of May 1968.

Before discussing this last paragraph, I should perhaps explain how the "ludic" principle works in practice. *Project for a Revolution* is not, of course, a documentary or "realistic" account of an actual or imagined revolution in New York, any more than *Le Voyeur* was a description of the mind of a pathological killer or *La Jalousie* an explanation of the psychology of a jealous husband in a tropical bungalow. Robbe-Grillet's method is to take elements *that might have been present* in a traditional novel on the subject and then to orchestrate them according to his own rules.

In this instance, we can suppose that if a revolution were being organised in New York, an agent might emerge gingerly from the house in which he was living with his sister, walk

---

* *Ludique,* a now fashionable neologism, formed from *ludo,* "I play." "Ludic" is not in the *OED*, nor is "ludique" in *Littré.*

anxiously toward the nearest subway station, take a train to a place of assignation in a secret underground hall, and listen to a revolutionary pep talk from three spokesmen of the organisation. His duties might involve torturing a beautiful female half-caste to get information about a rival group. An intruder might break into his flat during his absence by climbing up the fire escape and shattering a pane of glass in a French window.

We have all read about episodes such as these, or seen them a thousand times in the cinema or on television. Robbe-Grillet does not want to do anything so banal as reorder them in the light of some value judgment about what the revolution might be, or should be. Instead, he uses them to make a pattern that is rather like a dream one might have on going to sleep after reading a thriller or attending a film. Certain details are seen with maniacal precision, although their relevance, if any, remains unexplained; incidents recur and are recounted in the same, or slightly different, words. All identities are in a state of flux, just as in a nightmare one may be both the pursuer and the pursued.

But it would be too simple to conclude that Robbe-Grillet has abandoned the rational organisation characteristic of the waking state to produce oneiric patterns, comparable, say, to the short stories of Edgar Allan Poe. His dreams, if they are dreams, are strangely refrigerated, because the prose carries no direct charge of emotion, either positive or negative, to make the pattern intelligible. In *Project for a Revolution*, the overtones are undeniably sombre, because the "characters" are spying on each other or torturing each other (there is no suggestion of any joyful revolutionary excitement). Yet no sinister vibration is allowed to creep into the language, which always moves at the same measured pace to describe everything with the same calm objectivity. Thus, there is no rhetorical difference between one of the recurrent descriptions of the broken windowpane:

Le choc a produit un son net et clair. En même temps est apparue, s'étendant à toute la surface du rectangle, une fêlure en étoile à multiples rayons. Mais aucun morceau ne s'en détache, si ce n'est, avec un retard notable, un petit triangle de verre très pointu, long de cinq ou six centimètres, qui bascule lentement vers l'intérieur et choit sur le carrelage avec un bruit cristallin, se brisant à son tour en trois fragments plus menus. . . .

and one of the high points of a torture scene, where the operator
sets fire to a bundle of horse-hair glued to his victim's vagina:

> *Je craque une allumette, prise dans la boîte qui se trouve dans ma poche et j'en-
> flamme le buisson roux. Cette fois le corps aux courbes voluptueuses bouge davantage,
> dans le rougoiement de la torche vivante, ses liens ayant sans doute pris un peu de
> lâche, à force d'être tiraillés en tous sens par la fille qui se tord au paroxysme de la
> souffrance. Une sorte de râle sort de sa gorge, avec des halètements et des cris de
> plus en plus précipités, jusqu'au long gémissement rauque final qui se prolonge encore
> après l'extinction totale des flammes, dont une gerbe d'étincelles a marqué l'achève-
> ment.**

These are two very neat pieces of writing, and in their context
they seem to imply that the breaking of a windowpane and the
mangling of a body are similar phenomena. This is undoubtedly
true from the strictly scientific point of view; torture is merely a
particular exploitation of the senses, which can be described as
a time-and-motion study with chemical and physiological
incidents. Robbe-Grillet's peculiarity is that he places the
tortured female bodies at intervals in the pattern, very much as
an architect might use anguished caryatids to support symmetrical coping stones. The deliberate flatness of all the
elements—whether normally of slight human significance, as in
the case of a windowpane, or of intense significance, as in the
case of torture—is offset by the extreme complexity of the
pattern.

* Mr Howard translates the passages as follows; it will be seen that his
rendering is sometimes inaccurate and does not reproduce the sense of
careful linguistic control characteristic of the French:

> The impact has produced a loud, distinct noise. At the same time has
> appeared, extending across the entire surface of the rectangle, a star-
> shaped fracture. But no piece of glass falls out, unless, much later, it is a
> tiny pointed triangle about half an inch long, which slowly leans inward
> and falls on the tiles with a crystalline sound, breaking in its turn into
> three smaller fragments.

> I strike a match, taken out of the box which is in my pocket, and I set
> fire to the red tuft. This time the body with its voluptuous curves moves
> more, in the reddening explosions of the living torch, its bonds having
> doubtless grown a little loose, having been tugged in every direction by
> the girl twisting in a paroxysm of suffering. A kind of rattle emerges
> from her throat, with gasps and increasingly frequent screams, until the
> long final harsh moan which still continues after the total extinction of
> the flames, whose conclusion is marked by a shower of sparks.

This complexity is not inherent in the language, which always remains simple, but lies in the multiplicity of the items manipulated and their polyvalent relations with each other. For instance, in the opening pages, the anonymous "I" of the narrator is both inside and outside a door; he has a key in his pocket, or he has put it on a marble shelf, or it has fallen into the stairwell; he is the brother, the lover, or the assailant of a secluded woman or little girl, who may also later be a female gangster in the subway, and so on. The pattern is so involved that I cannot hold it in my mind while I am reading, and it fades away again as soon as I close the book. I am left with wraithlike impressions of contorted bodies, staircases, and the movement of underground trains.

Robbe-Grillet seems to be suggesting that since the stuff of experience is undifferentiated through the universal collapse of value judgments, all the writer can do is make playful arrangements of ready-made data. In his case, although the arrangements are unintelligible to me, they are recognisably similar from one novel to the next, at least from *Le Voyeur* onward. Since they are so alike, in spite of the differences in "subject", they presumably correspond in one sense to a necessity of his temperament, just as people who doodle always do so in the same way, because such "play", whether spontaneous or controlled, can only occur within certain individual limits.

What puzzles me in the first place is why the necessity of Robbe-Grillet's temperament should be so remote from that of mine. His patterns can only interest me as objects of study through a sense of duty, because he handles French well and is obviously a man of parts; they do not appeal to me of their own accord.* But then I reflect that there are many abstract

* Nor, incidentally, do his films, but I consider them to be inferior to the books, because the obtrusive "realism" of photography does not allow anything like the interlocking ambiguities of language. Robbe-Grillet can write French, but he seems quite mediocre with the camera; and I have seen no genuinely enthusiastic account of the films he has made on his own, since *L'Année dernière à Marienbad*, directed by Alain Resnais. Could it be that Robbe-Grillet has bamboozled himself into using the camera through a confusion between *le regard* of the camera lens and *le regard* as expressed in language?

pictures that leave me unmoved, as if I were dealing with a totally foreign sensibility.

If I appreciated Robbe-Grillet's novels, I might see that the apparently gratuitous patterning had, in fact, a significance. It could possibly be an arrangement corresponding to the needs of a sadistic temperament, in which case, of course, it is not truly "ludic". Certainly, sadistic features are always very prominent, and in this last book, in so far as the word revolution is given any meaning, it is taken as a pure synonym of destruction, centred on the three "major liberating actions connected with the colour red: rape, arson, and murder". The revolutionary pep talk is concerned not with politics but with defining the perfect crime:

> . . . le crime parfait, qui combine les trois éléments étudiés ici, serait la défloration opérée de force sur une fille vierge, choisie de préférence à la peau laiteuse et aux cheveux très blonds, la victime étant ensuite immolée par éventration ou égorgement, son corps nu ensanglanté devant être brûlé pour finir sur un bûcher arrosé de pétrole, embrasant de proche en proche toute la maison.

> (. . . the perfect crime, combining the three elements already discussed, would be the forcible deflowering of a virgin, chosen preferably for her milk-white skin and very fair hair, and her subsequent immolation by disembowelling or throat-cutting, after which her naked and bloody body would finally be burnt on a paraffin-soaked pyre, which would gradually set the whole house ablaze.) [My translation.]

I am puzzled in the second place by Robbe-Grillet's categorical assertion that this ludic pattern (if it is really ludic) is the only valid linguistic activity at the present time. It reduces language to the level of the inarticulate, so that a "novel" is no more translatable into a series of statements than an abstract painting might be; however, the innovation is more striking, since figurative painting was never articulate in the linguistic sense. True, since this "novel" maintains intelligibility sentence by sentence, it does not go so far, say, as concrete poetry, which replaces language by collocations of sounds invented by the individual sensibility and therefore almost entirely solipsistic in relation to that sensibility. But it does not correspond to Barthes's definition of literature as a question minus an answer, since it does not put any question. Balzac, Tolstoy, Proust, etc., may not give any final answers, but they certainly raise lots of issues, since their use of language is generally significant.

Robbe-Grillet produces a series of question marks in the reader's mind (or at least in this reader's), because he has deliberately arranged his pattern so that it is opaque. This is not to deal with the real, or supposed, opaqueness of life, but to parody it, which is quite a different matter. The traditional novelist has often been accused of rivalling God by simulating omniscience. One might accuse Robbe-Grillet of trying to rival God by carefully creating a little unintelligible universe, in which to entrap his readers. But whereas we have no way of opting out of God's incomprehensible universe, we are not obliged to accept Robbe-Grillet's, any more than we are obliged to do the *Times* crossword puzzle.

This brings me back to the problem of necessity and gratuitousness, and its relation to the "game", a word which has both a precise meaning and a loose, metaphorical one. I used to believe that no one with a genuine metaphysical interest could have any patience with games; but I have come across philosophers who were football fans, so I am obliged to conclude that the mind is not always all of a piece. The point about a game, in the literal sense, is that it relieves general emotional and intellectual tension by creating a small, clearly defined area in which the rules are man-created, obvious, and stable, so that human endeavour acquires an immediate pseudo-meaning, instead of becoming lost in the general struggle with the universe. In this sense, fishing and hunting, if one's livelihood does not depend upon them, are just as much games as any other form of "sport". Conversely, a game that is played professionally, or that involves a death risk, ceases to be ludic in the simple sense, because it becomes part of the general battle with existence.

But, even though we may greatly admire the intellectual stamina of an outstanding professional sportsman (*e.g.*, the jockey Lester Piggott or the racing driver Jackie Stewart), the fact remains that his activities are inferior to serious art or serious thought, because they take place within a given narrow and arbitrarily defined field. Art has to obey certain rules, of course, in order to achieve form; but the artist, unlike the games-player or sportsman, is facing the general problem of life.

It would be wrong, for instance, to argue that Beethoven's *Diabelli* Variations are fundamentally ludic, although they take a simple waltz tune and juggle with it in thirty-three different ways, as if the composer were playing some technical game with consummate skill, as a tennis player might demonstrate various placings of the ball. All the variations, even the humorous ones, have a complex human solidity which shows that the *Diabelli* waltz is only the starting-point for different forays into significance. One may be unable to translate the meaningfulness of the music into words, but it is still obviously there, rich and necessary, at the hundredth hearing. In this sense, good art, in its discovery of meaning, is exactly the opposite of a game. When Robbe-Grillet says that everything is a game, either he is indulging in a mystificatory paradox or he wants to convince himself that gratuitous structures are an adequate response to the confusions of life. In the absence, or assumed absence, of necessary human principles, he is consoling himself by inventing pseudo-necessary rules.

But is it true that there are no necessary human principles? I have never been able to understand sweeping statements such as "After the bankruptcy of the divine order (of bourgeois society) and, following that, of the rationalistic order (of bureaucratic socialism)...." They are just cliché-like reformulations of the misleading "God is dead" metaphor. Similarly, I have never understood why, in Sartrian Existentialism, to which the New Novelists are heavily indebted, the non-existence of God is taken to prove the non-existence of "human nature". The assumption seems to be that there was once a form of God-supported human necessity that has now collapsed, leaving us floundering. But the order of bourgeois society (which, to be historically accurate, was secular rather than divine, and came after the full-blooded, God-centred order) was never anything more than an imperfect human attempt at organisation. The various divine orders which preceded it were just as imperfect and never had any objective necessity because, if God is now a fiction, He always was, and religious certainty was a subjective mirage.

In other words, with respect to necessity, human nature, and value judgments we are objectively no worse off now than humanity has ever been. The complication is that we now see more clearly that man's "nature" (if we insist on using the term), is fluid, evolves historically, and remains unpredictable. But since this has always been the case, we are not in a new situation where only gratuitous or ludic responses are possible; and I am pretty certain that Robbe-Grillet himself does not adopt a truly ludic or gratuitous attitude about his position on the French literary scene or his general conduct of life.

We may grant that human nature is indeterminate without jumping to the conclusion that it does not exist, and we may agree that value judgments are changeable and always invented by man without assuming that they are therefore devoid of necessity and can be discarded. If I can indulge in a paradox myself, I would say that, at any historical moment, there must be a *relative* necessity of human nature that it is the function of art to discover and express. In so far as the New Novel is genuinely "ludic", it seems to be doodling, rather self-indulgently, off the point.